ALL-CHANGE IN THE CITY

Also by Margaret Reid and published by Macmillan

THE SECONDARY BANKING CRISIS, 1973–75: Its Causes and Course

All-Change in the City

The Revolution in Britain's Financial Sector

Margaret Reid

MACMILLAN
PRESS

First published 1988

Published by
THE MACMILLAN PRESS LTD
Houndmills, Basingstoke, Hampshire RG21 2XS
and London
Companies and representatives
throughout the world

Typesetting by Footnote Graphics,
Warminster, Wilts

Printed in Great Britain by
Richard Clay Ltd, Bungay, Suffolk

British Library Cataloguing in Publication Data
Reid, Margaret
All-change in the City: the revolution in
Britain's financial sector.
1. London (City). Financial institutions
& money markets
I. Title
332.1′09421′2
ISBN 0–333–36234–9

To the memory of my parents, Marcus and Winifred Mary Reid

Contents

Preface   vii

PART I   THE CITY REVOLUTION   1

1   The City's Place in the World   3
2   The Government–Stock Exchange Accord   23
3   City Restructuring for Big Bang   51
4   The Pay Explosion   71

PART II   MARKETS AND INSTITUTIONS   87

5   City Markets after Big Bang   89
6   Clearing Banks: Business   123
7   Clearing Banks: Organisation   149
8   Other Banks: Merchant, Investment and Foreign   169
9   Investing Institutions   189

PART III   POLICING THE CITY: THE WATCHDOGS   203

10   Bank of England   205
11   Protecting Investors and Users   243
12   Lessons and Reflections   261

Notes   267
Index   274

Preface

It would be difficult at the most static of times to write about the City of London without talking to the participants in its varied areas. But to have done so in the present age of rapid evolution would have been impossible. I am therefore particularly grateful to the many City people who have been good enough to give me interviews, from some of which I have quoted, in connection with this book. They have been most generous with their time and their perceptions of the changes that have swept Britain's financial centre and I thank them all most warmly.

In what follows, I have attempted to focus on some highlights of City events in the present decade, which has seen not only the Big Bang stock market revolution but significant developments in other fields also. One problem with writing about the City is the difficulty of knowing whether to tackle the subject by markets or by institutions. For better or worse, I decided to mix the two approaches. One chapter has therefore been devoted to a look round the different markets and others, in more detail, to a consideration of various types of institutions. In the book as a whole, I have concentrated on certain subjects, including the stock market's reshaping and recent changes in the banks and investing institutions, dwelling more lightly on other sectors. If this has meant some aspects of the City being passed over too briefly, my excuse must be the limitations inevitably imposed by the restricted capacity of a single volume and author.

I should like next to express my grateful thanks to Miss Gillian O'Connor, Editor of the *Investors Chronicle*, for which I write, for her permission to me to use the resources of the magazine's library. I am most appreciative too of the help of the librarians, Mr John Pearce and Mr David Hall.

I also wish to record my thanks to Mr Geoffrey Owen, Editor of the *Financial Times*, on whose editorial staff I formerly worked, for most kindly allowing me to use the newspaper's library. My thanks are due, in addition, to Mrs Elizabeth Marsh, the library manager, and Miss Mary Batten, the library administration officer, for guiding me to different sources.

The appearance of this book gives me an opportunity to say how grateful I am to Mr Philip Warland, head of the Bank of England's Information Division, and to his present and former Press Office colleagues, for much valuable help to me down the years. I am very much beholden as well to Mr Paul Mortimer-Lee of the Bank of England's Gilt-Edged Division for the generous assistance he has given me over statistics of government bond markets.

Finally, I am most indebted to Mrs Kathleen Rogers of Oxford for her excellent typing of my manuscripts, sometimes in most rushed conditions. I thank her most warmly for her help and her invariably kind and cheerful support of my endeavours.

London   MARGARET REID

Part I
The City Revolution

1 The City's Place in the World

The 1980s have witnessed advances in technology that have allowed [catered] for the geographical separation of borrower and lender, growing trade imbalances and a trend towards deregulated markets unparalleled in history.

Securities Industry Association of the US.[1]

New York and Tokyo matter because of the domestic economies they serve. London, by contrast, serves the world community.

The Economist.[2]

It is no accident that the recent radical shake-up in Britain's financial structure has occurred during the premiership of that tough challenger of established practices, Mrs Margaret Thatcher. Reshaping the City of London was scarcely a top aim when Mrs Thatcher's Conservative government won power in 1979, though another financial objective, squeezing inflation through 'monetary' means, was. But questioning of long-established systems generally stood high on the agenda of this first British woman Prime Minister who, asked after ten years of party leadership what she had changed, answered simply, 'Everything'.

The Thatcher approach, springing from dislike of controls and competition-curbing equality ideas, had early and famous outcomes. Public utilities were 'privatised' and trade union powers restricted. A linked disapproval of price-fixing caused pressures for freeing-up of charges competition among professionals like solicitors. Reaction against 'left-wing interventionism', even in the cause of guided economic growth; dislike of cost-boosting union strength; matching discouragement of price-propping cartels – all these emerged as part of the Conservative spirit of the age in the eighties. It was a spirit which Reaganism in the United States shared with Thatcherism in Britain, and which captured electorates disenchanted with the disappointments of the seventies' 'stagflation'.

Its key aim was the fight against inflation – no matter if at the cost of lost growth – and its crucial instrument the fostering of deregulation or, as it might be put, liberating the consumer to seek out the best bargain. Highlighted early on by the freeing of United States airline charges and by Britain's ending of exchange control, deregulation became the ideology of the time and gradually surged through many sectors and continents.

As it has happened, many influences have combined to make the impact of deregulation most dramatic in the financial industry throughout the world. The ideological climate has sharpened the appetite of businesses, bank customers and savers alike for a wider range of choice of services. Rising prosperity has led investors to look beyond their own markets in quest of fresh outlets, and stock market firms to range more widely to serve them. At the same time, financial companies of all kinds have seized the opportunity to search for business outside their home areas. And rapidly developing technology has assisted the process by making many old-style barriers between countries obsolescent.

The result has been that cosily protected markets, long shut off from each other, have been opened up and become more closely linked in a wider world system. And nowhere has the shake-up been greater than in Britain, whose growingly sophisticated City of London markets need to be understood in their global context.

London has opened its Stock Exchange doors to newcomers, home and foreign, in a process which has caused vast reshaping of its financial industry, mainly under large banks with the capital to play in today's top-league markets. And this 'Big Bang' initiative has been echoed in many countries.

Japan is letting in foreign competition with a controversial slowness born of its long isolation, but as the price of Tokyo's staying one of the world's key money centres, with London and New York. In the United States, interest curbs which distorted the banking system have been scrapped. The Glass-Steagall law which, since the troubled thirties, has banned commercial banks in the US from taking on some of the risks of stock market business is still in force, but banking across state bounds is growing somewhat easier.

Action elsewhere has gone the same deregulating way, with most advanced nations having abandoned exchange control. Canada is following up earlier easements by letting its banks break into securities – stock market – business and France has embarked on a similar 'Big Bang'. West Germany has steadily loosened remaining controls. With the United States and others it now allows interest payments without tax deduction on bonds owned overseas: in Germany's case this is more a move to open its markets than, as with

America, to woo foreign funds to finance its deficits. And, Down Under, Australia's bank fraternity has felt the shock of new foreign bank rivals in its long-sheltered markets.

If all this, and far more, change is in the ideological interest of more competition, it also suits aggressive financial groups nearing saturation point in their existing markets and wanting to break into new ones. There is, too, the point that, as one stock market centre, London, goes competitive and cuts its charges, others feel a need to follow suit lest inroads be made into their own markets. As one British banker says: 'Most of the Continental markets have been highly regulated, much more so than the United Kingdom's, and rather introverted. But they are suddenly changing, very rapidly. The reason is that they are very worried about losing the business they've got to London.'

It is not only that world money centres are now less no-go areas to each other. Who-does-what divides between activities are dissolving. In Britain, for instance, you can now just as easily get your home loan from a bank as from a building society, while at the same time the societies are vying with the banks to give personal credit. If you buy shares, the deal is as likely to go via a bank- or foreign-owned investment house as through a small family stockbroker.

For companies, the changes are as great. Corporate (company) treasurers want the best terms when they raise cash or place out funds and increasingly go to whoever – whether British or foreign – offers the best 'buy', rather than just to the merchant banker whose father and grandfather served them. This is known as 'transaction' rather than 'relationship' banking.

Types of business are altering too. It is no longer simply a question of borrowing and lending, with the banker occupying his 'intermediating' role of taking in deposits and handing out loans. Where large-scale company needs are concerned, finance is frequently now supplied more cheaply direct from investors, like large pension funds, against the company's 'promise to repay' paper or bonds. A bank then acts as arranger, not lender, and the issued paper is tradable if the holder wants to exchange it for cash. The whole fashion for more of the finance which is industry's and commerce's life-blood to be put up in this way has been labelled 'securitisation'. And the fact that the system cuts down the traditional loan role of the bank makes the latter regretfully tag it 'disintermediation'.

In the consumer field, much mortgage lending is, in the United States, no longer left on the lender's books but is 'packaged up' and sold to – and perhaps also traded among – big investors, through a practice beginning to spread to Britain. The same 'packaging' technique is also applied in America to other 'streams of income', such as those to repay instalment car finance. And these are only some of many novel arrangements in today's innovating markets.

The whole deregulating process has been given strong impetus by the concurrent explosion of the new telecommunications and computer technology, making it possible to flash information – on prices, trading and companies – swiftly round the globe. When such data, and orders to deal, can be passed instantly, any distance, frontiers shrink in importance: the electronic beam simply skips them. It is almost by accident that such high-tech gadgetry has staged a swift advance in the era of deregulation. But as matters have turned out, it has reinforced the boost towards more interlinked world markets and, on the way, transformed the nature of banking. Looking back on his chairmanship of Britain's Barclays Bank from 1981–7, Sir Timothy Bevan stresses how much, in that time, 'banking has become an information industry'.[3]

Certainly the new technology has been crucial in knitting up the markets into globally connected ones. And, as trade once followed the flag, so the world's ambitious financial and securities groups have been broadening their networks to match the reach of the electronic eye. Many of the biggest, wherever their base may be, now have important footholds in Tokyo, London, New York and other centres. Thus they deal almost continuously, as the clock revolves, by passing their 'book' – their trading position of stocks and shares – round the globe electronically. It is more or less true that the sun never sets on the stock market business of such as Nomura, Japan's largest securities house, America's Salomon Brothers, Britain's Barclays' BZW and Warburg, and Union Bank of Switzerland. Smart dealers do not, like other mortals, adjust their watches when travelling: instead they call up, on their Japanese dial, the current time in key markets. It is an almost non-stop stock market since there is a scant four-hour lull after the United States closes and before Sydney and Tokyo take up the next day's dealing action. And London's Greenwich Meridian position in the time zone between Tokyo and New York has proved a lucky natural resource, enhancing the City's importance, and the opportunities created for it, in the new 'global village' market.

Though the City of London is sited in a smaller economy than its big rival financial centres, Tokyo and New York, it has long enjoyed prominence through serving a wider world beyond its domestic markets. And the City's long-standing role as financial services supplier to the globe has been revivified at intervals by the addition of new services, of which its strengthened post-Big Bang stock market is just the latest.

For centuries, as a trading nation at the heart of a far-flung empire, Britain led in the finance of world commerce, while its commodity markets and insurance services – dating back three centuries to Edward Lloyd's coffee house – served a wide international custom. Through the nineteenth and early twentieth centuries, capital from the surpluses of a Britain in the high noon of its power – raised through its banks and stock market – financed the Empire and developments from Argentinian railways to Russian mines. The pound sterling was long the dominant currency and, even since national power has waned, it has remained significant in world markets. As to financial techniques, British money men have long prided themselves on their inventiveness. They gave the world the bill of exchange to serve as a medium of short-term credit provision, often used to finance sales of raw materials until repayment was made from the finished product. As negotiable 'promises to pay', bills are 'accepted' (guaranteed), traditionally by London merchant banks (accepting houses), then becoming tradable for cash, at a discount, reflecting interest, through the City's specialist discount houses. Bill finance, though now complemented by numerous more modern credit-giving facilities, remains in changed conditions an important mode of money provision.

The financial drain of two world wars left Britain unable to afford to continue channelling its own capital, in the shape of former-style sterling bond issues, to projects world-wide. Just how squeezed resources became is shown by the fact that there was no net rise in the country's real wealth between 1913 and 1951 because a 50 per cent increase in domestic assets was offset by sales of foreign assets and the shouldering of more debt to finance war and recovery needs.[4] Consequently, a strict exchange control was enforced to protect the United Kingdom's scarce national reserves for forty years from the outbreak of the Second World War until it was scrapped in 1979 as one of the Thatcher government's first free-market moves.

But even in this long-restricted period, the City's outward-looking stance was maintained and exchange controls were modified to allow as big a continuing role as possible for the City in international finance. Partly this involved banks being active in advisory work and in the arrangement of export project and similar finance. But it also, in time, made possible a vastly more important initiative, the setting up of the Euromarket.

This was far and away the biggest City development in the mid-twentieth century, since what was in question was the establishment of a completely new forum for the trading of the large and growing pool of internationally mobile funds. The new market's creation, by financiers aiming to build a fresh business that came to terms with prevailing controls, was actively fostered by the Bank of England and has been of the first importance for the City's survival and prosperity as a leading money centre. This 'offshore' market, so called because it exists separately from Britain's domestic banking sector, has over the past thirty years brought a massive volume of business to the City. And that in turn has attracted to London an unprecedented international financial community, including the operations of over four hundred foreign banks and many other overseas money companies.

Dating from the late 1950s, the Euromarket got its start because big quantities of dollars, paid abroad by the Americans for investment and other purposes, remained held by their owners, as dollars, in banks 'offshore' to the United States. This was partly because they could earn more interest there than in the tightly controlled United States home banking market. Also, Communist countries preferred to hold dollars outside, not in, the United States to protect them from seizure should the Cold War hot up. Reputedly, some Russian funds were held through a French concern, Banque Commerciale pour l'Europe du Nord, whose 'Euro-bank' telex name gave the new market its title. But the name could just as well have been the 'offshore dollar', rather than the 'Eurodollar', market. The resultant expanding reservoir of cash came to be traded around to finance much medium-term bank lending, never touching the United States. London gave the new mart a home, affording it favourable treatment, with no exchange control on non-resident business and a mellow tax régime.

Vast sums now change hands in this international market, which has spread out among various centres and through which the world's banks lend their cash surpluses to each other. Alternatively called the international capital market, it is also the source banks tap to fund their substantial 'cross-border' lending. A huge boost was given to its growth in the middle and later seventies, when hundreds of billions of dollars' worth of 'petro' surpluses were 'recycled' by the newly-rich oil nations to the leading countries' banks and on-lent by them, often to the later troubled third world. From millions only in the late fifties, the entire international credit pool, now in various key currencies, had by the end of 1987 reached a massive $5.3 trillion (£2800bn).[5] London still accounts for between a fifth and a quarter of Euromarket business, despite the creation of 'offshore' facilities in New York, Tokyo and elsewhere as well as in certain Caribbean and Far East areas.

Parallel to the Euromarket as used by the banks is the associated market in Eurobonds – 'offshore' instruments devised in 1962 by the London merchant bank S. G. Warburg – through which high-grade companies and governments raise medium- or longer-term finance in the international capital markets. By definition, a Eurobond is denominated in a currency other than that of the centre in which it is issued: bonds launched in London are therefore expressed in dollars, yen or other leading foreign currencies. They may carry fixed interest (straights), or variable interest (floating rate notes) or they may be exchangeable into shares of the issuing company (convertibles) or contain warrants to subscribe for the shares. All manner of complex variations of bonds can be derived from these basics. In true 'offshore' style, interest on the bonds is paid without tax deduction and the bonds are anonymous 'bearer' ones, both features which appeal to the investors putting up the funds who may be wealthy individuals or certain institutions. Issues of bonds are arranged through major international banks and investment houses (many non-British), which form part of the London financial community and which also trade in the bonds via a telephone market. Deals are 'cleared' (settled) through two specialist companies.

The Eurobond market is very large, as it is a prominent source of finance for high-status entities the world over, and highly active. There are some $650bn bonds outstanding and total turnover in 1987 was a huge $4·7 trillion.[6] Lately the severity of competition to handle bond issues has made participation in the market unprofitable for many participant houses and some have withdrawn. But the flexibility and confidentiality of capital-raising and investment through it should assure the Eurobond market's continued appeal to issuers and investors alike.

In recent years there has been some blurring of the division between bank loans and finance put up against bonds. Many of the world's big companies enjoy a higher credit rating than do the banks themselves (shaken by third-world debt troubles) and so can raise finance more cheaply against the direct issue of their own bonds than by bank borrowing, a fact which has boosted total issues of the former. But sometimes banks hold in their portfolios bonds issued against cash, while they also guarantee the repayment of some company finance raised against 'securitised' tradable paper, so the borderlines between types of financing can become indistinct. Times of financial upset, like those after the October 1987 stock market crash, can also make investors warier of providing cash direct to companies, with the result that more resort is had to borrowing from banks. Altogether, as has been said, the bond markets are not likely to supersede the banks as providers of finance in the same way as the car displaced the horse and buggy.

There has been no lack of grist to the City of London's mill in the form of new developments in recent years. One has been the trend for investors, both personal and institutional, to raise their eyes beyond their own domestic stock markets and diversify their port-folios by purchasing foreign shares. Removal of exchange controls, the general buoyancy of stock markets in the eighties, the easier access to overseas markets with the new technology and the greater research effort stockbrokers now give to foreign companies, have all promoted this major movement. So far from its seeming hazardous to invest abroad, a wide geographical spread is now often seen as diversifying risks in a world of fluctuating exchange rates. This is the more so since uncertainties can be hedged against through the futures and options markets which have also been added to the spectrum of world financial services in the last fifteen years.

The new practice of offering parts of big privatisation issues (like those of Britain's British Telecom and British Gas) in overseas markets has enlarged the ready availability of foreign shares, often now labelled 'Euro-equities', to world investors. Eurobond houses are turning their attention to 'Euro-equities', often arranging not only new issues but 'secondary' sales of existing shares abroad, though upsets have attended some such operations, notably the 1986 disposal of Fiat shares, sold on behalf of Libya, and the United Kingdom government's disposal of its BP holding just before the October 1987 stock market crash. Certainly the habit of international share investment has generally been rapidly spreading. It has been estimated that, altogether, the world over, in 1986 $750bn of share deals, a significant minority proportion of total turnover, took place across national borders and that the 1987 figure may have topped $1 trillion.[7] Growing pension funds, probably the biggest group of investors, are to the fore in this trend and Mr David Booher, European director of InterSec Research Corporation, an international consultancy, predicts that the world's private pension funds, which had just 7½ per cent of their resources invested abroad at the end of 1986, will raise this proportion to 12½ per cent by 1990, more than doubling such non-domestic pension investment from $145bn to $320 bn in four years.[8] As the American Securities Industry Association noted in July 1987 'the equity market is quickly moving from a basically domestic market to an international one'.[9]

The opportunities created by this trend towards international share dealing form part of the backdrop to Britain's revolutionary Big Bang, involving a huge ownership shake-up and recapitalising of its stock market, along with major trading and rule changes. This crucial event in October 1986, the City's most historic happening for decades, was designed to make London's securities markets as a whole more prominent and competitive internationally. The sweeping changes, particularly in strengthening equity market capacity and placing the sterling government bond (gilt) market on a new more American-type basis, have been consciously aimed at establishing London as one of the world's top three stock market centres, along with New York and Tokyo. Just how much London stockbrokers needed to boost their international competitiveness is shown by the fact that in 1979–85, when Britain's annual flow of investment abroad multiplied from £1bn to £18bn following the end of exchange control, overseas brokers handled more than 90 per cent of the business.[10]

A further key development of financial services in recent years in which the City participates, though it did not invent it, is the modern market in 'swaps', which has been described as the biggest market innovation since the Euromarket's invention. Created from virtually nothing since 1982, the swaps market can be considered a by-product of exchange control freedom, coupled with market imperfections which can never be ironed out. What is involved is the exchange of interest or currency payment obligations between two parties. In other words, one borrower (company or government agency) fixes up a loan in a market where, because it is specially strong or welcome, it can raise funds on favourable terms, and then 'swaps' the servicing costs with another doing likewise. In this way the benefits to which each can gain advantageous access – say, because its name means a lot in, or it has made little use of, such-and-such a market – are shared to their mutual advantage. Very often swaps take place between variable (floating) and fixed-rate loans and between those initially raised by large and smaller borrowers. The importance of these arrangements is that a company can, in effect, use a swap as a stepping-stone from the type of loan and currency it can most easily raise itself to any other in which it would rather be. Put another way, parties can 'redistribute risk', perhaps also using the equally booming futures and options markets in Chicago, London and elsewhere to hedge risks.

Already the swaps system has made its own major contribution towards converting the various separate financial markets of the globe into a more linked-up world-wide market in which the borrower can choose the kind of currency or interest rate risks it prefers to shoulder, and on the best terms. Many swaps are part of long chains of deals to achieve the best effect: the Swiss-owned Union Bank of Switzerland (Securities), of London, decorated the cover of its 1986 annual report with the outline of a twenty-part swap network. In fact swaps have done more to knit up world markets with each other than almost any other single trend. Globally, well over $350bn of interest swaps are outstanding: with a smaller currency swaps total, the joint figure is probably now over $500bn. Swaps in these modern senses were an American rather than a British innovation but the service is widely available from banks in London, as elsewhere.

How do the City of London's various activities rank in scale compared with world markets as a whole? As will be seen, Britain is well outsized by its two big competitors, the United States and Japan, in the trading of stocks and shares. But in banking it can claim primacy, since the proportion banks in Britain (local and foreign) have in international banking business via the Euromarket 22 per cent – $1143bn of liabilities out of a $5285bn world total – is probably the largest for any country. The City is also the undoubted centre of the Eurobond market.

In the different field of foreign exchange, the trading of currencies against each other, London also remains the premier market. Studies have shown that *daily* foreign exchange business through London in mid-1986 was a huge $90bn, compared with New York's $50bn and Tokyo's $48bn.[11] These figures are almost double those recorded as recently as 1984, when London was reckoned to have a third of world business.[12] Current figures can only be guessed at, but, allowing for recent growth, total world foreign exchange trade daily is probably now up to around $300bn, implying that some $80 trillion ($80 000bn) is washing through the world's exchanges during the total business days of each year. Since this is roughly forty times world goods trade of about $2 trillion – or perhaps thirty times trade plus 'invisibles', such as insurance – it is a vivid reminder of the frenetic activity generated in today's free money markets beyond the volume of underlying 'business'. Busy trading in the Euro credit market, numerous swap deals, Eurobond and other securities market turnover, together with further investment, speculative and other activity, must account for the excess. The awesome figures underline the magnitude of the task central banks face in influencing world-wide currency markets without exchange controls.

With stock and share dealing becoming more international, as investors look across frontiers for the best buys, the world's stock markets are now viewed increasingly as parts of a single whole. Where each was once largely isolated from the others, they are now brought together under the analysts' microscopes and their scale, activity and peformance constantly compared.

While cash investment can be in shares, in government or other bonds in national markets, or in 'offshore' Eurobonds, it is the equity (share) markets which dominate the headlines. There are some 20 000 companies which have their shares listed on one or more stock markets around the world and of these perhaps a tenth, 2000, representing 70 per cent of values, are big enough to be 'international equities' of interest to overseas investors.[13] And what stands out is the huge scale and buoyancy of these equity markets after their long rise in the favourable low-inflation and falling-interest rate conditions of the 1980s, which have heightened the relative attractions of holding financial, compared with physical, assets.

The October 1987 upsets notwithstanding, world equity markets stand at the start of 1988 at historically lofty levels, having reached, in July 1987, a peak total value of $7·8 trillion ($7800bn).[14] This was almost double their $4 trillion figure at the end of 1985 and was just down to $6·8 trillion in United States dollar terms even after the first (October) ravages of the autumn turmoil. Throughout 1987 the American and British share markets stood at least ten times higher than in the depressed mid-seventies, the rise being due far more to higher prices than to new share issues.

At the end of 1987, the United States accounted for only 31 per cent of share market values world wide, expressed in dollars, compared with 61 per cent twelve years earlier. The fall in the American proportion reflected the decline in the dollar, along with the surge in numerous other world markets which have grown more prominent with the new eighties cult of the equity internationally. Japan overtook the United States for top place during 1987, reaching a 42 per cent share. Britain took third size position, with 9 per cent. No other country held as much as a 4 per cent proportion, Germany having just over 3 per cent and Canada just under that level.[15]

While Britain's share market is less than a third of that of the United States, it is already notably international, which is encouraging for City ambitions that its next big act should be to promote itself as a world equity, or 'Euro-equity', market. Investors' dealings in foreign shares (much in 1987 still outside the Stock Exchange) are often in busy times about £1bn a day, not a great deal less than those in United Kingdom domestic shares.

Prominent world equities include America's IBM and General Motors, France's Peugeot, Germany's Hoechst, Italy's Fiat, Japan's Sony and Hitachi, and Britain's BP and ICI. Of London dealings in foreign shares in the first half of 1987, the biggest slice (21 per cent) was in Japanese shares, but trade in European issues was also large. In May London turnover in Holland's Royal Dutch was almost half that done in Amsterdam.[16] Salomon Brothers has estimated that foreign investors account for 36 per cent of share turnover in Britain.[17] For their part, leading British shares are actively traded in New York, packaged into convenient dollar form as ADRs (American Depositary Receipts), while United Kingdom investors show enough interest in United States markets to have invested $5bn there in 1986.[18]

Generally speaking, yearly trading in shares in the various national markets adds up to less than the values outstanding. It was approaching $3 trillion, about half of quoted market values at the time, in 1986, and, remarkably, was slightly less than that year's $3·6 trillion activity in the smaller-value, but most hectically traded, Eurobond market. This suggests that many ordinary equity investors are prepared to stick quietly with their shareholdings, however busily others speculate. Morgan Stanley, the American investment bank, has calculated[19] on 1986 figures that yearly turnover ranges down from 65 per cent of outstanding share values in Japan, through a comparable 63 per cent in Germany and 62 per cent in the United States to only 33 per cent in Britain and a mere 19 per cent in patient Singapore. This suggests that British investors on average alter their shareholdings once, and Americans, twice, every three years.

The separate government bond markets also loom large for investors and among them by far the biggest is that in United States Treasury bonds and notes, known in shorthand as T-bonds. The marketable portion of the T-bond issue exceeds $1·6 trillion, which compares with Britain's £133bn ($198bn) gilts and Japan's outstanding government bond issue at the equivalent of $1 trillion or so. West Germany's corresponding issue is equal to $152bn, all the figures in this paragraph being as at the end of 1986.

As the American budget deficit has yawned from $23bn in 1972 to $221bn (1986), more and more bonds have been issued to finance it and have increasingly been bought by Japanese and other foreign investors, who now hold some 15 per cent of this huge debt. The result is that the United States T-bond market is now highly international, regarded as a key indicator of world interest rates, and hugely active. Turnover in it far exceeds that in all the world share markets put together and also that in Eurobonds: indeed, foreign activity alone in T-bonds is over $2 trillion a year[20] and the total, including United States dealings, is more than ten times as high.

An important part in this market is played by the City of London, which in 1986 saw $444bn of dealings conducted in T-bonds,[21] some $1·75bn on average each business day. 'Derivatives' like zero-coupon bonds, where the principal is dealt in separately from the stream of interest entitlement, are busily traded adjuncts, in London as in New York. Part of the reason for the scale of this trading through the City is that Britain's time zone position enables it to provide an instant dealing service to investors when the New York market is closed. T-bond trading forms a big part of the activity of the much enlarged community of United States securities and investment houses in London, which also contend for international equity business. One sizeable American investment bank boasted as long ago as 1986 that its City telephone bill was larger than that of one of the two main United Kingdom stock jobbers.

As markets have changed, so have investors and, while once

individuals were the main shareholders, now the large institutions have succeeded to that role in advanced countries. Big funds representing millions of present and future pensioners in companies throughout the world exercise major investment sway, as do insurance groups on behalf of numerous policyholders. InterSec estimates put pension fund assets round the globe at the end of 1986 at a huge $3·1 trillion[22] which, though a good deal of it will be in bonds and property, must account for a fair slice of the $7 trillion or so global share capitalisation. Insurance funds, another large savings medium, may almost rival pension holdings in some countries, while other pooled investing through unit trusts (mutual funds in the United States) and further routes is, though smaller, substantial also. Portfolios run by professional managers for wealthy people, affectionately known as HINWIES (high net-worth individuals) are a further investment segment. For instance, Union Bank of Switzerland – largest of the Swiss banks which are beloved of the world's rich on account of their skill and secrecy – has been credited with managing investments of about $200bn.

Altogether, direct investment by individuals has now been far outstripped by the activities of the investing institutions, the new market mammoths. In Britain, while a quarter of a century ago personal investors held 54 per cent of United Kingdom shares and institutions 30 per cent, the roles have now been firmly reversed. The individuals' share had dropped by 1981 to only 28 per cent and that of the institutional proportion had climbed to 58 per cent,[23] from which it has since risen to over 60 per cent. (Foreign, charity and other additional holdings make up the balance.) Despite the Thatcher government's efforts to widen shareholding, the direct personal stake remains proportionately modest. For, although nearly 20 per cent of people in Britain, against only 7 per cent in 1979, are now reckoned to own some shares, more than half the new investors only hold privatisation stocks, such as British Gas. In the wealthier United States, only just over a quarter of adults are direct investors.

The position is different in the 'offshore' Eurobond market, to which wealthy individuals have traditionally been the main suppliers of funds as investors. The shy international rich value the absence of tax deduction from interest and the bonds' discreetly bearer character. They also welcome the high-quality character of the issuers, which means that defaults are almost unknown, so that bonds can be locked away with safety. Although the relative attraction of United States T-bonds to world investors has been somewhat strengthened with the introduction of untaxed interest payments to foreign holders, the comparative appeal of Eurobonds has been sustained by their anonymity and the fact that they come in a wide choice of currency and other forms. A number of institutions, including 'captive' insurance firms handling the in-house risks of United States corporations from 'offshore' tax havens and inhibited from buying United States T-bonds, invest in Eurobonds. But there have been recent signs that the dominance of the private investor is reasserting itself in the market. Buyers range from that classic well-off personal saver, the Belgian dentist, through Eastern magnates, Latin American farmers and successful United States businessmen to numerous non-taxpaying expatriates throughout the globe.

With its extensive banking activity, including 'merchant banking' advisory and investment management work, a wide span of securities trading and a big insurance industry, along with commodity, bullion and other markets, the City embraces a spectrum of almost bewildering variety. It is thus not surprising that a crowded financial community now clusters together in and around its narrow confines, vying for shares of the wide-ranging business. Around about 500 foreign banks, including 59 American and 47 Japanese, now have a presence in London out of a United Kingdom total, with native British groups, of some six hundred banks. On top of that, a much increased total of 121 securities houses, among them 38 from the United States and 37 from Japan, also cram into the City and its environs.[24] The breadth of the international flavour can constantly be glimpsed, as in King William Street, across which the USSR's Moscow Narodny Bank, in London since 1919, just after the Russian revolution, faces France's largest bank, Banque Nationale de Paris, which first came to the City in 1867. Since the Big Bang expansion in the stock market, conditions have grown so congested and floor space so dear that some offices have spilt out of the Square Mile heartland of the financial district. Further-flung offices in peripheral sites, which are acceptable in today's electronic markets, range from Salomon Brothers' new glass palace at Victoria Plaza in the west to the Isle of Dogs' giant new docklands Canary Wharf structure eastwards.

The City doubles as the focus of Britain's own financial industry, which radiates out in networks of bank, insurance and building society branches through the country, and as an international money centre. Of the 2·3m (some 10 per cent of the United Kingdom's working population) people employed in banking, finance and insurance in Britain in 1987, compared with 1·9m two years earlier, the City employs up to half a million. The foreign banks and securities houses alone have a work-force of over 72 000 people, a figure increased by 34 per cent in 1987, following a 26 per cent rise the previous year.[25] These figures suggest that, even if the staff shake-out at United States and other houses following the October 1987 market crash goes further, the City's employment total after the big recruitment drive, which sent salaries soaring before Big Bang, will stay high, short of any market Armageddon.

The very multiplicity of institutions is a strength to the City because the fact that each rubs shoulders with so many others means it has convenient access to needed services. Bullion traders, for example, require insurance and securities dealers foreign exchange and various hedging facilities. And the City too has such a reservoir of what supports a financial market – from lawyers to skilled clerks and from office space to restaurants and wine bars – that it would not be easy for the most determined competitor to emulate it elsewhere. This helps explain way, although other cities have set up 'offshore' markets with tax concessions – New York's International Business Facilities (IBF) in 1982 and more recently in Tokyo's offshore market – they have not stolen London's thunder as an all-purpose international financial centre.

The City in its broadest sense is also a major 'invisible exporter', its net earnings of foreign exchange for Britain's payments balance having reached £9·4bn in 1986, against only £1·5bn ten years earlier. Insurance is the biggest contributor, with £4·3bn, followed by banking with £2·3bn. This important input to a private sector 'invisibles' balance of £12bn helps explain why the government and the Bank of England have so strongly fostered the City's business development, though considerations of national pride are also involved.

The present, more one-world, financial system has many merits, often including ones of efficiency and cheaper charges to users as a result of competition and economies brought by the new technology. But the increasingly integrated structure also has dangers which national authorities cannot ignore. For crises can ripple more quickly through a linked-up system. The outbreak of the third-world debt crisis in 1982, when Mexico and others could not repay billions of dollars of debt to hundreds of banks, posed a threat to the world's bank groups. The dangers were only stemmed because the central banks of the Western countries stepped in to mobilise rescue action. Since then the Bank of England and its counterparts abroad have nudged commercial banks into new precautionary measures.

In parallel, stock markets also need supervision against both malpractice and imprudence, whose consequences could be direr than ever in the freer-market world. While the United States has its statutory Securities and Exchange Commission (SEC), Britain is experimenting with a fresh watchdog body combining law and self-regulation, but with the legal muscle increasingly apparent. Time will show how this system, based on the private Securities and Investments Board (SIB), operating through delegated legal powers and with a group of five sector self-regulating organisations (SROs), works out in practice. It remains to be seen whether SIB, with its unusual hybrid structure, will be firm enough to ensure fair treatment of investors, without unduly shackling enterprise or getting bogged down in a legal quagmire. There are senior City people who feel that the high standards needed in modern markets will in the end necessitate a fully legal SEC-style regulator.

Since the build-up to the major changes involved in London's 1986 Big Bang stock market revolution to meet modern conditions began, the City has changed character, culturally as well as organisationally. A more transatlantic, or mid-Atlantic, accent is evident, with the adjustment to an increasingly standardised world market norm. 'The City has changed. It's very, very American', says a chief of one of the biggest British-owned securities houses. The average age of staff seems lower, as the revamped markets place a greater premium on youth and energy and less value on experience as old skills grow obsolescent. Even appearance is different. The formal days, when City gentlemen came to the office in a bowler hat, changed it for a top hat to go round the market, then changed back for lunch and the journey home, are fading, though the top hat survives in the gilts and linked discount markets. Most people – including Americans – go hatless and the bowler seems to be on its way out. At the launch of the TSB share issue – advertised with a bowler-hatted mob of improbable-looking investors – one journalist protested that bowlers were only now worn by bookies and butchers. (It is different, though, in Whitehall where, they say, nothing can move in a bowler hat without being smartly saluted as a possible officer of Her Majesty's Forces.)

As working rhythms adapt to the need to link in with other centres, life-styles have been transformed. The once leisurely City tenor of activity and exclusive club atmosphere have been replaced by the brasher, more hectic atmosphere suited to the global market-place. Business days stretch out up to twelve hours. 'Virtually everybody's in the office by 7.30 am, nobody later than 8.15', says one boss 'and nobody leaves before 6.30. Also, somebody has to be on tap round the clock for the international markets. Stress and strain? We watch for signs of it and try when appropriate to get our people away for short holidays.' Some senior managers are getting used to being telephoned in the night by nervous young dealers wanting authority for especially big deals with New York or Tokyo.

A widely felt regret is that, with the replacement of the Stock Exchange trading floor by the post-Big Bang screen-based market, brokers no longer meet other members and swap gossip throughout the day. Some also argue the change impedes smooth functioning of the market at the margin. There are, for instance, now no half-commission men standing around, as before, to absorb unwanted remnants of offered blocks of shares. Lack of a floor meeting-place makes the new market less companionable, as it is also less convivial.

Certainly it is widely claimed that there is now less eating and drinking in the City. And though the claret and port lunch cannot be said to have vanished, 'there are probably', as a leading American points out, 'more breakfasts than lunches now served in the Square Mile'. The breakfast meeting to assess global developments overnight and fix the day's strategy is indeed one of the City's important recent innovations. One bank chairman compares his chief dealer's briefing of his forces before a day's trading in the aftermath of the October 1987 crash with Henry V's exhortation to his troops before Agincourt.

The vocabulary too is altering. 'Fast buck', even 'fast money' sound dated, though 'slow money', meaning remuneration falling due over time, is in. So is 'serious money', a term which has given its name to a play (by Caryl Churchill), or, still more sophisticatedly, 'grown-up money', both meaning cash in substantial quantity. And the new glossary extends further, with such expressions relevant to employment deals as 'golden hello', 'golden handcuffs' and 'golden parachute' now more used than the long-familiar 'golden handshake'.

This chapter has been designed to sketch a broad setting, against which the City's recent development can be further considered. A closer look will now be taken at the complex and curious process by which the Big Bang stock market revolution came about, and the dramatic nature of the City's restructuring and its spin-offs, including the enrichment of many stockbrokers. An outline will follow of the securities market changes and their first effects, along with a glance at other markets in the City to show the ambit of its main services.

It is not only the securities markets which have evolved almost out of recognition in the changes that have swept the world financial scene, and Britain's City in its broad sense as the United Kingdom's financial industry, in recent years. Much in the banking world has also been transformed, as will be discussed in chapters covering the big British high street clearing bank groups, the merchant banks and other banking sectors. The investing institutions, now the chief users of securities market services and powerful influences on the markets, are next considered. Some important further institutions, such as the insurance industry and the building societies, are glanced at more briefly.

The Bank of England, at the summit of the City and in impalpable and changing relationships with the government, is the next subject, followed by a review of the new arrangements for City regulation. The book then ends with some commentary on recent events.

2 The Government–Stock Exchange Accord

> Having this monopolistic market [the Stock Exchange] fixing its own prices ... it couldn't go on.
>
> A banker.

The story of how Britain's City revolution – a pace-setter in the global money shake-up – came about is an instructive example of how big events in national affairs can happen in a largely unplanned way. Strands of development intertwined, disparate forces contended over years and the outcome was what nobody had at first foreseen. Yet, as the drama unfolded, a degree of creative guidance was imposed and events were finally shaped to harmonise with the spirit of the time and the less than half-formulated instincts of Britain's new Conservative leaders. Along the way, money men were spectacularly enriched, hallowed procedures were flouted and some official feelings were deeply bruised. It is a tale of how the unthinkable – a total about-turn in the Stock Exchange's system and ownership – became the actual and how an era of stability gave way to one of helter-skelter change. The trigger to the revolution was a pact with the government in late July 1983 for reform of the Exchange's rules.

Yet, to most eyes, there was little as late as the festive midsummer of 1983 to hint that the City of London was on the eve of a financial earthquake. The atmosphere was one of relaxed cheer among investors and stock market men alike. And with good reason. Less than a month earlier, Mrs Margaret Thatcher's Conservatives, traditionally the businessman's friend, had been triumphantly voted back to power in a general election. Stockbrokers let their attention stray to Ascot races and Wimbledon tennis, knowing that business was prospering.

The past year, 1982–3, had been a vintage one, the best on record, for the Stock Exchange, helped by a climb of over 20 per cent in share prices and buoyancy in gilt-edged government bonds. Several broker moguls were authoritatively reported to have earned over £1 million and employees to have doubled their salaries with bonuses.[1] The seventy-year-old fixed commission pattern of charges for stock market dealing was working in brokers' favour, since it operated as a

23

sliding-scale percentage tariff on what was proving growing business
volume at rising prices.

Stocks and shares could only be bought or sold on the Stock
Exchange, whether by the humblest pensioner or the richest investing
institution, through a stockbroker. The broker acted as an agent,
dealing on his client's behalf with the 'wholesaler', the stockjobber,
who traded from a 'book' of stocks and shares. For this service, the
broker made a charge, known as commission, to the investor.
Commission income accounted for the bulk of the takings of
stockbroking firms, the partnerships – sometimes private companies
– in which brokers were organised.

There was, and still is, more dealing volume on the Exchange in
gilt-edged stocks than in British shares and this was particularly so in
the 1970s and early 1980s when British governments were churning
out new gilts to finance big Budget deficits. Dealings in gilts by
institutions like insurance groups and pension funds being very large
and frequent – it is worth being active in big amounts to profit from
small market changes – the brokers' business in this field tended to be
particularly profitable at fixed commission rates and several broker
firms made a speciality of gilts. The fact that there was a floor under
commission rates – save those on short gilts, which were negotiable –
meant that, in booming markets, broking firms' revenue went
soaring. The opposite was of course also true, as had been shown in
the mid-1970s' crash when steep falls in stock prices slashed revenue
and profits and the Exchange's total work-force was cut by nearly a
third.[2]

Shyly, the Stock Exchange did not publish estimates of broker and
jobber firms' revenue, nor did these overwhelmingly private businesses reveal their own figures. None the less, clues are available
from which it is clear that, in 1983, commission takings had for some
time been rising sharply. For, since the troubled mid-seventies, a
'general service' charge towards the Exchange's own increasing costs
had been levied at varying rates. From the yield of this, which *is*
published, it is possible to make a rough rule-of-thumb calculation[3]
of the total revenue, the largest part of it derived from commissions
on dealing for clients, of the Stock Exchange's firms. Thus revenue
looks to have risen from some £190m in the drab year of 1976–7 to
around £265m in 1979–80, the first mainly 'Thatcher' year, which saw
better markets. There was a levelling-off in 1980–81, when interest
rates jumped discouragingly and share prices ebbed accordingly.
Next there followed new rises to some £490m in 1981–2 and then, in

1982–3, just before the big changes were to be set in train, to perhaps £580m. Of these figures, up to three-quarters was attributable to broking firms, most of it for share deals, but a significant part for gilts business. A further record in commission take was to be set in the following year, 1983–4, the best, up to that time, in the Exchange's history.[4] Thereafter, the upward trend was maintained as the stock market continued booming.

These rising revenues were clearly making a lucrative living for the Exchange's firms, most of which had to meet only moderate costs. A prosperous year meant a generous pay-out to the partners who owned the Stock Exchange businesses and a rise too in the worth of their investment, in so far as profit was ploughed back into the firm. Employees too would collect useful bonuses. The jobber firms did not have their earnings as neatly geared to market price and volume as did the far more numerous brokers. Unpredictable price gyrations could hit their 'books', though, generally, rising markets helped them. Accounts of the larger of the two jobbers whose own shares were quoted, Akroyd & Smithers, show that its pre-tax profits tumbled in the difficult year 1980–81 to £5·9 million from £20·5 million, then bounced up to £25·0 million in 1981–2, easing the next year to £16·0 million. All told, though, profits were going very well in mid-1983 for the Exchange's 4269 members spread among 225 firms.

But the basis on which they were earned – the fixed commission tariff – had not gone uncriticised. Indeed a major legal challenge to it as a restrictive practice had for some time been impending and was due to come to court in a few months' time. Its purpose was nothing less than to bring the breath of competition into the pricing of stock and share deals, as had happened in New York's 1975 'Mayday' commission rates unfixing, and to introduce other reforms.

The action, however, had horrified the stock market men, who saw their income threatened through a resultant squeeze on their commission rates, and their whole way of life menaced. The prospect was particularly galling for the powerful brokers specialising in gilts. 'The main problem', a critical member of the Exchange fraternity remarked in retrospect, 'was the vast profits being made by the gilt brokers, who said: "Don't rock the boat; it [the current fixed commission system] will see us out".'

Commission revenue and profits on gilts broking was particularly contentious in the early eighties when they ran at a very high level because of the big volume of deficit-financing government stocks. For instance, gilts accounted for some 30 per cent of all commission revenue in 1980 and 1981, against only 10 per cent in the more tightly budgeted 1986, and the gilts takings in question were concentrated in a handful of major broking houses. Gilts dealing was highly profitable compared with other forms of broking, as was clearly indicated in a later Stock Exchange paper which noted: 'The huge growth in Government Funding over the past ten years may have led to dealing operations in the UK equities market as a whole being subsidised by the profits generated by the gilt market.'[5]

The looming legal challenge had its roots in initiatives stretching some way back, under mainly Conservative governments. There is a certain piquancy in that the protectionism which the Exchange displayed in defending its system is as dear to Conservative hearts – such as those found nearly exclusively in the Stock Exchange – as is the competitive principle which prompted the developing case. Indeed, these two warring concepts have been vying for Tory loyalties ever since the free trade–tariff reform strife of a century ago.

The postwar Tory competition crusade dates back to the Restrictive Trade Practices Act 1956, associated with the name of Mr Edward Heath, which de-fixed the prices of many goods previously pegged by 'resale price maintenance'. Then, in the Fair Trading Act 1973, the Conservative government of which Mr Heath was Prime Minister took power to extend the RTP control to services. This was done by the successor Labour government – competition policy tended to be bi-partisan – in the Restrictive Trade Practices (Services) Order 1976. The Stock Exchange failed to make a successful case for getting its rules clawed out of this Order when others, like some of the building societies' agreements, were exempted.[6] The Stock Exchange was accordingly required to register its 170-item 'rule book' of restrictions, including its fixed commissions and the 'single capacity' system under which brokers acted as investors' agents, jobbers made markets, and neither could trespass on the other's territory. 'A massive amount of paper', including numerous circulars to members, was involved in this registration procedure, somebody concerned remembers.

It was then for the Director General of Fair Trading, entrusted under the 1973 Act with administering the restrictive practices and monopolies and mergers law through his Office of Fair Trading (OFT), to consider whether the contents of the Stock Exchange rule-book should next be referred to the Restrictive Practices Court. If they were so referred, it would be for the Court to judge whether they should be scrapped or given a seal of approval as justified in the public interest.

The Director General, Sir (then Mr) Gordon Borrie, took the view that the rule-book clearly contained restrictive practices, including the minimum commission tariff, and should be referred. This was done, in February 1979, after a Stock Exchange appeal to Mr Roy Hattersley, the Labour Minister responsible for the OFT (an associate of the Trade Ministry), to abort the process had failed. Thus the competitive challenge was cleared to proceed. Then began a lengthy process of preparation for the case on both sides – by the OFT as plaintiff and the Stock Exchange as defendant – which involved a cost of millions of pounds in legal and other expenses and made a heavy call on the time, energy and expertise of many people in the Stock Exchange, the OFT and elsewhere. It not only led the Exchange and the OFT to scrutinise the existing system deeply, but caused others, notably the Bank of England, eventually to take a fresh look at the City's role in a changing world in a way that was to have revolutionary consequences.

Well as the Stock Exchange's members, including its influential 47-member ruling Council, knew their own market at working level, they were little practised, before the late seventies, in surveying and discussing it in detail for the public eye. For its part, the Office of Fair Trading had amassed detailed skills in assessing trade monopolies and considering mergers. But services in general were a newer field to it, while the finer points of stock market practice were not easy to penetrate. Nor was the Exchange noted for admitting outsiders to its inner workings and thinking or for unveiling all its vital statistics. Even textbooks did not tell the full story of an ever-evolving market, while, as to academic studies, these seemed more plentiful across the Atlantic – where New York's 1975 changes had been much studied – than in the United Kingdom. For both the Exchange and the OFT, therefore, much work lay ahead in preparing for what would be a landmark case. Yet each had, one way or another, been approaching the task for some two years when the formal reference of the Exchange's 'rule-book' was made to the Restrictive Practices Court in early 1979.

As it happened, the Stock Exchange had then just been gaining vital experience in publicly explaining its structures. Not so long before the OFT challenge was launched, it had been called on to give evidence on its own market and organisation to the Wilson committee appointed in 1977 by the Labour Prime Minister, Lord (then Mr James) Callaghan, to review Britain's financial institutions. Many at the time saw the creation of the committee, chaired by the former Prime Minister, Lord Wilson of Rievaulx (at that time Sir Harold Wilson) as chiefly aimed at side-tracking left-wing Labour pressure for the nationalisation of banks. In the event, the Wilson committee, after taking extensive evidence, made a very wide-ranging investigation into the financial system, helped by detailed material provided from many quarters. Though its practical consequences were slight the committee's report[7] threw much useful light on the system.

To prepare its evidence to Wilson, the Stock Exchange chose a small committee chaired by one of its best brains, a member of its Council and a former deputy chairman, Mr David LeRoy-Lewis, who was also chairman of the large jobber Akroyd & Smithers. Mr LeRoy-Lewis, an Old Etonian, at once courteous and brisk and with a considerable sense of humour, was used to running an efficient business and proved a good choice for this special role. Others in the high-level group included three colleagues who were all later to be deputy chairmen of the Exchange. They were Mr George Nissen, chief of brokers Pember & Boyle, Mr Peter Wills of Sheppards & Chase, brokers, and Mr Patrick Mitford-Slade, of Cazenove, one of the larger broking firms, which is active as a broker to big companies and has legendary 'placing' power in distributing shares to major clients. They were joined in 1978 by Mr John Young, who had been voted a broker member of the Council and who later, in 1982, became the Exchange's policy and planning director.

Members of this expert group recall the daunting nature of the task of describing their Exchange in all its aspects for Wilson as they gazed at blank sheets of paper at their first meeting. However, the assignment was successfully completed and the committee was next asked to work on the Exchange's defence against the OFT challenge in the Restrictive Practices Court. From the first, the Exchange had to face the fact that its fixed commission structure, and perhaps other aspects of its rule-book, *were* in the nature of restrictive practices. Consultations ensued with the Exchange's legal advisers – their leading Counsel was Mr Anthony Graham-Dixon QC and their solicitors were Linklaters & Paines, a leading City firm – and with their outside specialist advisers, who included academics. The Stock Exchange men took their advisers down to the market floor in

Throgmorton Street on occasion, to instruct them, it is said, on some matters of practice which were not always quite as represented in economic textbooks.

The author has been told that, quite early on, advisers to the Exchange began to come to the conclusion that the chances of winning on the fixed commission structure alone were poor – that it would be 'almost a miracle', in the memory of one close to the scene, if the case for its defence in isolation succeeded. How, after all, could one justify this fixed-charge practice, when the whole restrictive trade practices law was aimed at furthering a freer market?

But of course fixed commissions were only part of what was at issue. If they could be understood as an essential feature of a valuable market structure, the position would look far different. Mr LeRoy-Lewis then took the problem away over a weekend early in 1979 and wrote a detailed paper to demonstrate that fixed commissions were, in fact, inseparable from the single-capacity market, with its broker–jobber split, which had long made for stability and which worked against conflicts of interest.

The argument was in essence that this desirable separation of function could not survive a free-for-all on commission charges. For, were fixed commissions to go, the brokers, with their revenue squeezed by competition, would seek an increasing dealing role for themselves in quest of compensating profits. Existing pressures for brokers effectively to make 'matched bargains' between buyers and sellers among their own clients, and to hold stock for trading, would be immeasurably, irresistibly increased. But, if this development occurred, it would drain business from the jobbers who, in turn, would seek to trade direct with the public. The whole 'single capacity' system that had stood investors and the City in good stead for seventy years would crumble.

This persuasive line of reasoning became known as the 'link argument' and was soon embraced by the Exchange as the cornerstone of its defence. Mr LeRoy-Lewis, from then known in the City as the 'father of the link argument', later stressed that the analysis was not simply constructed as a justification of minimum commissions. It was an elucidation of the position as it was, a 'stringing together of the facts that were there, but had never been linked in that way'.[8] The premise that supported the link argument was, of course, that the single capacity system was itself meritorious, not least because under it the broker's interests were the same as his client's, which they might not have been had he been running a 'book' of shares himself. A City banker later remarked: 'All the case rested on was the moral rectitude of single capacity.'

Other important parts of the case to be deployed by the Exchange in defence of its whole structure concerned the speed and efficiency of its existing settlement systems, its 'listing' agreement of conditions for share quotation, and its supervision of its markets and members.

If extensive descriptions and defences of the Stock Exchange's system made testing demands on its own top people, the task for the challenger of its alleged restrictive practices – the Office of Fair Trading – was yet more formidable. Despite all the resources of the Office, its experts and advisers, the assembling of needed facts on the somewhat secretive Stock Exchange, let alone the wider background necessary to persuade the Court that the Exchange's restrictions should, in the public interest, be dropped, was no light task. In the late 1970s, even the Wilson report, with considerable descriptions of the stock market's workings, had not been published, relevant up-to-date textbooks and surveys were few, and the Exchange, perhaps understandably, gave the impression of wishing to keep itself to itself. The preliminary building of a stock of all relevant information, British and overseas, was in itself a major undertaking, quite apart from the extensive programme, also carried out by OFT officials, of discussions within the City and enquiry into practice abroad.

Under the Director General of Fair Trading, Sir Gordon Borrie, the leader of the team working on the case from 1977 to 1983 was the Assistant Secretary in charge of the restrictive practices side of the OFT, Lady (Olive) Wood. The widow of a former top Defence Ministry official, Sir Frank Wood, she had, after an earlier stint in Whitehall, returned there following her husband's death. Upon this woman civil servant in her early fifties, a history graduate with an outgoing personality and no want of determination, rested much of the responsibility for challenging the basic rules of one of the City's most august institutions. Another member of the OFT staff much concerned was an Australian, Mr Maxwell Hill, an economist with the Aussie's downright manner and characteristic lack of reverence for established institutions. The Treasury Solicitor acted for the OFT, whose chief counsel was, first, Mr Christopher Staughton QC. When he soon afterwards became a Judge, he was succeeded by Mr Leonard Hoffmann QC (now Mr Justice Hoffman) for the main period of the case. Like the Stock Exchange, the OFT also had outside advisers, chiefly academics.

Lady Wood recalled in later years:

> We did start off in some ignorance of the Stock Exchange system.
> There was great difficulty in finding out exactly how it worked –
> even understanding something like the dealing glossary of the
> Exchange – from books and so forth. But we pressed on, and all
> the time we were educating ourselves by gaining knowledge abroad
> as well as at home and talking as widely as we could in the City.[9]

The work – and it was merely one part, though an important one, of
the OFT's Restrictive Practices duties – extended over six years and
involved detailed scrutiny and appraisal of numerous 'rule-book'
restrictions, their effects and the results the scrapping of similar curbs
in North America. Gradually dossiers of relevant information were
assembled on a wide range of markets in the United Kingdom and
overseas, including Europe, the United States, Canada, Australia,
the Far East and elsewhere. Visits were made, particularly to the
United States, where the sequel to New York's 1975 abolition of its
fixed commissions – heavy cuts in the cost of transacting large
institutional deals – was specially relevant, and to Canada, where
some restrictions had also been eased. Certain detailed studies were
commissioned and the case was gradually built up, under Sir Gordon
Borrie's direction, in consultation with the legal advisers.

The two sides saw very little of each other, but it is worth recalling
a story about one occasion. The OFT and its advisers had sought a
meeting with Stock Exchange experts to expand their background
knowledge, and this was fixed up, along with visits to a member firm's
premises and to the trading floor of the Exchange. The arrangements
were made through the good offices of the Exchange's first-ever chief
executive, the former senior Civil Servant, Mr Robert Fell, who after
a successful spell at the Exchange later went on to a distinguished role
as Hong Kong's chief regulator, first of securities markets and then of
banks.

At this unusual gathering, unique in bringing together representatives of the plaintiff – the OFT's staff and its legal and other advisers
– with those of the defendant Exchange, there was a detectable sense
of opposed viewpoints, even cultures. And Mr LeRoy-Lewis, who
had been pressed, rather against his feelings, to give the OFT party a
discourse on the workings of the jobbing system, prefaced his
remarks – jocularly, but perhaps not quite jokingly – by saying he
was not used to helping the enemy.

When this was recalled some years afterwards, Mr LeRoy-Lewis voiced astonishment that it should have been remembered, but clearly recalled the occasion:

> Some of us were asked to give a half an hour's talk on certain aspects of the Stock Exchange. I was invited to talk about jobbers and what jobbers did and why jobbers were there and everything about jobbing. Now, I thought that this was a slightly remarkable way of going about it and, although I knew something about the legal principle of discovery, I scarcely felt comfortable about it. I did, I think, say, now I am reminded of it, that I hoped that I was going to give them the right sort of – the right amount of – information, but I was *inclined*, having regard to their role in the affair, to tell them nothing![10]

Whether or not further enlightened by this meeting, the OFT team, with its lawyers, continued with its scrutiny of the long list of rules and agreements which the Stock Exchange had registered as the first stage in the whole legal process.

Very far from all the Stock Exchange restrictions were to be challenged: 'It was always recognised', an OFT official said afterwards, 'that you don't run a market without restrictions.' But on each of the very many that were up for rulings under the Act, an OFT judgment, for the purpose of the 'pleadings', had to be made on whether a 'restriction' was to be 'denied' (opposed outright), 'admitted' (no objection being raised), or placed in the more indeterminate category of 'not admitted', implying to the Court some reserve on the Office's part about the practice.

The chief restrictions singled out for attack were the tapering tariffs of minimum commissions rates, which meant that brokers could not compete to provide cheaper dealing, the 'single capacity' system of separation between broker and jobber, and the fact that brokers could not trade on their own account. Certain other restrictions also caused concern, as the Office's knowledge of them developed. It was widely reported later that the OFT felt strongly that the Exchange should be opened up to new entrants, and it seems likely that this was so.

Under the law, the Stock Exchange's defence of the challenged rules could be through several 'gateways', grounds which the Act set out on which defendants could seek to justify their 'restrictions'. The gateway that would probably have to be opened up if the Exchange were to win was that of a demonstration that abolition of the 'restrictions' would deny the public, as purchasers, benefits or advantages. In other words, the Exchange would have to prove that its restrictive rules were helpful rather than the reverse to the investing public, and so not against the public interest.

A lengthy and closely argued case, ranging widely, but centred importantly on the link argument, was put into the Court by the Exchange in defence of its system in 1981. The OFT responded and preparatory argument continued, with the case due to be heard before Mr Justice Lincoln early in 1984. Unusually, the hearing would have a 'predictive' character, in that it would revolve round the likely consequences of various possible changes, rather than centring on known facts, as in many judicial proceedings.

One of the Exchange's complaints from early on was that a chaotic situation, disrupting market business disastrously, would result if the Court were to come down against its rule-book, requiring its abandonment before anything could be worked out to replace it. To meet this point, the new Conservative government included in the Competition Act 1980 a section enabling the Restrictive Practices Court to postpone the coming into force of a declaration that an agreement was contrary to the public interest so that those concerned could work out, and submit for its approval, an alternative arrangement. This provision facilitated the negotiation of a compromise solution in another OFT case before the Court, that affecting the Association of British Travel Agents (ABTA), and would have made possible a similar procedure in the far more prominent Stock Exchange affair.

From the late-seventies, as the OFT case loomed ever larger as a key issue, the then relatively new Stock Exchange chairman, Sir (at that time, Mr) Nicholas Goodison, became increasingly concerned in preparations for it. Important as it was, though, the OFT's action was only one among a cluster of difficult, and often related, questions then preoccupying Sir Nicholas and the Exchange's ruling Council in a rapidly changing world. Another problem was that Stock Exchange firms, being held to dealing as either brokers or jobbers, were increasingly losing business in international shares to American and other foreign 'dual capacity' houses which could both collect and themselves transact orders. After exchange control was dropped in 1979, this difficulty grew more acute since the great majority of United Kingdom investors' swiftly growing overseas share-buying business was captured by foreign dealers. Minor easements were made to Exchange rules to let members deal more flexibly abroad but these did not put the United Kingdom firms on an even footing with their overseas competitors. And more radical change was eschewed since it was always feared that this could imply a breach in the single-capacity principle and undermine the main defence to the OFT challenge.

An earlier scheme for the Exchange to grow more competitive internationally by making commissions negotiable on international share trades only had also been shelved as its effects would have seeped through to domestic shares: by drastically slashing their charges on overseas share deals, brokers could indirectly have been subsidising those on home business too and so effectively 'unfixing' them. And these were just some of the problems – others concerned the adequacy of Exchange firms' capital and the possibility of in some way admitting foreign members – which confronted the Exchange's chairman and his colleagues at the start of the decade.

Sir Nicholas was to have a central role as head of the governing Council in debating, negotiating, and defending numerous crucial changes at the heart of the City revolution which has now transformed Britain's financial industry. It is one of the fortuitous aspects of the City's recent development that this growingly influential figure came when he did to be in the Exchange's top role. Voted in on the sudden death after a short tenure of his predecessor, Mr Michael Marriott, Sir Nicholas, senior partner of his medium-sized family broking firm, took over as the Exchange's youngest chairman in living memory, at the age of only 41, in 1976.

The new chairman contrasted in his relative youth and academic style with the traditional choice for the post of an older stockbroker nearing the end of his career. He is a significant scholar, an expert on antique clocks and an opera buff, being vice chairman of English National Opera. In a tenure that has unprecedentedly stretched well over twelve years into the late eighties, Sir Nicholas has demonstrated gifts of creative imagination, resolution and leadership that are akin to the qualities of a successful politician.

Lanky, cool, often aloof, he has a manner that warms to valued friendliness with those he knows well. But he has never seemed 'one of the boys' in the very clubby Stock Exchange and can on occasion look almost an isolated figure. 'Nicholas is one of those people it's not easy to get near to, personally or in any way. But that is perhaps no bad thing in a time of trial such as the Stock Exchange has gone through', a senior Exchange man said in the late eighties, when Sir Nicholas had guided his organisation through massive change. 'He's not that obviously popular among the members, but the vast majority – there's always a lunatic fringe – have an enormous respect for what he's done. Somebody who might have been a hail-fellow-well-met sort of chap would not have got us through these years. I think he was exactly the right man for the job – how clever we were to elect him!'

If coolness is an asset for leading a Stock Exchange through a revolution, Sir Nicholas's was certainly tested in one anguished moment before the main events of the eighties. In April 1981, his own firm, Quilter Hilton Goodison (later Quilter Goodison), was about to put into effect plans to take over the smaller stockbrokers Hedderwick Stirling Grumbar. However, at a very late stage, the result of studies which had been under way into Hedderwick threw up information which caused Quilter not to complete the deal. Sir Nicholas who, as it happened, was that day entertaining the Chancellor of the Exchequer, Sir Geoffrey Howe, to lunch at his firm's offices, found himself escorting this eminent guest to the door shortly before 3.00 pm., then summoning his staff in order to break the shock news that the merger was off. Hedderwick then, on Quilter's advice, reported to the Stock Exchange authorities the nature of its own position, which was that it was not then fully able to meet its obligations. As a consequence, late that Friday, 10 April, Hedderwick was 'hammered' – declared, in Stock Exchange terms, in default – and subsequently passed to a liquidator.

There was plentiful scope for Sir Nicholas' sagacity and diplomacy as his chairmanship got into its stride from the later seventies. After the Tory government succeeded Labour in May 1979, Sir Nicholas, having unsuccessfully asked the previous government to stop the OFT case being launched, appealed for the process of the court hearing to be called off and for matters to be approached in another way. But the new Minister concerned, the Secretary of State for Trade, Sir (then Mr) John Nott, was not sympathetic, clearly feeling it was right for the challenge under the law to a prima facie restrictive practice to take its course.

In August 1980, Sir Nicholas went to see Sir John Nott who, at what was a rather frigid meeting, on the Stock Exchange side at least, appeared to encourage the idea of an attempt at a negotiated solution between the Exchange and Sir Gordon Borrie, who was about to be reappointed as Director General of Fair Trading. But this hint about the pursuit of a compromise outcome was never taken up by the Exchange. An appeal by Sir Nicholas to the next Secretary of State, Mr John Biffen, for the calling off of the case was equally unavailing. This Minister, like his predecessors, was warned about the damage to the general standing of the Restrictive Practices legislation that could have been done by the withdrawal of such an important case as the Stock Exchange one.

In 1980, too, the Wilson committee reported, and gave another opening for a compromise. On the Stock Exchange case it queried whether the procedure via the Court was the best way to consider the matters at issue. Having suggested that there was cause to doubt whether the existing Stock Exchange system would be able to continue without substantial change, irrespective of the Court's decision, it went on:

> Public debate about possible alternatives has been muted by the Stock Exchange's understandable unwillingness to do anything which might weaken its position before the Court. We believe that consideration of alternatives is now urgent and suggest that the Council for the Securities Industry [the then top City watchdog] is the body to undertake this task.[11]

No new development followed this and in October 1980 Lord Wilson wrote to the new Prime Minister, Mrs Thatcher, raising the question of following up what his committee's report had said about the unsatisfactory situation over the Stock Exchange case. There was reference to possible alternatives and in particular to the idea of a small committee to consider the matter.

Mrs Thatcher replied in November, referring to the Exchange's rules involving significant restrictions on competition and noting that the Director General of Fair Trading had had a legal obligation to refer the case. As to possible exemption, the Prime Minister told her predecessor-but-one that her government had re-examined the case since coming to office but had decided, on balance, that such a course would not be justified. The idea of a small committee was not taken up.

As the years had gone by, things had not stood still over the actual business and workings of the Stock Exchange. One of the biggest long-run changes was the one under which the bulk of business had come to be done for the major investing institutions, rather than for the private investor. There were various consequences of this shift, one being that dealings were in larger, more 'lumpy', amounts. This meant that, if business swayed strongly one way – say, by many holders selling at a gloomy time – it might strain the resources of the jobbers who, by buying and selling stock, cushioned price changes and kept up a continuous market. Already such problems had caused jobbers to link in bigger groupings: there were just fourteen London jobbing firms, including five large ones, by 1978, against 187 in 1950. Some recourse was made to arrangements like agreed spreads – the gaps between buying and selling prices – and, on occasion, joint books between jobber firms to resist the pressures. It is interesting that agreements among jobbers were not themselves referrable to the Court under the Restrictive Trade Practices law, since they were not for the provision of services, but concerned the jobbers' handling of their own resources.

Concern about the adequacy of jobbers' capital persisted over the years. In 1975, one of the largest two jobbers, Akroyd & Smithers, went public, partly in order to have better access to fresh capital against new shares, should the need arise. The other, Wedd Durlacher Mordaunt, considered but rejected the same course, though it received new capital from a minority 10 per cent outside shareholder, Rothschild Investment Trust. Two more of the big five, Smith Brothers and Bisgood Bishop, planned a merger in the late-1970s but, though the deal was cleared by the Monopolies Commission, they did not go ahead with it. Then Smith, like Akroyd, went public.

One source of difficulty lay in the increasingly wide swings in gilt and share prices caused by the more active government monetary policies used, from the early 1970s, to fight rising inflation. The stock market slump accompanying the secondary banking and property crisis[12] of 1973–5, when share prices reached record lows and numbers of Stock Exchange firms, members and employees left the market, had accentuated the problems. Concern at the role of the jobber sector then deepened and, in the late 1970s, a committee of Stock Exchange senior partners, reporting on international dealings, made some ominous points. It warned that, while it should be possible for a structure of four or five main jobbing firms to continue over the coming five years, the entire dealing system was vulnerable. The withdrawal of only one of the four top firms would, the committee believed, render it very difficult to maintain public confidence in the competitive nature of the Exchange's market-making system. This was described as a conclusion of the utmost importance for the Exchange.[13] The report was not a signal of acute danger but an alert to the possible need for later change.

The Stock Exchange Council worried not only about the long-term adequacy of the jobbers' capital but about that of brokers, which differed sharply from firm to firm. Just how great these variations were was shown by an enquiry which revealed that some brokers were well enough provided to have capital equalling two years' expenses, while others got by on capital as slender as just six weeks' costs. It was true that brokers did not ordinarily need large capital since they were not position-taking, but they still required a cushion to absorb results fluctuating between good years and bad. Moreover, should the OFT win its case and a shift take place to dual capacity, additional capital to finance own-account dealing would be needed, the more so if foreign competition for clients stayed strong. At all events, the Exchange's Council, which from as early as 1969 had let outside 'sleeping partners' take a tenth of member firms' capital, decided in 1982 to step up the limit on a single external stake to 29·9 per cent. This was after still higher outside percentages, of 49·9 per cent for all firms or 50 per cent for jobbers – and even more – had been considered but rejected.

Meanwhile, as the City moved into the eighties, the investing institutions, like the pension funds and insurance companies, the main users of the Exchange's services, were increasingly unhappy about the nature of the fixed commission charges. After all, not so much more work was involved in the million-pound scale of many of their deals than in much smaller transactions, yet the – admittedly sliding-scale – commissions tariff hardly adequately recognised this. Charges on big deals, especially the frequent ones for 'switching' in gilts to take advantage of changing market opportunities, should be a lot cheaper, many felt. Moreover, the Exchange had twice actually raised its scale of charges, once in 1976 after a very troubled two years, and again – after considerable debate in the Council in which the wisdom, against the backdrop of the case, of the proposed gilts commission rates was strongly, though unsuccessfully, queried – in

1981. On the latter occasion, institutional managers, who had been given some scope to comment through the Stock Exchange chairman's 'Liaison Committee' with the City, fought the increases proposed, which were partly rolled back in certain respects. Yet many institutional managers still felt they had not as much say as they would have liked in such decisions.

A number of other adjustments and arrangements were also made in an effort to meet the institutions' sense that they were just simply paying too much into the pockets of the Stock Exchange members. One was for 'continuation', whereby one large client could lump together all transactions over a limited period, paying commission only at the lower rate applicable to large deals. If the institution was managing funds for several clients, though, it could still charge each the relevant higher rate for its smaller share of the total, and so itself collect a useful profit. This latter practice could benefit both City fund management businesses and stockbroking firms which themselves managed investment funds for clients. For the former it could considerably mitigate dislike of the fixed-charge system.

Then again, institutional clients who were prevented by the fixed commission rules from negotiating cut-price dealing costs were consoled in other ways. Research, in the shape of regular analyses of company performances and prospects, was thrown in without charge by various brokers and could save institutions the need to have expensive research departments themselves. Portfolio valuation was another free bait for large clients.

And the sweeteners (sometimes called 'soft dollars') did not end there. Travel facilities provided by brokers, enabling fund managers to visit, say, overseas companies which might be of investment interest, formed one example. And the Stock Exchange Council watched, trying to adjust its guidance to allow reasonable 'soft' services without seeing too large a hole blown in the principle of common charges. Apparently, where a broker escorted a party of fund managers abroad, it was acceptable for him to pay the bills, but he was not supposed just to hand out free air tickets to such travellers and pick up their hotel bills. Nearer to, or perhaps over, the margin of acceptability were presents, not only of screens related to dealing but of other furniture, too, to win and hold desirable custom. 'There was nothing dishonest about it, because the benefit went directly to the institutions. But it was one way of getting around fixed commissions', a senior pension-fund man recalls. 'So the broker might pay for a suite of furniture for the institution's office or send them some filing cabinets.' Such devices were all classic instances of the distortions thrown up by a tightly regulated structure.

Other more important practices emerged as symptoms of the strains in the system. Brokers, wanting to enhance their role, would match buyers and sellers among their own clients, merely 'passing the deal through the market' by checking the price with a jobber. These were 'put throughs', estimated in the Wilson enquiry at 10 per cent of all turnover.[14] To a degree they diverted real business from jobbers and demonstrated how large brokers could edge near to a trading role. From the other side, there were signs that jobbers would occasionally informally discuss deals with institutions, then put them (perhaps lumped into large sums for lower commissions) through friendly brokers. Such a practice was frowned on by the Council as against at least the spirit of the rules.

That not everybody was quite comfortable with everything that went on is suggested by the fact, of which the author has been told, that there were sometimes requests for recording machines to be switched off in talks by legal advisers round the City concerning evidence in the OFT case.

In an effort to avoid what were thought excessive commission charges, a number of large users, mainly merchant banks with a fund management business and insurance groups, including the largest, the Prudential, set up ARIEL (Automated Realtime Investments Exchange Ltd). This was a computer-based system for direct trading in shares outside the Stock Exchange and so was a potentially important threat to the Exchange's service. But ARIEL made little impact, mostly because the Bank of England, a big force in the gilts field, declined to use it, thereby giving welcome support to the Exchange. At its best, ARIEL only handled a trifling proportion of share deals.

As preparations for the OFT–Stock Exchange Court hearing went on, the delicate question arose of assembling witnesses on the two sides. On the face of it, the users – chiefly the investing institutions and fund-managing merchant banks – had a strong interest in seeing restrictive pricing for commissions ended and competition brought in. Yet the 'link' argument made many hesitant. Much as they wanted cheaper commissions, they found the total consequences of that course – with the scrapping of the time honoured single-capacity system – hard to foresee or worrying to contemplate. From 1982, Sir Nicholas Goodison and his senior Exchange colleagues held a series of dinners for institutional and other City personalities at which they explained the Exchange's viewpoint. These were friendly relaxed occasions, which showed up quite a degree of support among these users but also the existence of opposition to the Exchange's case.

One institutional investor who was firmly on the side of the established system was the outspoken Mr David Hopkinson, then chief of M & G, one of the largest unit trust groups, who feared the consequences of change in dissolving the protection for investors which was ensured by the split-capacity structure. Among other potential supporters within the institutional investor community, some grew less enthusiastic for the Exchange's case after the 1981 increases in commission rates.

Some people prepared to give evidence for the Exchange were viewed as unsuitable since they were not considered certain to sustain their argument convincingly in the witness box.

Given the clubby nature of the City atmosphere, there was certainly no rush of volunteers to stand up and be counted on the side of the OFT as challenger of the existing practice. But whatever support it might or might not find in the City, the OFT could look to the American experience, where United States commissions on institutional business had been sharply slashed after dealing charges went competitive there in 1975. Sir Gordon Borrie, who presided actively over his OFT's pursuit of the case and who is a barrister, QC and former university lecturer, had this to say later about obtaining evidence:

> I wouldn't say it was easy to find witnesses [in the City]. There is a certain family atmosphere and we noticed a certain reluctance to give evidence as a member of the family. Nonetheless, we had got sufficiently far in our preliminary work and there were a number of users of the Stock Exchange who were willing to give evidence that was critical of the restrictions. One cause of complaint was that major institutions with their own research facilities couldn't negotiate a commission with a broker for the deal alone, not including the broker's research service which the client didn't need. We also had witnesses from New York on the results of deregulation there.[15]

The OFT seems to have picked its way circumspectly in its quest for City witnesses, doubtless sensing that many might find it embarrassing to appear against the powerful Stock Exchange. It took very wide soundings, particularly among investing institutions, aiming to assess where it might find support if the case's development made fresh witnesses important. But it was evidently not keen to force the pace and risk inviting a downright 'No' at an early stage. Yet there was one highly influential quarter from which additional backing could almost certainly have been obtained if the crunch had come.

The Prudential, as a major force in the market, with over £27bn now invested, made it clear, in answer to an approach, that it could not support the Stock Exchange's defence. That it would have been likely to do the opposite, if pressed, appears from the following comment some years later by one of its senior people, Mr Ronald Artus, a director and the group's investment chief. When asked if the Pru would have given evidence for the OFT, he said: 'I think our position really would have been that we would have much preferred somebody else to do it but that if, at the end of the day, they had needed a substantial institution to make its views known, we would probably have been prepared to, yes.'[16] Discreet as these words from a top City person are, they represent what would have been a significant commitment to the free market cause in the then contentious atmosphere. It is possible to take the view that, had the case proceeded to Court and evidence for the OFT been forthcoming from such an eminent source as the Pru, some other City institutions would have come forward on the same side.

As the months went by, opinions varied in the Stock Exchange camp as to the chances of success in the OFT case. Some, including many Council members, remained rock-solid in their belief in the rightness of their cause and in the prospects of its prevailing. But still there were growing doubts in various quarters as to whether the defence could succeed, given changes in the world outside and the wavering of support among a number of City investors. One observer has described feeling in the stock market community as having evolved from a 'rallying round the flag' in the late seventies to steadily weakening confidence among many people by 1982 and early 1983.

In the autumn of 1982, one senior Stock Exchange official put the Exchange's chances of successfully fighting for fixed minimum commissions and single capacity at no better than one in three and quoted these words of W. B. Yeats:

> Things fall apart; the Centre cannot hold;
> Mere anarchy is loosed upon the world
>
> .   .   .   .   .   .
>
> The best lack all conviction, while the worst
> Are full of passionate intensity.

Elsewhere in the City too support for the Exchange was, in some places at least, eroding. One manager of a major pension fund recalled, speaking of the period running into 1983, when share prices were booming and the commission take with them: 'I sensed that the Stock Exchange were very much on a sticky wicket. They were losing friends very rapidly, I suspect.'

One other highly important aspect was the question of the line to be taken by the Bank of England, critically interested as a key player in the gilt-edged market, as well as because of its general concern for the City's well-being. A senior Exchange man later remembered: 'As we got down to working out whom we needed to give evidence, it became patently apparent that the Bank would have to come down off the fence. Because it's their market, the gilts market.'

As it happened, the Bank played a key role in what followed, this arising from its taking a fresh look at the whole situation of the OFT– Stock Exchange case in its wider City context from 1982. In that year, one of the Bank's top executives, Mr David Walker, a former Treasury high-flyer who had responded to an invitation to move to the Bank some years earlier, became the director concerned with City organisation.

In the review which then got under way the Bank came to feel that the arguments for lifting the case out of the Restrictive Practices Court had grown stronger with time. In the world outside things had been developing, helped by the newly blossoming technology, in a way that should be highly relevant for London's future. For one thing, the securities industry based in foreign centres like New York and Tokyo was becoming a bigger, more highly-capitalised international business and was looming, with uncomfortably strong muscle, over Britain's insular Stock Exchange.

In the United States, where deregulation in stock market commissions from 1975 had caused much protective restructuring, many of the old brokerage–investment bank partnerships were gaining powerful new owners and getting more strongly financed. Bache had been bought by the big Prudential Insurance (unconnected with Britain's Pru) and Dean Witter by the Sears Roebuck stores giant, while Salomon Brothers had linked with the Phibro commodities group and other ties had been forged in a process of take-over by major purchasers which continued for years. Strengthened afresh, the houses embarked on wider and larger activities, including those in the Eurodollar market: Salomon, for instance, multiplied the voume of corporate debt issues it managed or co-managed by ten times, from $9·6bn to $96bn, between 1975 and 1984. Transaction of major stock deals through their own books – 'block trading' – became an activity increasingly grafted onto regular stock market broking by the United States securities houses, which were also increasingly expanding overseas. The Japanese, too, through their big four securities houses, Nomura, Daiwa, Nikko and Yamaichi, were setting their sights more and more on international markets, which raised the prospect of an intensifying export drive by Japan in financial products, following its successes in cars and electronics. There was abroad a feeling that, once again, it would be necessary to get up pretty early in the morning to keep pace with the men from the Land of the Rising Sun. Altogether, by 1983, foreign broker rivals were looming formidably in a search for business on the international scene and were endowed with resources on a scale that left British houses far behind.

Indeed the total capital of United Kingdom Stock Exchange firms at the start of 1983 was very modest, probably not more than at most £150m–£200m. A good deal of this was held by the jobbing market, the sector most in need of capital, although Akroyd & Smithers, the biggest jobber, had no more than £37m of capital and reserves in September 1982. It was not unknown in a good year for some Exchange firms, and not just small ones, to make a 100 per cent return on their slender invested capital. All told, the combined capital of Stock Exchange members was less than that of the largest American brokerage house, Merrill Lynch. And Merrill, in turn, was outweighed by Japan's Nomura, with over £1bn equity at the end of 1982.

There were also other worrying indications that the United Kingdom Exchange was unequal to developing contemporary needs. As earlier indicated, the great bulk of the billions of pounds British investors had poured into investment abroad in the years after the 1979 scrapping of exchange controls had been handled by overseas, not British, brokers. Then again, considerable proportions of dealings in top United Kingdom shares were taking place in New York via 'share token' ADRs (American Depositary Receipts), at some stamp duty advantage, rather than in London. In fact, trading in securities was sprouting in all manner of places outside the Exchange, not excluding the Eurobond market and through ARIEL. The new London International Financial Futures Exchange (LIFFE) was also attracting gilts business at possible cost to that going through the Exchange.

All this, to the Bank, posed the threat that, without major reform, Britain's national Stock Exchange could become more isolated and be by-passed in an emergingly global securities market-place, where it was currently little fitted to handle future explosions in inter-national share dealing. And the Exchange's closed-entry system – it had no foreign firms and had admitted almost no new British ones for many years – was looking ever more anomalous.

Certainly, the Exchange had made some responses to the fresh world trends, such as in allowing 29·9 per cent outside stakes in member firms, and had wanted to do more. But it had been inhibited, particularly over international developments, by legal impediments connected with the OFT challenge.

The whole OFT case affair, in the Exchange's view, cast a blight on its own development. Or, as one close observer remarked, 'it was paralysed like a rabbit in the car headlights: it could not move'. Sir Nicholas Goodison, who had long pressed the case for change, was later quoted as saying that the gradual erosion of the jobbing system had been a subject for discussion in the Stock Exchange many times in the seventies and that he had wanted to throw the matter open for public debate because changes were inevitable. But the Exchange's legal advisers had warned him not to raise the matter in public in case this prejudiced their position in the Court case.[17]

A more critical outside view was, however, that to many brokers the OFT case served as a convenient excuse to avoid radical reform which would never have been undertaken spontaneously, given the high level of commission revenue under the fixed-rate system. 'They [the brokers] had such a good time domestically they didn't want to look abroad. It would have been no good telling somebody with a fabulous home market to change', one observer remarked.

From the winter of 1982–3, the Bank of England, moved by the global developments afoot, went into a secret new dialogue with chiefs of the two major interested Whitehall Ministries, the Treasury and the Department of Trade, though not with the OFT, the Trade

Department associate which was the legal proponent in the case. The Bank produced papers for the Treasury, discussing the pros and cons of a shift towards a more deregulated stock market system, and these were discussed at a series of official meetings, which also considered the OFT case.

There was, seemingly, some apprehension among officials about either total failure or total success as the outcome of OFT's challenge before the Court. Victory for the Stock Exchange would entrench a system felt to be becoming outmoded: it might leave Stock Exchange 'backwoodsmen' blocking change till the end of the century. On the other hand, triumph for the OFT could leave an undesirably uncertain prospect, in the view of various officials. The idea of a compromise being negotiated between Sir Gordon Borrie and Sir Nicholas Goodison under Section 25 of the Competition Act 1980 does not seem to have been explored in this set of confidential discussions. Perhaps the Bank of England would have wanted a tighter control over any change in the gilts market than that procedure might have given it. The concept of some quango-type 'public interest' body to judge Stock Exchange charges from time to time was considered but discarded. Sir Geoffrey Howe, the Chancellor of the Exchequer, who, as Solicitor General had been associated with anti-restrictive practices legislation in the early seventies, may have felt such a solution would not have done enough to assert the competitive principle. A Monopolies Commission or Royal Commission enquiry were other possible alternative procedures reviewed but dismissed.

The key issue was whether it was desirable to divert the course of events from the Court, and the central figure who would have to favour this if the government were to intervene was the Cabinet Minister responsible for competition policy, the Trade Secretary, an office held from 1982 by Lord Cockfield. Early in 1983 those with political antennae in Whitehall began to sense that Lord Cockfield, a one-time Inland Revenue official who had later made his name as a top industrialist running the Boots stores group before entering politics, was not as opposed as his predecessors had been to a new approach on the OFT matter. The signs are that the Bank of England's arguments for a fresh move in the whole matter had been successfully explained to him by the then Governor of the Bank, Lord Richardson. The two already knew each other, because Schroders, the merchant bank Lord Richardson had chaired before becoming Governor in 1973, had acted for Boots, a background which probably helped them to consult with mutual understanding. A further influential voice heard behind the scenes against letting the legal case proceed unchecked was that of Professor L. C. B. (Jim) Gower, the academic lawyer who was conducting an investigation for the government on the state of investor protection arrangements. In characteristically pithy style, he described the situation of the Stock Exchange restrictions being scrutinised by means of Court proceedings as 'dotty'.

All the signs are that, before the campaign leading to the General Election on 9 June 1983, the government had moved far towards the view that the Stock Exchange affair should be settled out of court, in return for concessions by the Exchange, including the eventual dismantling of the controversial fixed commissions, if these could be negotiated. This would be in line with the Thatcher government's growingly critical approach to long-privileged groups.

The election campaign of May–June 1983 brought an interlude of uncertainty, but the triumphant return of the Tories saw the tentative conclusion confirmed. The new Chancellor of the Exchequer, Mr Nigel Lawson, a former financial journalist, was all for the plan. And so was Mr Cecil Parkinson, appointed to the combined senior Cabinet post of Trade and Industry Secretary after a successful role as Conservative party chairman in the campaign. Behind the official scenes, matters now went ahead towards final decisions.

From the Stock Exchange, Sir Nicholas Goodison approached the government once more just after the election about the pending legal action. He took up with Mr Parkinson, as the new Secretary of State, the question whether the case against the Exchange could be stopped, and matters handled differently, in the general interest of the securities markets' development. By this stage, Sir Nicholas had gleaned some idea that the government's thinking on the subject had shifted. But, with the case due in court in a matter of months, and with the Parliamentary and legal summer breaks approaching, he was conscious of the urgency of any action that might be contemplated and pressed for a quick meeting. This was fixed for 1 July.

Then, in late June, the government's conclusions were revealed to Sir Gordon Borrie, the official who, under the law, had been masterminding the long, arduous and costly preparation of this major Restrictive Practices case. On Tuesday, 28 June, he received a visit, heralded by a telephone call only hours earlier, from two senior Department of Trade and Industry officials, from whom he gained his first inkling that government intervention in moves to terminate the case was intended. The following day he called, as requested, on Mr Parkinson for a brief meeting in which the government's plans were explained. The news came as a thunderbolt after the marathon six years' work on the case, then due for hearing within only months.

Sir Nicholas Goodison's approach to the government on this occasion seeking the calling off of the case proved the last of several he had made over the years on the subject and the one which had the most dramatic sequel. Ironically, on the very eve of his crucial meeting with Mr Parkinson, he presided over a Stock Exchange dinner to leading merchant bankers. A top banker who was among the guests later looked back on the occasion and recalled not the faintest hint that Sir Nicholas had any thought the OFT case might be aborted: 'If Nicholas then expected what subsequently happened, he's a great actor', he remarked.

At the following day's meeting between Mr Parkinson and Sir Nicholas, the government's intentions were explained and the way was opened for the Exchange to prepare proposals which would allow the Court case to be ended.

From the Stock Exchange's viewpoint, the prospect of such a deal as the government was canvassing – an end to the legal action on conditions including the dismantling of the fixed commission structure over time – had by now much appeal, given the rapid development in the world stock market industry. In the topmost reaches of the Exchange's government where the proposition became very secretly known, the first response was therefore clearly positive. It seems, however, that the Exchange's chiefs did not respond swiftly to an official hint that the single capacity system of broker–jobber separation might be perpetuated. Thus this aspect was left in uncertainty for a time.

On 19 July a leak in *The Guardian* newspaper that the government was preparing to settle out of court triggered a Commons statement that afternoon. The Prime Minister confirmed that she and her colleagues were willing to consider calling off the case on acceptable terms. The matter was still before the Court but 'that does not preclude the Stock Exchange Council from making proposals to settle the matter', Mrs Thatcher said.

After lengthy sessions in the next few days the Exchange's ruling Council agreed with little difficulty to a deal under which the fixed minimum commission tariff would be dismantled by the end of 1986 – in, at latest, three-and-a-half years' time – and that other changes would be made, notably to allow non-members to be non-executive directors of Exchange firms. Outsiders were also to be admitted to the Council. But at this time there was no arrangement to abolish the broker–jobber divide.

Mr Parkinson announced the deal in the Commons on 27 July 1983, noting at the same time that single capacity 'should be preserved for the time being in its present form'. There was sharp Opposition reaction, alleging that the government was 'selling out to and looking after its City friends'. It went down badly that the move came so soon after an election campaign in which the Conservatives had received generous City contributions and in which the new development had in no way been foreshadowed. The Minister was also accused of having undermined the position of Sir Gordon Borrie. Intense briefing of the Press did, however, bring out the wider background of changing world markets in which, it was hoped, the Stock Exchange would now be freer to evolve appropriately.

Some Press comment was very critical. *The Daily Telegraph's* City commentary said: 'Sir Gordon Borrie ... has every reason to resent the way that a government committed to free markets and untrammelled competition, has systematically abandoned its own guardian of competition policy.'[18] And *The Economist*, under the headline 'Doing the City a favour' said of the move: 'This retreat is a political mistake and may prove a worse financial one.'[19]

Following the government's decisions, Sir Gordon Borrie urged strongly that the case against the Stock Exchange should – indeed, could – only be called off by a new Act of Parliament and not just by an Order under an existing Act. In this way alone, he argued, could the standing of the Restrictive Practices legislation be properly preserved. After some debate, this was accepted and the matter was taken out of court by the Restrictive Practices (Stock Exchange) Act 1984, which became law on 13 March, Sir Gordon's fifty-third birthday, a coincidence he hardly rejoiced in.

One of the most controversial aspects of the story is that the OFT was excluded from all say in the formation of the drastically changed policy until the essential decisions had been taken. However diplomatically Sir Gordon responded, the sudden aborting of the case – after costs which, on the two sides, had altogether reached £3m – came as a great and totally unexpected shock in his Department. There was understandable regret in the OFT that the vast quantity of assembled material, on the United Kingdom and foreign scenes, which was relevant to the case should never see the light of day as part of the process by which decisions on the future arrangements of such an important national body as the Stock Exchange were reached. There was also some dismay that the rest of the official machine should have carried its plans so far before giving any hint of them to the official who, under the law, had so long prepared this most important of competition cases in the services sector. The opposite viewpoint is perhaps that Sir Gordon occupied a special position in the structure of administration by reason of the semi-independence of his Department and his duty to launch legal actions on competition matters, and that this justified his exclusion from the key stages of the 1983 policy-making on the subject. There is also no doubt that there was a very determined government drive behind the new turn in policy and probably a matching unwillingness to be deterred by any obstacles to it.

As it turned out, much of the change the OFT had fought for did come about, though by a very different route from the legal one first envisaged.

3 City Restructuring for Big Bang

Big Bang, hypothesis in cosmology, a view that the present apparent expansion of the universe started ... with the violent explosion of an originally highly compressed and intensely hot homogeneous material ... In some theoretical models of the future, the expansion will continue into an infinite dispersal. In other models, it will be slowed and eventually reversed by gravity and the universe will then collapse catastrophically upon itself ... This cycle of explosion and collapse may repeat itself, perhaps endlessly.

Encyclopaedia Britannica, Micropaedia.

When Sir Nicholas Goodison and Mr Parkinson shook hands on their pact for the dropping of the OFT case against the Stock Exchange in return for concessions, it was the end of the beginning, not the beginning of the end, of the City revolution. Vast changes lay ahead and many of them were not yet widely predicted in the City. For the Exchange, the priority obligation under the deal was to open up entry through admitting lay members to its ruling council and to create an appeals body to see that would-be newcomer members were not unreasonably barred. Yet more important, the council had to decide how to dismantle fixed commissions, within the promised three-and-a-half year time limit, and whether to do this by stages or in one go. And beyond this were ranged the further key questions whether single capacity should be preserved and what trading system should replace it if it was not.

Mr Parkinson had told Parliament that the jobber–broker split would persist at least for the time being and had seemed to bless it as protective of investors. But there was mounting doubt whether this feature could survive the ending of fixed commissions with which it had been essentially linked. Sir Nicholas Goodison had already hinted at the need for the further change by saying before the end of July: 'The abolition of commissions [fixing] may prove incompatible with the present system of separate capacity. We are entering uncharted waters.'[1] If there were change on both fronts, the

51

Exchange's seventy-year-old trading system would need remodelling from scratch.

Meanwhile, in the rest of the City, the realisation started to spread that new opportunities were dawning. Strongly capitalised banks, both British and foreign, saw scope opening before them for branching out into stockbroking, a field that had so far been blocked to them. Large banks had anyway been growing more like financial supermarkets, and the fall in entry barriers to the Stock Exchange offered them fresh scope for diversification.

After so many years with a City in watertight compartments, it was not easy for everyone to see the new potential. Yet a little reflection suggested there were neat matches to be made. On the one hand there were the banks, with large resources as well as expansion ambitions. On the other were over two hundred broker or jobber firms, whose capital had just sufficed for a closed, split-capacity market but would be far too scant in the open-entry international-style future the Exchange now faced. The question was whether these 'pools of capital and pools of talent', as somebody close to the scene expressed it, could link up. If they did, the result should be a pack of strong new players able to afford the large-scale stock and share trading operations needed to make London one of the world's top three securities centres, with New York and Tokyo.

The Bank of England saw a role for itself in actively fostering the idea of suitable unions. Discreetly and behind the scenes, the Bank, as custodian of that national asset, the City's financial centre, did all it could to nudge the get-together trend along. Already many Stock Exchange partners were seeing the possibilities in the coming, more liberated, market and considering their policies. 'Suddenly, there was a great ferment of strategic planning among Exchange firms, a great release of energy where creative talent had been bottled up during the no-change years', a banker who was much involved remembers.

For its part, the Bank had government blessing for its close concern in the way events were evolving. For Mr Parkinson had said in July that his Department and the Bank would 'monitor the implementation' of the government–Exchange pact 'and the evolution and development of the Stock Exchange as an efficient, competitive and suitably regulated market which affords proper protection to investors'.

Over a two-month period from September to November 1983, the Bank's executive director for City organisation, Mr David Walker, held conversations, often at the rate of two a day, with over forty senior partners of Exchange firms. The idea of this quiet 'talkathon' was to discuss the implications of recent events and to swap views on plans as well as, sometimes, on actual get-together possibilities. 'The people making all the running were the authorities', one senior partner recalls. 'David Walker steered a bit behind the scenes', another remembers. ' "Think the unthinkable, think radical", appeared to be the message from the Bank's HQ in Threadneedle Street, and they did', is one recollection in retrospect. The Bank saw what it did as helping to bring to birth the new City already there in embryo: 'We midwifed change', Mr Walker later observed.[2] It was not to be long before dramatic developments followed.

But first the Stock Exchange as an organisation had to plan a new framework for its future. And it was soon clear that London would move to dual-capacity of the American type – allowing firms not only to broke as agents but to deal in stock on their own account – as well as making commissions negotiable. Dramatic change, though, was not accepted without some rearguard action. Many brokers felt understandable worry, based on New York's 1975 experience of deregulation, that competition in commissions would slash revenue and squeeze out smaller or weaker firms. But, to protesting voices wanting the government's 'bluff called' and the July deal cancelled, Sir Nicholas Goodison replied that this would simply land the Exchange back before the Court. The changes towards opening up the Exchange's membership that were required to endorse the pact were overwhelmingly voted through by its members as early as October 1983, and the government then fulfilled its side of the bargain by launching the Act to call off the OFT case. In the new circumstances, the Exchange also took swift action to allow its member firms, from early 1984, to deal in dual capacity and without fixed commissions in international shares. It was hoped that this would stem the flow of such business to brokers abroad.

Acceptance of the need to end the long-sacrosanct single capacity took longer. Its demise had not been foreshadowed in the July accord and, moreover, many Exchange members had grown conditioned to it as the bedrock of the OFT case defence. 'It had become the Ark of the Covenant', an observer recalls of this view. But now the 'link argument' operated in reverse and the City Capital Markets Committee (CCMC), a top-level 'think tank', did much in a paper in October 1983 to drive home the logic that minimum commissions and single capacity stood or fell together.[3] There was also the factor that everything was changing as stockbroking grew international and that

Britain's brokers were now face-to-face with world competitors flexibly running broking and market-making in stocks and shares under one roof. 'I believe single capacity would have had to be given up in the end because of the trend to global trading', was a comment in the later 1980s from Mr David LeRoy-Lewis,[4] a CCMC member who earlier, as already noted, had been a key architect of the original 'link' reasoning.

With the coming phasing-out of the single capacity system, in which jobbers as 'wholesalers' of stocks and shares operated quite separately from brokers acting as investors' agents, it was clear that the Stock Exchange trading system itself was up for remodelling. To replace it, a structure was devised under which all Exchange firms would become broker–dealers able to trade for their own account if they wished, as well as to broke. Some would, however, also be registered as 'market-makers' in particular shares, with an obligation to stand ready to deal continuously in times good and bad. Price quotes would be via electronic screens and actual deals would be clinched by telephone or on the Exchange's trading floor.

This system would accommodate a much larger range of market-makers than the existing jobbing sector which consisted of five large jobbers, dominated by a 'big two', and several smaller ones. The prices would be disseminated through a SEAQ (Stock Exchange Automated Quotation) system, which would have the advantage of covering large and increasing numbers of shares, domestic and foreign. This would be particularly useful in view of a growing ambition on the Exchange's part to be, in its revamped form, the leading world trader in international shares. Elaborate arrangements were to be worked out as to just how deals done would be publicly reported, given the need that a market-maker's 'book' should not be too transparently revealed to the competition.

The planned new arrangements were known as the 'competing market-maker system' and were modelled on the NASDAQ (National Association of Securities Dealers Automated Quotation) screen market on which numerous American companies' shares are traded throughout the United States without a central market floor. It was picked in preference to the New York Stock Exchange's structure under which 'specialist' companies' assist in matching trades and, in certain circumstances, themselves intervene to deal. The fact that Britain's Stock Exchange lists shares of far more companies than are dealt in on the NYSE was one factor thought to make the screen-based market-maker arrangement most suitable for London.

At the same time, the opportunity was to be taken to reshape the separate and large gilt-edged market in United Kingdom government stocks onto a fresh American-style pattern, with much more capital and a broad range of competitive market-makers.

Also central to the Exchange's whole package of reforms was a plan that interests from outside the market, foreign as well as British, should be able to buy control of stock-broking firms and even to start their own from scratch. This was vital to the whole objective of reinforcing the stock market industry through the injection of major new capital. The scheme was that the initial stakes taken in Exchange firms would be restricted to 29·9 per cent, but that this limit would be removed, allowing full ownership, before the new type of market was launched.

The Exchange also came to the conclusion that it would scrap its minimum commission rules, not by instalments, but in one 'Big Bang', the term that came to symbolise the emerging wider City Revolution. Eventually 27 October 1986 was named as 'Big Bang day', when the major reforms would finally take effect.

Proposals along these lines matured rapidly and were formally submitted to the Exchange's membership in a crucial discussion paper in April 1984.[5] With some refinement of detail, they were later adopted. As it turned out, by the spring of 1984, many earlier doubts on the part of stockbrokers about the impending string of radical changes had been dispersed. Discontent had been much assuaged as it became clear that a bonanza buying spree for Stock Exchange firms was under way by long-pocketed big commercial and other banks which were seeking footholds in London's fast-evolving securities market.

As the get-together opportunities in the freer climate grew apparent, a rush to take new partners developed. From the late autumn of 1983, the City went through a huge flurry of match-making as big banks surveyed the stock market community for the best choices and Exchange firms looked about them for the most eligible marriages.

An early link that proved something of a role-model came early in November 1983 when Mercury Securities, the holding company of the big S. G. Warburg merchant bank, announced a tie with Akroyd & Smithers, the City's largest jobber. The prompt timing was no coincidence, since both parties had long been anticipating the deregulatory movement now taking place. Back in 1982, in the words of Mr Stephen Raven, then an influential director of the company, Akroyd had 'foreseen the end of the jobbing system and had thought matters would go in the US direction'. A major worry had been that a crumbling of single capacity would prompt big brokers to widen their function to the jobbers' detriment. In words that vividly portray the jobbing sector's anxieties at the time – worries already touched on in Chapter 2 – he told the author:

> The jobbers were quite fearful. We felt that if the brokers found it necessary to deal net [at prices with no separate commission], and to take block positions [buy stock on to their own books], the jobbers must have a similar freedom and deal net with the investing institutions.
>
> Otherwise, the jobbers would be by-passed and entombed in the Stock Exchange, only being used by brokers when the latter could not undo [complete] the business themselves. The jobbers would get the worst end of any particular deal. The cream of the business would be done by the brokers. Then we realised it would be necessary to move to dual capacity. At the same time we foresaw a move to a US-style situation with three vital components in a grouping, issuing [raising capital for companies], dealing, and distribution [making shares available to investors]. Issuing pointed to a merchant bank partner. We drew up a list of merchant banks and stockbrokers. The choice pointed to Warburgs, who were big in Eurobonds, an area where Akroyd were also active.[6]

The Warburg group had also been thinking ahead. Indeed, people in this internationally-minded organisation, founded by one of the City's outstanding postwar newcomers, the late Sir Siegmund Warburg, had for some years predicted change in the City's structure. The abolition of exchange control in 1979, opening up investment channels world wide for the British, had been one pointer in this direction and the OFT–Stock Exchange case had been another. Now Warburg aimed at expanding into a broad financial–securities business on the lines of an American investment bank, a project which called for the inclusion of a high-powered jobber.

Terms were swiftly worked out and Mercury injected £41m capital to take 29·9 per cent in the enlarged Akroyd, with a view to a full merger later. These terms implied a then £137m worth for the enriched Akroyd, or £96m for the business before the deal. Soon afterwards, Akroyd forged its first link, for international dealing, with Rowe & Pitman, the large firm which is the Queen's stockbroker and which itself both wanted the right associates and was considered an attractive buy. Then Mercury, Akroyd, Rowe & Pitman, and Mullens – whose role as Government Broker vanished in the gilt market changes – fully joined forces as Mercury International (later renamed S. G. Warburg Group), becoming a leading example of a modern-style British-owned investment bank.

Since the transition to the reformed Stock Exchange would call for a wider range of market-makers, the spotlight quickly fell on the few firms with expertise in this field, the jobbers. Following the Warburg–Akroyd tie, attention focussed on the other large jobber, Wedd Durlacher Mordaunt, a private partnership whose chiefs rapidly came to terms with the now inevitable loss of independence. Looking back later on this stage, Wedd's senior partner, Mr John Robertson, a former deputy chairman of the Stock Exchange, recalled the decisions his firm faced:

> Clearly, with the July 1983 events, the walls of Jericho tumbled. Once it was decided the knock-on effect was dual capacity, we and others needed to get our skates on and seek a strong-capital partner and one that would bring something else to the table. We needed something complementary that would lead us towards becoming an investment bank: we needed trading *and* a distribution arm.[7]

Wedd considered a number of possible purchasers, both British and foreign. It had a lengthy negotiation with a large merchant bank, Kleinwort Benson, as a potential buyer. Kleinwort, of comparable size to Warburg, obviously contemplated a deal that would have emulated the latter's with Akroyd. But that link was not to be. One impediment was that Kleinwort felt it would have been expected also to buy the largish broker de Zoete & Bevan, which Wedd perhaps envisaged as its 'distribution' associate. Moreover, it seems Wedd wanted to be assured of larger future new investment than a merchant bank of Kleinwort's size could guarantee.

The outcome was that Wedd went to the much larger Barclays – one of Britain's biggest high street clearing banks – which also bought de Zoete in a very major purchase package, with an initial total price tag which can be put at nearly £140m. Mr Robertson was happy with this result and glad his firm was going to a British buyer. 'When you're assessing a deal, you need to look at all aspects, the price and – a crucial part of it – how you'd operate together. I was happy that we settled on a British deal rather than an American one. I think most of our people preferred that', he later remarked. The exact price was not disclosed but probably valued Wedd and de Zoete respectively in the region of £90m and £50m.

This deal had some ironic sequels. To chair the £250m new BZW (Barclays de Zoete Wedd) investment bank it was creating from its purchases, as merged with its own Barclays Merchant Bank, the Barclays group recruited Sir Martin Jacomb, a well-known City figure from the upper reaches of Kleinwort Benson. But then, in a tit-for-tat move, Kleinwort, for its part, poached a prominent team of eight Wedd jobbers, led by partners Mr Charles Hue-Williams and Mr William Mellen, to be the nucleus of market-making at its own planned investment bank. The 'Wedd Eight' forwent some £7m–£8m they would have received under the Barclays purchase of Wedd, but were suitably compensated by their new employer. The purchase money Barclays paid for Wedd was accordingly abated and that bank's cost for the goodwill of its two acquisitions came out at about £129m. Kleinwort then bought the sizeable broker Grieveson Grant, a gilts and fund management specialist, for £44m and the little jobber Charlesworth for £800 000.

The National Westminster, the other of Britain's biggest two banks, went about its entry to the Stock Exchange in a more economical way. It chose a buy-and-build policy and spent some £30m to acquire Bisgood Bishop, one of the smaller among the top five jobbers, and the modest-sized broker Fielding Newson-Smith, by way of an initial market toehold. The strategy was to expand by purchasing just 'the minimum critical mass to which we would add building blocks', as Mr Charles Villiers, the NatWest senior man in charge of the operation, explained.[8] A total of £300m capital was apportioned to allow heavy new investment in the planned NatWest Investment Bank, to be built from the acquisitions, as combined with the group's existing County Bank merchant bank arm. Later experience suggested that the initial purchases had been inconveniently small for their purpose and in 1987 NatWest also acquired the stockbroker Wood Mackenzie which in 1984 had been sold for £21m to the Hill Samuel merchant bank, itself later taken over by the TSB Group clearing bank. But although NatWest had problems because of its limited starting stock market base, it had spent on the goodwill of these purchases far less than Barclays' corresponding outlay – and, as Mr Villiers drily commented, 'goodwill is not tax-deductable'.

The Midland Bank, another big clearer, meanwhile bought into the prominent broker W. Greenwell, best known for gilts, with the idea of developing it also as a market-maker. This proved successful on the gilts side, though the equity side was later closed. Among merchant banks in the United Kingdom, Morgan Grenfell – one of the big three, along with Kleinwort and Warburg – acquired a medium-sized jobber and a broker, Pinchin Denny and Pember & Boyle, respectively for £21m and £10m.

Foreign buyers were well to the fore also, attracted by the opening up of what promised to be a new global stock market centre in London. They too were soon shopping actively. Citicorp, the largest United States bank, bought up, for £60m-plus, two stockbrokers, the biggish Scrimgeour Kemp-Gee and Vickers da Costa, the latter being a Far East specialist, then chaired by Sir Kenneth Berrill, the former government 'think tank' chief who later chaired the City 'watchdog', the Securities and Investments Board (SIB). Citicorp also acquired the discount house Seccombe Marshall Campion and earmarked £250m as the capital for its combined United Kingdom investment bank venture. Chase Manhattan, America's third largest bank, snapped up two more London brokers, Laurie Milbank and Simon & Coates. Among other United States bank groups, Security Pacific, which in 1982 had far-sightedly bought 29·9 per cent of a leading broker, Hoare Govett, now agreed more fully to buy Hoare, with a £78m value tag.

Altogether flirtations, negotiations and persuasive proposals abounded as rich banks proffered lucrative dowries to clinch matches with desired stock market firms. 'You didn't need to hawk yourself around', recalls one leading broker, who finds it hard to remember from how many would-be buyers his firm picked the one to which to sell out. 'You never knew in those days if people were calling with a deal in mind or just to talk about the market. Everybody was sussing things out.'

Among the largest prizes was Phillips & Drew, which went to Union Bank of Switzerland – biggest of the Swiss big three banks – in what was perhaps the costliest broker purchase in the City's restructuring. UBS also acquired a small jobber, Moulsdale. Another expensive buy was Hongkong and Shanghai Banking Corporation's take-over of a leading broker, James Capel, which has noted Far East expertise. Sir Michael Sandberg, Hongkong Bank's then chairman, said in 1986 of this acquisition: 'I said, well, we'll buy provided we can buy the top of the pops. I'm not going to buy second league. And I think we've got the top of the pops. We give them [Capel] an enormous amount of autonomy, as we do with our banking subsidiaries around the world.'[9]

The spate of deals continued into 1984 and beyond, each week bringing a fresh crop of purchase pacts, with overseas buyers prominent. Kitcat & Aitken, the broker linked with Rothschild Investment Trust (now J. Rothschild Holdings), passed to Royal Bank of Canada for some £8m–£9m, Crédit Suisse bought the Buckmaster & Moore broking firm, while Banque Arabe et Internationale d'Investissement took over Sheppards & Chase, and North Carolina National Bank acquired another broker, Panmure Gordon.

These were just some among numerous buy-out arrangements, certain of which were made more complex when one purchaser succeeded another. Sir Nicholas Goodison's firm, Quilter Goodison, first linked with the Swedish insurance group Skandia but was then sold to France's Paribas bank. The broker Savory Milln, having first tied with Dow Scandia, was bought by Royal Trust of Canada and then, afterwards, by Swiss Bank Corporation. Yet another complicated series of changes followed after Mercantile House Holdings (MHH), the money-broking conglomerate, first bought the stockbroker Laing & Cruickshank, together with Alexanders and another discount house. These were combined in the investment bank Alexanders Laing & Cruickshank (ALC). But when MHH was later bought by the rapidly expanding financial group British & Commonwealth and broken up, ALC was sold on, for approaching £100m, as the nucleus of its London investment bank, to the French bank Crédit Lyonnais.

Marriage brokers naturally did well from the avalanche of attachments. One of the liveliest go-betweens was Phoenix Securities, a private firm created by Mr John Craven, a banker formerly with Warburgs. Mr Craven's early awareness of the scope for get-togethers in the restructuring City led him to develop an active advisory role which won him the name of 'Mr Fixit'. Among the deals he advised on was Wedd's sale and Chase Manhattan's purchases. The going fee for such work is often thought to be one per cent of the consideration. Was something approaching £1m – one per cent of nearly £100m – paid to Phoenix for its advice to Wedd? 'I can't say', answers Wedd's former head, Mr John Robertson, afterwards a senior BZW man. 'All I can say is that they did an excellent job.'[10]

Phoenix was later bought for £15m by Morgan Grenfell, of which Mr Craven became chief executive following high-level departures from Morgan in the wake of the 1986–7 scandal at Guinness which the merchant bank had advised.

In the background, the Bank of England continued to watch over the take-over rush which was reshaping the City's houses into bigger conglomerates, British and foreign, for the emerging new deregulated securities market. In the spring of 1984 the Bank's blessing for what was under way was openly confirmed in a speech by the new Governor, Mr Robin Leigh-Pemberton. But at the same time the Governor gave a delicate hint that it would not be welcome if foreign purchasers were to swamp the City scene with their buying power. However, his accent was not on tough protectionism but rather on the need for United Kingdom firms to be reinforced to meet all comers in the liberalised global markets. 'We would not contemplate with equanimity a stock exchange in which British-owned member firms played a clearly subordinate role', he told an Edinburgh audience on 6 March 1984. 'If this is to be avoided, and yet the door to foreign participation – and the vigour and fresh experience that it brings – is to be open, it will be necessary for British firms to be substantially strengthened so that they can compete on an even-handed basis.'[11] This message was not lost on those whom it concerned, for in the run-up to the Big Bang changes a reasonable balance was maintained between the numbers of the British and foreign groups being put together for the new market.

Busily as many large groups were buying, enthusiasm in the banking community for plunging into the uncharted new stock market world was by no means uniform. While among Britain's biggest banks Barclays purchased on a large scale and Midland and NatWest more modestly, Lloyds Bank did not acquire any Stock Exchange firm: instead it started its own gilt-edged operation (later closing it). Standard Chartered Bank did not venture into the newly-opening securities terrain and among the Scottish banks only Royal Bank ventured forth, buying the Liverpool-based broker Tilney. Distinct caution was observable too in the United Kingdom merchant bank field, for, while the biggest three groups there all bought into the stock market, the sizeable Schroders merely, in the United Kingdom, launched a small broking firm begun from scratch. Hill Samuel's bolder strategy of buying Wood Mackenzie and embarking on gilts trading proved over-ambitious and was largely responsible for its later agreeing to being taken over by TSB. Hambros contented itself with a limited stake in the broker Strauss Turnbull. N. M. Rothschild took a large minority stake in the jobber Smith Brothers which, as Smith New Court, was destined for a prominent marketing-making role in the post-Big Bang world. Some others made modest purchases.

Sometimes mere caution about the unknown, or inability to afford the cash to stake a presence in what would be a big-league revamped stock market, kept off potential entrants. And well-reasoned arguments against involvement were heard. 'Why pay heavily to buy into a market where deregulation of commissions is about to squeeze profits?' was one theme. And there were fears of spending money to buy the goodwill of Exchange firms, which in effect meant taking over organisations and staffs, since the people might not stay or their skills could grow obsolescent. 'Why buy yesterday's expertise?' was one explanation for holding off. Another justification for not joining the buying rush ran thus: 'A number of the partners you'd be acquiring might not be very good and their capabilities are anyway growing less relevant with the new technology. And, as to brokers thinking themselves valuable because of their institutional business, what price that when rivals snatch it away in future by offering cheaper terms?' And dissent was openly recorded by one of the City's leading personalities, Sir Ian Fraser, chairman of the Lazard Brothers merchant bank and, as once the City Takeover Panel's first director general, a noted expert on the financial scene: 'I think a lot of these conglomerations will end in tears', he warned in 1985, talking of the new securities market groupings. 'We [Lazard] are not thinking of buying goodwill which is two-legged and walks out as quickly as it walks in.'[12] The same policy of non-involvement in stockbroking was continued by Sir Ian's successor, Sir (formerly Mr) John Nott, who had been Trade Secretary in the early days of the Thatcher government.

The approach of foreign groups varied too. While some top American banks moved deeply into London's securities market, others held off. German groups made very little move to join in, but French and Swiss banks bought substantial City interests. The larger American investment banks and brokerage houses naturally showed much interest as they had been getting globally-minded, particularly since New York's deregulation of commissions in 1975. Even among them, though, tactics varied. Merrill Lynch, the largest

United States brokerage group, known as the 'thundering herd' and already with a world-wide branch network, bought a small gilts jobber, Giles & Cresswell, and through it rapidly carved out a sizeable share of the gilts market, though this was later reduced. Beyond this, Merrill planned to build its London broking business through a business started by itself from scratch. Shearson Lehman, another sizeable group, bought the substantial broker L. Messel. A further strong American securities group, Prudential-Bache, made history in late 1983 by persuading the Stock Exchange to let it start a completely new broking firm, with several ex-partners from James Capel. The discount house Clive, and new gilts and corporate finance interests, were added to Pru-Bache's London securities grouping.

Some leading United States investment banks eschewed purchases of Stock Exchange firms but have made major incursions into the reshaped City securities scene through heavy new recruitment and investment to expand their existing London footholds. Salomon Brothers, Wall Street's leading bond house, and Goldman Sachs, another prominent firm, are both in this category. A somewhat comparable strategy has also been followed by the expanding Japanese securities groups, including Nomura and Daiwa, which have developed with some deliberation in London, conscious that the United Kingdom government wants access for British brokers in Tokyo to accompany progress by Japan's houses in London.

A notable feature of prominent foreign groups' attitude to the new-style City has been their interest in the broadened and reshaped gilt-edged market which the Bank of England and the Stock Exchange were meanwhile framing ahead of Big Bang.

Once great change was under way in the stock market's ownership and trading methods, it made sense for the gilt-edged (government bond) sector to undergo its own reform. So the opportunity was seized to remodel this important part of securities activity more closely on the American system, in which over forty 'primary dealers' do a vast and increasingly international business in US Treasury bonds. The reshaping of the United Kingdom gilts market, in which the government has the closest interest because its own borrowing takes place there, was master-minded, in association with the Stock Exchange, by an executive director of the Bank of England, Mr Eddie George.

In the early eighties, approaching four-fifths of dealing in gilts was handled through London's two largest jobbers, Akroyd and Wedd Durlacher Mordaunt and, while their capital had sufficed to date, the market looked undercapitalised for what could be an increasingly international market and could do with strengthening. More generally also, it was, in the post-Big Bang situation, desired, in tune with the competitive spirit of the times, to admit to the gilts market as many suitable participants as wished to operate there – and many would-be newcomers, British and foreign, did so desire. The more the merrier was broadly the attitude of the Bank, which felt the depth and liquidity of the market – its capacity to be active and smooth-working – could only benefit from new competition and capital.

The structure devised was much akin to the United States system, allowing as it did for a broad span of competing market-makers. But the design, first unfolded in 1984, was for a 'primary dealer' system with a difference, in that it would, unlike its American counterpart, operate through the Stock Exchange. Participants would also be closely supervised by the Bank of England, as a safeguard against the upsets which had rocked the United States bond market in the volatile conditions of the early 1980s. As a further assurance of their strength, gilts operations would have to be run through separate companies provided by their parent groups with their own capital.

Another contrast with United States practice was that the established British system of blocks of new government stock being kept on official books and subsequently sold off by 'tap' was to be retained. Experimentation with the contrasting United States issue method by which a new stock is knocked down by auction at the outset to the best bidders was, however, envisaged later. The revamped gilt market, like the new Stock Exchange system generally, would be screen-based, though with somewhat different quotation arrangements, to cater for the distinctive character of government bond trading.

Finally, the age-old practice whereby the Government Broker – the senior partner of stockbrokers Mullens – served as the Bank's link with the market would be phased out, with a Central Gilts Office in the Bank itself taking over the role. The new gilts 'primary dealers', the jobbers' more numerous replacements as gilts traders, would have a duty to make markets continuously, but would enjoy certain tax and other privileges, including entitlement to deal with the Bank as the heart of the gilts market.

When the Bank in 1985 invited applications for the role of gilt market-maker, an impressive line-up of thirty-one big names, British and foreign, came forward. It was clear that United Kingdom gilt 'primary dealer' operation was seen as something of a status symbol. After two had withdrawn, twenty-nine groups were designated, having committed capital ranging between under £10m and £50m. (Chase Manhattan Bank put up about the latter big sum.) Altogether £600m-plus of capital was dedicated to trading in the new market, probably at least six times what the existing jobbers had employed. This multiple vividly illustrates the greatly enhanced strength of the City's emerging new post-Big Bang securities markets, the equity sector of which probably also became, in a broadly similar manner, recapitalised to much the same level.

The parade of gilt market-makers included the big four United Kingdom banks and leading merchant banks, together with prominent American commercial and investment banks and securities houses, some other leading overseas groups and a range of smaller British houses. The names were mainly those of groups already expanding in London stock broking, through purchase or otherwise, but they included the large United States bank Morgan Guaranty (part of J. P. Morgan), which had shown no expansion ambitions in equities, and Crédit Suisse–First Boston, the Swiss–American concern which is a leader in Eurobonds. While at first the British and American names were roughly evenly matched in number, the foreigners, as a result of take-overs, new admissions and departures, afterwards predominated. Much surprise was expressed that the UK 'primary dealers' were so numerous although their market was far smaller than America's with its forty-plus dealers – and ominous predictions of competitive gilt market 'bloodbath' were heard.

Meanwhile, the Stock Exchange, as well as agreeing the gilts arrangements, was preparing over a wide field for the coming revolutionary shake-up. A new form of corporate membership was introduced, now that companies would predominate over individuals as owners in the market. Unlimited personal liability ceased to operate in its old form and compensation fund arrangements were adjusted. From 1 March 1986 – some eight months before the main all-change package of reforms was due to take effect on Big Bang day, 27 October 1986 – 100 per cent ownership of Stock Exchange firms by newcomer outside interests became possible. At that time, two leading foreign houses, America's Merrill Lynch and Japan's Nomura, launched their own new fully-owned broking firms. And

from the same date, the numerous purchasers which had so far held
only minority interests in Exchange firms, started stepping up their
control, usually to total ownership.

Altogether during the stock market's reshaping to its new form, over
a hundred Stock Exchange firms were bought up in the biggest and
swiftest take-over spree in the financial industry's history. Virtually
all the large and medium-sized concerns lost their independence in
the huge sell-out, which continued with a trickle of deals even after
the Big Bang trading changes in October 1986. One large broker,
Cazenove, alone among the leaders, stood out against all buyers. Of
those now remaining unlinked to new owners, the majority are
smaller London or provincial brokers with a personal business which
has been little affected by the freeing of commission rates. And some
such firms have teamed up in new partnership groupings.

All told, in the giant buy-up movement, more than £1·5bn has been
laid out on the purchases of Exchange firms which have given
numerous banks entry to the City's deregulated stock market. And
this money, being paid personally to the selling partners as owners of
the businesses, has gone into private pockets and so vanished from
the financial sector itself.

The total take-over figure has never been revealed but its order of
magnitude can be estimated. The biggest single set of deals was
Warburg's three-part absorption of the £100m-plus Akroyd, along
with Rowe & Pitman (£60m) and the smaller Mullens, total
consideration of some £200m. Then Barclays' take-over of Wedd and
de Zoete was worth £129m. The several other jobbers bought,
including Pinchin, for £21m, must have accounted for at least a
further £50m. Then five brokers, Hoare (for £78m), Phillips & Drew
and James Capel, both at probably rather more, Scrimgeour, and
Grieveson Grant (£44m) cost around an additional £350m together.
Another twenty medium-to-larger brokers must have fetched between £15m and £40m each, say an average of £27m, or £540m in
total. Numerous further firms, some quite sizeable, probably changed
hands for no less than £250m in aggregate. These amounts, some of
which may be under-estimates, add up to over £1·5bn.

On top of this outlay – 'lost' as far as the continuing market was
concerned – the new owners have channelled in probably something
like as much again to recapitalise their acquisitions and fit them for

their role in the City's revamped stock trading forum. The gilt market alone was endowed with over £500m fresh capital and the equity sector with probably as much. The published target sizes for such investment bank ventures as Barclays', the NatWest's and Citicorp's show how much investment, beyond buy-out-costs, was involved. And the first two of the three just named had major fresh capital injected after the October 1987 share crash. Again, firms like Salomon Brothers have multiplied their staffs and capacity several times over in the past few years, which implies heavy capitalisation.

Outlay on building has often been involved and many firms have spent heavily on vast new dealing rooms which, with their gleaming multi-coloured screens and endless miles of cable, cost up to £18m–£20m apiece for the largest. One observer who commented that the big dealing halls looked as large as the vast meeting chamber in the Doges' Palace at Venice evoked the response: 'Ah, but the investment banks are today's Doges.'

It is worth pausing to review the way the take-over prices of Exchange firms were fixed. Many were set at multiples of between ten and fifteen times earnings (taxed profits). Little detail was revealed except by those quoted merchant banks (Warburg, Kleinwort, Morgan Grenfell and Hill Samuel), whose purchases were large enough in relation to their business to require a detailed circular to shareholders. Kleinwort's price for Grieveson, for instance, was 10·4 times the latter's 1983–4 earnings.

The buy-out prices were essentially for goodwill – a ticket of entry to the market for the buyers – since few, if any, assets changed hands. The partners who were cashing their interest customarily withdrew their cash reserves before the sale. The Morgan Grenfell flotation prospectus notes, with reference to the bank's purchases of Pinchin Denny and Pember & Boyle: 'Partners' funds including taxation reserves withdrawn prior to completion.' The 1986 listing particulars for the planned new Mercury International (Warburg) group refers to 'funds of £17·9m proposed to be withdrawn by the general partners of Rowe & Pitman'.

Most Stock Exchange firms had been organised as partnerships, a type of association offering substantial tax advantage if profits fluctuate over the years. In the take-over movement the previous partnerships were generally converted into companies, a convenient form for purchase, as a preliminary to their sale.

The new bank owners' stake money for their investment in the remoulded stock market has been high indeed at some £3bn, of which

£1·5bn was withdrawn and so 'dead' money no longer employed in the businesses. To win a reasonable return on such a vast outlay, the investing banks would need to earn, say, £450m net (15 per cent after tax) a year on £3bn. That looks a highly demanding target – an unattainable one in the short term, some would say – and explains why certain groups, such as the very profit-conscious Lloyds Bank, have held largely aloof from the game.

Given that the firms making up the bulk of the Stock Exchange were bought out for ten to fifteen times 1984 earnings at some £1·5bn, those earnings would only have been £100m–£150m. To triple that figure even in the reformed and enlarged – but more competitive – market promises to be a vast task. It is true profits rose strongly in the mid-eighties and were reasonable, despite heavy running costs, in the eighteen months from the spring of 1986, when the new owners took full control ahead of Big Bang. Yet a great deal of previous profit was then wiped out in the October 1987 share crash, as later loss announcements, cutbacks and injections of new capital showed.

It is therefore clear that the massive £3bn or so laid out on the restyled London stock market must be viewed as a long-term investment, which will at best take a considerable time to earn its keep. The huge spending is eloquent testimony to the worth many world groups put on a place at the City securities table, but not all of them are likely to be able to sustain their first ambitions.

For the partners in the firms which sold out, the big take-over rush was a Klondike-like strike of gold. Concerns with partners totalling some 1 500 in 1983 received £1·5bn or so of purchase money. But it would not be correct to do a simple division sum and say that 1 500 people got £1m each. Some partners had only a small equity stake in their firm and so were not entitled to much, though many, on the other hand, received much more than £1m. The actual numbers of partners sharing the sales proceeds also grew a good deal between 1983 and 1986, which made for some thinner spread of benefits. This was because various middle-rank employees were going to be much needed in the bigger market and it was desired that they should receive the encouragement and tangible advantages of partner status at this critical time.

In addition, steps were sometimes taken to allot some of the purchase cash to employees in the 'marzipan layer', the next tier down from the 'icing level' of the partners. This was, for instance, done by a distribution to certain such staff of Wedd and de Zoete just before Barclays took over and formed BZW in June 1986. Sir Martin Jacomb, BZW's chairman, later commented on this arrangement: 'The partners recognised that the dividing line between the partners getting consideration amounting to significant sums and the next layer down getting nothing was too extreme. So in both cases [Wedd and de Zoete] it was the partners' decision to pass on chunks of consideration to the marzipan layer.'[13] It was reported in one newspaper[14] that in early June 1986 cheques for between £150 000 and £200 000 had been despatched to a number of BZW salesmen and analysts.

Even allowing for such distributions, probably as many as five hundred or more millionaires were created by the Stock Exchange take-over bonanza. At the big Wedd Durlacher Mordaunt some twenty-five partners received at least £1m each – some more – while substantial, if usually smaller, numbers were similarly enriched at numerous other purchased firms. This great unleashing of wealth helps explain the rush of new investments by British brokers, some of it in farms from Gloucestershire to the Dordogne and in villas from the South of France to the Caribbean. At a more modest level, it accounts for the spread of heated swimming pools all over Surrey.

In most cases the consideration for the purchased firms was disbursed by instalments ('slow money') over some three to five years. Payment of the full amount was usually linked, too, with an understanding (known as 'golden handcuffs') that the recipient would stay with the acquired firm at least for that time. Occasionally the 'handcuffs' were unlocked early by agreement. Often the consideration was in loan stock, maturing for repayment over time and in some cases it was in shares, perhaps with restrictions on their early sale. In some cases, selling working partners retained some claim on part of the profits of the firm transferred, at any rate for a while.

As to taxation on the large profits thrown up by the purchase prices, the general position appears to be that tax only at the then standard 30 per cent rate of capital gains tax was due. One delicate question for the selling partners and their accountants arose, however, over whether an element in the purchase payments could be considered to be in respect of – given in order to retain – the future services of the recipients and so taxable as income, usually at the top, until recently 60 per cent, marginal rate. But this view does not seem to have been taken by the Inland Revenue, closely as it has monitored the scene and actively as it has watched 'golden hello' recruitment payments, on which (see Chapter 4) a more stringent view has usually been taken.

Altogether, therefore, in the event, the restructuring of London's stock market brought, not worry, but a cornucopia of benefits to its former owners, as it was also to do to the many needed new recruits.

4 The Pay Explosion

To me, a company's biggest asset is its people, or its greatest
liability is its people, and nobody ever weighs up the assets and
liabilities related to people.

Mr Michael Silverman, Chairman,
Merton Associates, executive
search consultants.[1]

If it's only money keeping you at a firm, then you're bound to leave
– someone always offers you more.[2]

Mr David Smith, equity market-maker,
Smith New Court.

If the banks' race to buy up Stock Exchange firms developed into a
scramble, it was matched by the succeeding stampede as the new
combines fought for scarce talent to staff their groups. Never before
had it been so much the right time for those with the right expertise in
the right place to capitalise on their assets.

Young executives of a few years' standing could frequently double
their pay overnight if they switched to a rival house. And they were
sometimes able to treble it in swiftly-growing areas like gilts
market-making. At the top end of the scale, a few people coaxed over
to head key new ventures could command £1m-a-year packages.
Incentives and baits to change jobs proliferated. Youth, and the
ability to stay the punishing pace in a near-round-the-clock market,
were at a premium, while life-long experience counted for less in
trading so fast-changing that past knowledge could seem irrelevant.
'Age has become less meaningful: chaps of 25 to 27 have made huge
sums of money', a recruitment expert recalls. And it was true that the
nature of desired skills was changing with the move to electronic
dealing with which youthful City people felt at home. 'The young are
very screen-literate', while 'Some older brokers' talents are now less
germane' are further comments.

Even lords of old can scarcely have been more sought in marriage,
with big dowries, than were bright gilt and Eurobond traders who
had left school at eighteen and graduated through a few years in the
City, pursued by would-be employers. Thousands swapped jobs in a
three-year free-for-all as big money to switch posts was offered on a

scale to overbear old loyalties. The richest game of musical chairs in history was played out in an amazing version where virtually none lost and almost all had prizes. Even the tougher environment following the late 1987 share crash left the much above-average pay levels intact.

How did it happen that people often far from intellectual giants – the streetwise trader with 'feel' for his market, the well-connected salesman with good contacts – commanded rewards well into six figures? And that the exceptional ones, along with many top Eurobond specialists, could do better than that? After all, none were nuclear – sorry, high-energy – physicists or brain surgeons, scarce talents whose development requires long years of post-graduate study.

The answer lies in the simple law of supply and demand, that where there is a shortage, the price of the wanted commodity soars. As the City prepared for its role as the European time-zone securities centre, numerous houses were growing simultaneously and all questing for fresh staff. So, in the London of 1983 to 1986, skilled experts were about as easily available as foie gras in a famine. Organisations had often to double or treble in scale, with their payrolls lengthening dramatically, if they were to be fitted for the post-Big Bang world. But most were at least reinforced with big capital, from which they could afford to shop for recruits in what soon became very much a sellers' market.

The unbridled rush to sign up fresh staff with greatly increased rewards did not occur without leaving some sense of disquiet. This was particularly so since the Thatcher government, and notably the Chancellor of the Exchequer, Mr Nigel Lawson, was at the same time urging ordinary workers to curb pay demands or even take reduced wages to price themselves into jobs. The City loomed embarrassingly in the background when Mr Rodney Bickerstaffe, general secretary of the public service workers' union NUPE, demanded: 'Why is it necessary to pay the rich more – and the poor less – to get them to work?'

But delicacy of feeling was more than the City could afford as it hustled to build greatly expanded, sometimes almost completely fresh, investment houses. Moreover, the searchers-for-staff had to allow for another major factor forcing up rewards: that they were trawling – often guided by international head-hunters – in a global pool of talent. Higher United States pay levels further helped force up London rates as deregulation trends made the staff market more of a world-wide forum. One leading recruitment agent says the activity of international head-hunters in London in winkling out top talent in the early eighties 'increased the competition for top performers, resulting in more competitive salaries for high flyers'. The head-hunter industry has, of course, itself enjoyed a bonanza time in the great City staff-seeking race, just as has that of City company marriage-brokers. Its fees are often around a third, payable by the employer, of the new employee's first year basic salary.

As the newly structured City houses were planned out, crucial managing and other top posts had to be filled swiftly. One of the most high-level moves came when Sir Martin Jacomb left Kleinwort Benson where he had been a vice chairman, and had masterminded British Telecom's flotation, to chair Barclays' combined new Barclays de Zoete Wedd (BZW). America's Merrill Lynch signalled how serious its City venture would be by attracting a well-known banker, Mr Stanislas Yassukovich, an American, from European Banking (which was passing under Holland's big Amro Bank), to head its European operations from London. Merrill also hired a top Euro-bond figure, Mr Michael Von Clemm, who had just left the prominent Crédit Suisse–First Boston. Mr Peregrine Moncreiffe switched from American Express's Shearson Lehman to run the London capital markets business of E. F. Hutton, a large United States brokerage house (later bought by Shearson), at reported pay of £1m.[3] A later high-level switch came when, in 1987, Mr John Craven move into the top executive job at the merchant bank Morgan Grenfell.

Considering that, in the post-Big Bang markets, a greatly enlarged crowd of gilts companies were to act as market-makers, the pressure for staff was at first most intense in the fields of gilts and market-making. Gilts people woke up to the fact they were in high demand and able to command much improved pay conditions. 'Many had been where they were a fairly long time and were grossly underpaid for what they did: suddenly one could put a value on their market worth. That was market forces', a recruitment expert recalls. Job switches between firms escalated, and prevailing pay rates shot up. One harassed top gilts broker, when asked in 1985 if it was true that salaries had doubled within a few months, groaned: 'The flaming things have trebled.'

Equity jobbing talent was also wanted and in scarce supply, as was shown by one of the most dramatic events, the departure for Kleinwort Benson of the 'Wedd eight', as described in Chapter 3. This move in force sent shock waves through the City, alerting all concerned to the new dangers of staff losses. Nothing, it soon seemed, could stop the rush of staff poaching. A telephone invitation to have a drink or lunch, often away from the gossipy City, with a key man from a rival house or a head-hunter was turned down by some but found irresistible by many.

The general post, first focussed on gilts – for which discount houses, specialists in short-term money and skilled in bill-dealing, were also a recruitment ground – spread rapidly through new sectors. Enough fresh groups were branching out into equity-market-making – where over thirty groups trading in alpha (top line) shares alone would replace far fewer jobbers – for demand to quickly build up there, too. And Eurobond staffs, usually highly-paid because of the big profits made (at least until lately) in their vast market, were much sought-after since developing groups often added Eurobond capability to round out their activities.

Then the hiring wave surged on to analyst-research staff at the bigger brokers. New investment banks saw research as a key sales bait for their services and scarce talent in this field grew much sought-after. The movement also spread to economists, a specialist academic group wanted to provide background studies to clients and as instant interpreters of world events to their group's in-house dealers. Several of an élite group switched posts at climbing salaries, Mr Gavyn Davies leaving Simon & Coates (now part of Chase Manhattan) for the expanding United States house Goldman Sachs, Mr Malcolm Roberts moving from Laing & Cruickshank to Salomon Brothers and Mr Roger Bootle switching from Capel-Cure Myers to Lloyds Merchant Bank. Mr Brendan Brown joined part of the NatWest Investment Bank (NWIB) from Phillips & Drew and the former Treasury economist Mr Neil MacKinnon moved to Japan's Nomura. Others stayed put, but with a bigger role in a widening organisation, Phillips & Drew's gilts expert, Mr Stephen Lewis, being one example.

Slightly lower-profile, but still in strong demand, were the fund managers who staff some of the City merchant banks' most profitable activities, the handling of big clients' investments. Just how much scarcity and rising pay rates were felt here was illustrated when the big British Rail Pension Fund largely wound up its own management team and farmed the work out to City houses, since it could not afford to hire and retain needed staff.

Another, already well-paid, sector of City expertise, the corporate finance advisory work of the merchant banks was less directly affected by Big Bang. But with some groups adding this service to fill out their ventures, talent in the field stayed much in demand. Among notable moves was Mr John MacArthur's switch from Kleinwort to head a new department at Pru-Bache.

Later, after Big Bang, when the City was acclimatising itself to the new screen-based trading and related procedures, paperwork backlogs built up and this meant increased demand, and pay, for the normally less generously rewarded backroom 'settlement' staffs skilled in documentation handling.

Senior job changes hit the headlines most. But the recruitment trend spread rapidly, focussing on the 'marzipan layer', the people next down from partner status who bore much responsibility in Stock Exchange firms. Here was a fruitful source of talent and, as it began to be wooed, many skilled employees switched firms for very lucrative pay packages. Existing employers then soon realised that their experienced 'marzipan' people were such an obvious recruitment target that their conditions needed to be radically improved if they were not to be left vulnerable to the head-hunters' blandishments.

The feelings and ambitions of the 'marzipan' people are understandable, considering how sharp a divide the old City caste system often meant between the smart partners and the experienced staff below them. One observant recruitment expert thus portrayed the attitude, and readiness to be poached, of certain 'marzipan' people early in the staff-switch merry-go-round: 'If your boss spends two hours at lunch and returns well-oiled, is often in committee meetings, and just occasionally tells you what to do – when you can do it better and (though he's collecting a million pounds) you reckon *you* make the profit – you're not going to have a very happy relationship with him.' While this doubtless does less than justice to many dedicated City top people, it still reflects conditions that did sometimes exist.

Certainly the City Revolution did wonders in winning recognition for 'marzipan' staffs, who were often either moved up into partnerships, ahead of Big Bang, and so given access to a share in a firm's take-over price, or were, at least, enabled to climb rapidly up their firm's promotion ladder. Indeed, so intense was the poaching spree that considerable persuasions were exercised to retain even mediocre staff where they were for fear of a spreading rash of empty desks. 'A year ago I would have been glad to be rid of them: now I must offer extra to keep them', sighed an anxious boss after lunching some acknowledged third-raters. All this produced the odd result that many City 'yuppies' of moderate gifts were soon earning several times as much as some of their more talented former fellow-students or schoolfellows were getting in less privileged sectors.

The exits and entrances between firms often took place *en bloc* as whole teams moved together. The new hirer could thus fill a major need in one go and perhaps obtain an intake whose whole was worth more than its parts individually. For the group used to working together, there was the advantage that terms could be worked out in a single negotiation, but the practice magnified the blow to the firm deserted. The revolving doors could whirl swiftly, too: in one recorded case, a recruit arrived at Chase Manhattan Bank one Monday and by the end of the week was on the move once more as part of a team shift.[4]

With the intense pressure for staff as groupings expanded in unison, new sources outside the securities industry were actively tapped by alert head-hunters for open-handed clients. Talent in the legal and accountancy profession was often persuaded to join the financial sector. And another, previously narrow path, from Whitehall to the City, was far more frequently trodden, as the gap between soaring pay levels in the financial world and those in the shrinking and somewhat disenchanted Civil Service widened sharply. And the recruitment process quickened as, with the spread of City–Whitehall consultations on such issues as privatisations, the money men realised what a reservoir of good, modestly-paid, university-trained talent lurked, little-recognised, in government Ministries. There had for some years been a small brain drain to the merchant banks from that prestigious bastion of Whitehall, the Treasury, but from 1983–4 this outflow became a flood. No fewer than forty-four officials of the medium-senior Principal grade and above quit the Treasury in the three years to mid-1986, mostly for the City. Many swiftly doubled their salaries and some upped their pay to yet higher levels, bonuses included. As the success of this recruitment became known, the trend spread to other Ministries, including the Department of Trade and Industry, some of whose staff moved east to man the City's new self-regulatory watchdog bodies.[5]

People switching from one City house to a rival were usually expected to clear their desk and leave as soon as their move was announced. This was not so much due to resentment on the first boss's part – the realities of the City general post were well understood – as because of the need for the departing person to be distanced as quickly as possible from the secrets of his old group. In some cases a *cordon sanitaire* of some months' gap between the two jobs was demanded by the former employer.

Exasperating as key staff losses through 'poaching' were to firms losing staff, and lucrative as were the rewards offered to woo staff over, there were almost no cases of soccer-style 'transfer payments' being made by the gaining to the losing company. In one never-publicised case, however, a claim for compensation for something like enticement was made – when, in 1985, the money broker–financial conglomerate Exco lost two directors of its WICO Far East broking offshoot to Wall Street's Salomon Brothers, whose international network has been much enlarged. Exco took the view that the departure was not in line with the individuals' existing contracts. The matter was resolved with a £500 000 payment to Exco from Salomon, which made no admission of liability.[6] Without this being revealed, shareholders at Exco's annual meeting in June 1986 were told that the intensifying competition for financial services (in Japan in this case) had made it difficult for WICO to retain its staff. In the previous year, it was added, the firm had lost two key directors to Salomon Brothers for salaries of around £500 000 a year each and others had threatened to follow.[7]

It is now part of folklore far beyond the Square Mile that City people's earnings burst skywards in the mid-eighties. As the prominent accountants Coopers & Lybrand said in 1986, summing up their survey on City salaries the previous year: 'There is now a general perception that the City is experiencing a pay explosion.'[8]

Remuneration in Britain's financial sector was also taking on a transatlantic-like complexity, so that simple words like 'salary' no longer captured the totality of reward packages. Bonuses – some geared to the individual's 'performance' – share options, cheap mortgages, pensions, cars and other perks became familiar parts of what the Americans call employee 'compensation'. Such multi-part packages have in fact been rapidly spreading for some time in the upper echelons of United Kingdom industry, where it has been estimated that extra benefits on average add 45 per cent to directors' actual salaries.[9] But in the City the additions can top up basic pay by considerably more.

Performance-geared pay arrangements, whereby those seen as generating most profit themselves benefit personally, have some odd results in the City. For this system brings very high rewards to those in the front line of a securities business, whether as dealers or brokers bringing in custom. 'Star' merchant bankers acting for clients in take-over fights, where vast sums can turn on the outcome, may also see the steep fees such work brings their employers reflected in their own remuneration.

But this tying of individuals' earnings to the profits they are credited with being instrumental in making up-ends salary structures, often leaving top people making less than those junior to them in the pyramid. 'If a trader can quickly earn a million dollars, one has to pay him more than one is getting oneself', the director of a Eurobond house notes resignedly. And the head of a big investment bank admits calmly: 'I don't regard it as an anomaly if people in my firm get paid more than I do. You have to respond to the market-place, not go by a predetermined hierarchical salary structure.'

A prominent American presiding over a big United States securities house in London admits to being in a similar position, which he finds shocks British traditionalists but in which he sees some consoling aspects. 'I have working for me at least fifteen people who earn more than I do', he says. 'I once remarked to a senior person at a UK clearing bank that one of the ways my performance is measured by my own bosses is according to how many people I have whose earnings are higher than mine. The banker answered in surprise: "You mean you actually have staff under you paid more than you are?" And I explained: "Yes, of course, the more the merrier. The more of such people there are, the better I am perceived to be doing."' Such are the consequences of a strongly 'paid by results' system. For completeness it should be added that the American maestro probably made up at least some of the salary discrepancy through his own shareholding in the firm.

Some British City people, however, cannot come to terms with the idea of such paradoxical pay patterns. As a foreign exchange manager argues: 'a dealer is only part of a team, and couldn't operate without it, so an exceptional reward is unfitting'. And some merchant bankers dislike the concept of 'star' advisor earners, thinking it productive of jealousies, generally stressful to the organisation's morale and perhaps prejudicial to good order and discipline. There is also the controversial issue of how matters work out when star traders turn in losses instead of profits.

Many City firms distribute bonuses widely to staff (not just to star earners), but keep these flexible to avoid being locked into irreducible overhead costs and so retain scope for making savings, other than through sackings, if trade turns sour. The practice of fixing bonus rates at a late stage in the light of a firm's results is now widespread, even if, in the mid-eighties recruitment turmoil, some minimum bonuses were fixed for a time. The general approach was explained by Sir Martin Jacomb, chairman of Barclays Bank's recently-created BZW investment bank:

> The important thing about the payroll is to make sure you can adjust it downwards as well as upwards and that means that a big element in everybody's pay, including my own, is non-pensionable bonus, so that, if business goes down through lack of volume or lack of success, that can be cut – and I would expect it, in those circumstances, to be cut. Of course, in the initial years, it has to be guaranteed – but that only lasts for one, two or at the maximum three years.

And, summing up BZW's salary approach, which would be quite separate from its parent bank's, he added: 'Our salary policy is to be market-related, independent of Barclays plc, not extravagant, and heavily bonus-oriented so as to avoid being trapped into permanent fixed overheads.'[10]

While the American preference for high, and often performance-related, pay has much influenced the City, there are still some differences between the employment packages of United States-owned and British firms. Often the Americans provide rather more in actual cash but accord shorter contracts and fewer perks. 'It's your decision whether to have a Rolls-Royce of a Mini, a £100000 or a £1m house', says one recruitment expert. Another feature is the American insistence on parting quickly with unsatisfactory employees. 'Shape up or ship out' is the attitude. And when sackings are made to cut overheads, United States houses complete the process swiftly.

A facet of the City jobs general post which has found a place in the language is the practice of paying 'golden hellos' as baits to wanted employees to change firms. The term is now as voguish as 'telephone number salaries', meaning those in seven figures. Golden hellos are, as a staff seeker explains, 'mainly related to unshackling golden handcuffs'. In other words, they are to coax the prospective recruit to quit his existing group, where he is probably still due, if he stays, to collect some benefit connected with that concern's purchase by a bank. Sometimes, though, joining fees are paid to those entering the City from outside, including new university graduates. Golden hellos may themselves create new 'handcuffs', by being payable over time and subject to reduction should the newcomer leave quickly.

Tax on golden hellos is, in the view of the Inland Revenue and of many accountants, due at the traditionally higher rate applicable (for the well-off) to income, rather than – more advantageously – liable only to the capital gains tax levied on proceeds of sales of Stock Exchange firms. This is because these payments have been generally seen as in respect of future services. The 1988 Budget, however, ironed out many of these rate differentials.

This whole subject is, though, important enough for the Inland Revenue to have established a special office to keep track of developments in the City Revolution and to watch that the State receives the tax it should. What is notable is that, despite the very large sums flowing to individuals during the City's huge shake-up, it was decided that no special tax levy should be made on the various transactions, although (see page 83) there was some expectation that such action would be taken.

Just how high City pay levels had climbed even by 1985 was shown by the Coopers & Lybrand study[11] quoted above. This revealed that, even those few years ago, a formidable array of six-figure cash salaries was already being paid. And that was the position despite the fact that the survey did not cover the pay of heads of firms but only that of chiefs of departments and lower ranking staff. Moreover, the findings almost certainly understated actual maximum salaries, since some of the largest houses – with the highest pay rates – had declined to take part in the study. Even so, the findings were remarkable by previous British, if not transatlantic, standards.

City groups' capital markets departments, those arranging Euro-bond and similar finance, were the best paid, according to Coopers' report. Over 60 per cent of department heads in that sector had total 1985 cash earnings of over £100 000, the highest-paid employee identified receiving £300 000, half in basic salary and half in bonus.

Even junior bond traders could earn as much as £57 000, though a number in this category were on less than £30 000.

Outside the top-paying capital markets, the fields where the largest proportions of department heads were getting over £100 000 were the gilts and merchant banks' take-over advice sectors, where the figure in each case was some 40 per cent. A rather lower 25 per cent of chiefs of departments in investment management were into six figures. But these fund managers did well as to cars and other benefits, as indeed did most of the groups surveyed. Further increases in all the areas studied will doubtless have taken place with the general salary uptrend since 1985, when the evidence just described was collected.

The Coopers survey also found that a very high proportion of the City's securities and investment bank-type jobs – up to 93 per cent of those in the Eurobond sales and swaps areas – were attracting bonuses. But the ratio of bonus to salary varied greatly, ranging up to 78 per cent of pay for swaps specialists. Confirmation of the prevalence of 'golden hellos' came in a finding that 'substantial lump sum inducements, over and above the normal remuneration package' were being made 'to recruit and retain staff'. These could be either 'golden hellos' on joining or 'guaranteed bonus payments, often not obviously related to performance, as an inducement to stay'. In some cases contracts provided for guaranteed bonuses, in certain instances up to late 1987, 'to lock in the staff concerned during the period of adjustment to deregulation'. Finally, a variety of non-salary benefits, in the shape of pensions, share options, mortgages and loans, insurance and cars was, the survey reported, also provided.

A year on, in 1986, six-figure salaries were very widespread in the City and seven-figure ones were not unknown as time went on. It was revealed in 1987 that Mr Christopher Heath, managing director of Baring Securities, an offshoot of the merchant bank Baring Brothers, had had a pay and benefits package of £2·5m,[12] allowing for a linkage to the profitability of the group's successful Far East venture. At the fund management concern Mercury Asset Management, controlled by the S. G. Warburg merchant bank group, the chairman, Mr Peter Stormonth Darling, received £1 051 000 in 1986–7 and that firm's unnamed highest-paid director £1 265 000. Both these latter figures included substantial 'non-recurring long-term performance related remuneration which has accrued over five years'; the figures exclude pension contributions for the directors. At S. G. Warburg itself, the chairman, Sir David Scholey, received

£355 000 and sixteen further directors each over £100 000, in 1986–7.[13] But such figures were not exceptional in the mid-eighties City. For it is partly a matter of chance that much salary detail emerges in the accounts of quoted merchant banks which directly employ their most high-powered people. In other cases, numerous top earners are on the books of operating subsidiaries, with the result that their pay is not disclosed in the published accounts of the listed owning commercial bank or holding company.

Generally, the very high pay levels prevailing in the new City are defended as both rewards for skill, hard work and long hours in demanding conditions and as necessary to retain high-quality people in a competitive international market. None the less, the figures cited provide a very stark contrast with the average British employee's earnings of £9 604 a year in (April) 1986.

How has all this outpouring of wealth been seen by statesmen and politicians and the City Fathers themselves? The evidence is that, despite some unease, it has been accepted as a necessary price for the City's revamping to an international model. In a newspaper interview in March 1986,[14] the Governor of the Bank of England, Mr Robin Leigh-Pemberton, said:

I can understand it is distasteful for someone who is unemployed to read of these high City wages offered to talented young people at a time of great pressure and competition. But I can also understand employers putting great pressure on such people. They have to compete in the world markets and they do a very specialised job.

Then, alluding to the point often made about sportsmen, actors and authors with supposedly limited years of 'peak' performances, he added: 'In addition there is a shortness of career which is comparable with pop singers and athletes. Indeed, this trend may not be sustained, some salaries may come down and some of these high-flyers may even be redundant.'

A slight difference of emphasis, reflecting more anxiety, characterised the comments on the subject of his colleague, the then Deputy Governor, Sir Kit McMahon, now chairman of Midland Bank. 'One of the means by which any company can strengthen its management or introduce new skills is to seek out staff and attract them from their existing employers', he told a conference in Switzerland in 1985.

This is certainly a much used technique in the City at present and, while it may not be inherently undesirable when used in moderation, the scale it is now assuming has important implications not only for the individual firms – at both the losing and receiving ends of particular high-cost transfers – but also much more widely. There is, after all, only a limited pool of talent available in the short term and if it is being sought out by too many firms the consequences are inevitable: a significant escalation of salaries generally and a lack of stability in staffing.

Both of these developments are worrying ... If key staff – and even, on occasion, whole teams – can be offered inducements to move suddenly from one institution to another, it becomes very difficult for any bank to rely on the commitment individuals will give to implementing its plans.[15]

For his part, the chairman of the Stock Exchange, Sir Nicholas Goodison, justified the salary surge by saying, in a BBC interview, that 'good peoples' salaries are rising to international levels'.[16]

There were some reports of government concern on the subject of the pay explosion. 'Senior political figures are claiming that Margaret Thatcher is considering how to tax the City's new wealthy', *The Sunday Times* said soon before the 1986 Budget under the headline 'Super-pay tax threat'.

It is widely thought within Whitehall that she feels acutely embarrassed that with the deregulation of the Square Mile, some 25 year olds are now earning six figure salaries while the dole queue is measured in seven figures. Last week Mrs Thatcher told senior City executives that she felt 'great concern' about the surge in City pay.[17]

But, in the event, as already noted, the 1986 Budget unveiled shortly afterwards contained no new measures to tax the rich rewards.

Some hope that the City salary boom will in time abate, leaving rewards in this part of the financial world less outstandingly high compared with other sectors. BZW's chairman, Sir Martin Jacomb, says: 'The amount of remuneration reflects the excess of demand over supply, but that won't be of indefinite duration. You saw the same thing with the foreign exchange market when fixed exchange rates were abandoned. Then new people moved up and that will happen here to some extent.'[18] The recruitment expert Mr Michael Silverman of Merton Associates remarks: 'My view is that the salaries will get re-balanced over the next five years and then you will not have this tremendous divergence between rewards in different sectors. That's what happened in New York: you've got a much more balanced salary structure there.'[19] There are some signs of the start of this more sedate trend following the share price crash of October 1987.

How have the new City conglomerates, in which Stock Exchange firms have been merged with merchant bank interests to form new-style investment banks, settled down in practice? There was much talk early on about cultural differences and potential clashes between what might prove discordant personalities. 'The banks [the new owners] are risk-averse, while we are natural risk-takers', former jobbers and brokers often commented, warning of misunderstandings to come.

Worries over incompatibilities persisted during the long 1983-6 phase, when the banks had only minority stakes in the Exchange firms as a prelude to the full ownership they took before Big Bang. But once the get-togethers were consummated, the anxieties often eased. A banker who watched over developments from an eminent position recalls some of the problems of the adjustment process:

What was extremely difficult was trying to blend three cultures, those of jobber, broker and merchant bank. And then you had to consider all three, in total, *vis-à-vis* the owning clearing bank. A particular problem was, I think, that it took abut three years from taking the initial stakes to getting all the people into the same building. Once people are working under the same roof, they get to know each other and it gels reasonably quickly. But in the interim, when they were all working semi-independently, in different buildings, everybody was extremely suspicious and no-one actually bothered very much about getting to know the others. That *was* difficult. And then you had the cultural problem: the regular banker would say: 'Don't look at those investment banking boys, they're just plain spivs.' And the investment banking boys would regard the clearing bankers as just a rather stupid form of elephant.

Various people still lament the changed tone and atmosphere the new City trends have brought. There are even lingering regrets about the switch from former cautious recruiting approaches to the present aggressive methods. 'When I came into the Stock Exchange', says somebody from a stockbroking dynasty 'my father wouldn't let me hire somebody from another firm without first ringing up to check that it was all right. But that kind of courtesy stopped ten to fifteen years ago. I think we've lost a lot of the nicer aspects of City relationships, ethics and so forth, and I think the rest will disappear in the aggro of competition.' Such traditional practices are, indeed, unlikely to return to a City where business is business and competition has overcome old-style inhibitions.

Part II
Markets and Institutions

5 City Markets after Big Bang

A bull market is a great shock absorber of the penalties of experimentation.

Sir David Scholey, Chairman of S.G.
Warburg Group.[1]

By and large, we feel better served now than under a system which required us to use brokers and jobbers. We seem more relaxed as our own price gatherers.

Mr Mick Newmarch, Chief Executive,
Prudential Portfolio Managers, and
Director, Prudential Corporation.[2]

It's often said that futures are frightfully risky, but putting people into stocks and shares can be just as risky.

Mr Michael Jenkins, Chief Executive,
London International Financial
Futures Exchange.[3]

The City's Big Bang day, 27 October 1986, when Britain's glossy, modern-style stock market made its bow, may have dawned like just another Monday. But there was soon no doubt it had ushered in a new age. Business at once burgeoned and within a year trade with customers in United Kingdom shares was nearly double what it had been before the reforms. The soaring trend owed something to the climb in share prices, which rose 46 per cent in the first seven months of 1987 after a near-one quarter increase in 1986, and to the launch of privatisation issues. But the much enlarged market, where thirty-five well-capitalised market-makers replaced thirteen jobbers, with its greater depth – facilitating large deals – and its cheaper costs, was clearly the trigger to the volume leap. By September 1987, customer business in domestic British equities was running at over £1·1bn a day, against £0·6bn in 1986, with £0·8bn of further deals taking place among the market-makers.

In short, competition had arrived, bringing its natural consequence of benefiting the main users, the investing institutions, while also pressuring the stockbroking community's profit margins. 'You've ended a monopoly and we're getting a much cheaper and better service. From the institutional point of view, things have definitely improved. From the broker's standpoint, they tend to be worse', a manager of one of the biggest institutions summed up. Another top investor, Mr Mick Newmarch, chief of the Prudential Portfolio Managers, said: 'For too long, we felt, those whose affairs we are employed to manage had been denied the benefit which would flow . . . from the introduction of serious competition into the affairs of the Stock Exchange . . . [Now] we are certainly dealing substantially more cheaply than prior to Big Bang.'[4]

Under the new system, which made the Stock Exchange the first traditional bourse to go electronic, the market-makers feed onto the SEAQ screen network the two-way (bid and offer) prices at which they stand ready to deal. Brokers acting for clients survey the screen for the most promising quotes, then ring up to transact orders. As the quotes may be only for smallish numbers of shares (1000 even for the larger 'alpha' companies), a degree of shopping around and price negotiation for the normally much larger institutional deals may well be involved. However, an important aspect of the new market is that, in normal times, the screen quotes in practice hold good for much larger deals than the minimum. Also, market-makers can signal, by indicating 'LXL' on the screen, that their price is firm for at least a 100 000 share block. Each share has a screen 'page' that sets out the quotes of the various houses, from which can be seen the 'touch', the narrowest gap between available buying and selling prices.

Using letters of the Greek alphabet, the Exchange splits the British shares it lists into four categories, the top one being alphas, those of over 130 of the leading companies most widely dealt in. There have to be ten or more market-makers in an alpha – in fact the average is sixteen – while the companies must have at least a market worth of £625m and quarterly turnover of £100m. Betas, the next in size, have four or more market-makers willing to quote firm prices. 'Indicative' quotations only are put out for the smaller gammas but firm prices must be named on request from the minimum two traders in these shares. Firm quotations are also given, on enquiry, for the lesser deltas.

To ensure a well-informed market, the Exchange requires the price and size of deals in alphas to be reported within five minutes, following which these details are relayed on the screen 'pages' to show the 'last trade'. Companies that are the subject of bids, are, if necessary, promoted to being 'temporary alphas' for this purpose. Correspondingly less demanding rules apply to the lower tiers so that, while beta deals must be as quickly reported, their particulars (like those of alphas, for the record) are published only in the next day's Stock Exchange Daily Official List (SEDOL), along with the same data for gammas and deltas. The slower dissemination of trade particulars for the less actively traded stocks occurs because the 'positions' of the limited number of traders in them might be damagingly illumined if deals were immediately published. The size and price of block trades in alphas 'matched' by brokers which are not market-makers have also to be at once reported and publicised for the sake of a fair market.

The effect of the greater competition and larger capital in the revamped market is that it has generally been possible for investors to transact quite large deals without moving prices against themselves. An early 1987 Stock Exchange survey showed that more than three-quarters of the big orders in between half a million and one million alpha shares were being transacted at or better than prices quoted for 100 000-share amounts.[5] This is, however, the sort of position that can, and does, change rapidly in turbulent markets, like those prevailing after the share price crash in October 1987.

A major feature of the Big Bang changes has been the cut in the cost of transacting large share deals. This has come about in various ways but has, overall, slimmed the cost for major institutional business by about a half. There are several major adjustments which have produced this result.

For one thing, a substantial proportion of larger deals is now transacted with market-makers 'net', with no commission charge. (The market-maker would hope to gain something by itself on-selling for more than it has bought at, or buying in more cheaply than the price at which it has sold shares.) In the autumn of 1987, just over a quarter of all deals, by value, were in this form, though a higher one-third of those over £250 000 were done net,[6] as was a yet greater percentage of still bigger deals. Moreover, although the overall rate of commission, when it is charged, is still, at first sight surprisingly, little changed since Big Bang at 0·45 per cent, this is because the costlier small private investor business has spurted, raising the average. For big institutional deals between £250 000 and £1m, commission rates are much lower, at 0·25 per cent, compared with 0·31 per cent before October, 1986, while for over £1m the charge is 0.2 per cent or less. At the other end of the scale, though, the small investor has seen minimum commission rates raised. Allowing for the fact that a substantial proportion of business is now done net, the average commission on all deals works out at 0·33 per cent.[7]

Another factor in dealing costs is the 'touch', the gap between the most favourable buying and selling prices that can be picked out from the bid–offer quotes of the various market-makers. Average touches in mid 1987 were little changed from before Big Bang at 0·76 per cent for big alpha deals.[8] On the largest trades, where dealers are at greatest risk, the touch can be rather more, and in 1987 was higher still, though less than before Big Bang, in the lower-tier beta and other categories. But here again a dramatic widening takes place in disturbed markets: in the month after the October 1987 crash, touches in alphas and betas widened two-and-a-half times as dealers sought to protect themselves.[9]

Considering that Stamp Duty was also halved at Big Bang by a Chancellor keen to give the City revolution a fair wind, investors stood overall to gain significantly from the late 1986 changes. Some shift to net trading, the squeeze on commission rates for larger deals, and the reduced Stamp Duty, all helped. Putting all these together, the Bank of England calculated early in 1987 that a big institutional deal of £500 000 would have cost 0·9 per cent to 1·1 per cent of its value to put through after Big Bang, a cost almost halved from the previous 1·8 per cent. Even a £1000 trade for an individual was estimated to be costing modestly less, at 2·3 per cent, against 3·1 per cent.[10]

Meanwhile, London's fledgling market in international shares showed such growth through most of 1987, as the vogue for foreign investment spread, that by the autumn daily dealing in this popular sector was little short of that in United Kingdom equities. Before the October price tumble caused a fit of panic repatriation, international equity trade through the Stock Exchange had reached £510m a day. And on top of that about as much again was transacted outside the Exchange through major United States and other City houses, making a London total of £1bn. A market-making system somewhat similar to that for United Kingdom shares, but less developed, is run through SEAQ International, an arm of the Exchange's electronic system, with the participation of 45 market-makers, United Kingdom and foreign. SEAQ International carries price quotes for some 700 foreign shares, but trading can and does range over several thousand issues, even though it is concentrated on a few hundred familiar international names. In the autumn of 1987, about half the international share trade – rather more than for domestic equities – was done net of commission. Average commission, where charged, worked out at 0·25 per cent, a lower rate than on home business, largely because international deals come in blocks on average five times as large. By contrast with the United Kingdom domestic equity area, there is little dealing between market-makers in the more diffuse and scattered international sector.[11]

In the important gilt-edged market, which will be reviewed in more detail later, the year following Big Bang also saw a big rise in business and cheaper transaction costs. Trade for customers was up by a half at £1·8bn daily, with as much again done in new-style business between market-makers. Later both quantities rose afresh. The fourth and much smaller side of Exchange activity, that in traded options, through which investors and speculators seek to protect themselves against, or profit from, price movements, also saw noted expansion to almost three times pre-Big Bang levels.

Of a number of features which stand out about the first experience of the remoulded, competitive, Stock Exchange system, a notable one is the tussle that has occurred between big clients and securities houses on whether commission should be paid. Initially there was heavy pressure from large institutional users for maximum benefits from the freer system. One observant market-maker recalls: 'In the first few weeks after Big Bang, all the institutions wanted to play the new game, which was dealing as much as they possibly could on a net basis. But there has been some move back now.'

Some fund managers recall the tension that developed in the tussle over dealing terms soon after Big Bang. One who had guaranteed certain business to several brokers in return for halved 0·2 per cent commission remarks of the succeeding weeks: 'We stuck by our bargain, but others [institutional investors] haven't: they have pushed for further concessions or gone off and dealt with somebody else on even finer terms.' Another reports: 'There has been a tremendous fight [among securities houses] for market share.'

At first the pressures led to as much as half of all institutional business being done without commission, with fund managers often by-passing broker firms, or giving them less business, and going direct to market-makers. But later a swing back towards more extensive payment of commission took place. A large part of the reason for this was worry lest the flow of research (analyses and advisory reports on companies) from brokers given insufficient business might dry up, leaving an institutional client feeling short of this desired material. 'This sort of organisation doesn't have its own in-house research and so is quite dependent on the market for it', admits one major institution, explaining how it was reconciled to considerable cum-commission dealing to ensure this service. Another rationalises a decision not to squeeze commission rates by saying it would have been foolish to risk driving broking firms out of business: 'We enjoy net trading. But there are brokers whose advice we value that we think need to be around.' Thus in time a higher average proportion of around 75 per cent of business came to be done on commission, but with some bias towards concentrating it through houses offering top-quality research.

The very biggest institutions with the strongest negotiating muscle continue, however, to enjoy particularly favourable dealing terms. The big Prudential has reckoned that, allowing for the fact that over half its business is on net terms, it now pays average commission of only 0·1 per cent on all its United Kingdom equity business, compared with an average pre-Big Bang agency commission rate of 0·36 per cent.[12] Large institutions also welcome the new screen market for the closer way in which it lets them track market conditions in reaching investment decisions.

The high proportion of much institutional business still done on commission sometimes surprises the securities houses themselves. The chief of a prominent and broadly ranging one, embracing market-making and broking, admits candidly: 'I find it fascinating that we are not more of a net market. A lot of our clients insist on paying us a commission as well as our [dealing] spread. They want visibly to pay for research. They think that, by paying commission, they will get the first calls with our analysts' recommendations and they are right.' But the same expert thinks the trend towards more net trading will return, in effect warning that the big houses with the most competitive market-making could fight to gain new ground from rivals which are essentially broker operations.

The deeper and more capital-rich market has proved able, in stable times at least, to transact outsize share deals that would have been too big to handle before Big Bang and the preceding capital strengthening. For instance, in 1986, the large United States securities house Salomon Brothers partnered London's big broker Hoare Govett (owned by the United States bank Security Pacific) in a £100m-plus placing of BP shares in Europe, the United States and the Far East. The transaction was described as the first global block trade on record. Even in more day to day-type trades, very big deals can be handled, and quickly, in normal conditions. Mr Michael Marks, chief executive of Smith New Court, says: 'We like to quote quickly and make very fast decisions on major trades. We don't like to say to a client who comes with, say, a £10m deal: "We'll take quarter of an hour and phone you back." '[13]

Another novel form of major business, first seen in London after Big Bang, is that of 'portfolio reorganisation' or 'basket' trades. These are made to meet the needs of investment managers desiring to reshape a whole portfolio when, say, they take on a fresh fund and want to sell a long list of its existing holdings. Some of the larger securities houses then bid to buy all the shares, which may be worth perhaps £50m, sight unseen, simply on the basis of the information that the content is well spread, with alphas, betas and so on in stated ratios. In the boom days of early 1987 such trades were done at or near middle-market prices (half-way between bid and offer), leaving the dealer with a very narrow gain if he passed on the shares at his quoted offer (selling) price. But such terms scarcely recognised the risks involved and in time 'basket' trades grew a little costlier, before, not surprisingly, fading in the fraught environment of late 1987.

One of the Stock Exchange's earliest decisions after Big Bang was to close its trading floor for all business save traded options, leaving the new electronic market to operate solely on a screen and telephone basis. Although this arrangement has worked smoothly in normal times, it can magnify discontent, and suspicion that telephones are being deliberately left unanswered, in difficult conditions. And that can create nostalgia for the former market with its fixed trading place. 'In the good old days, you could go down to the Floor and look the jobber in the eye and he had to deal', laments one City person. 'No longer. Come back jobber: all is forgiven.'

The sheer volume upsurge under the new market did bring some problems, the worst of which was the pressure on settlements systems and severe delays in completing transactions. The result was the build-up of a paper mountain of contracts uncompleted because faulty recording under an unfamiliar system, or some other mischance, prevented their being matched and the deals paid for. The difficulty was, in a sense, the price of success, in that larger trading turnover, and the appearance of millions of new 'privatisation' shareholders, multiplied the actual numbers of deals, each of which generated paperwork. One unfortunate by-product of the problem was that many houses faced costly interest bills through borrowing to pay clients before they were themselves paid. Unsettled deals could run into hundreds of millions of pounds at a single firm and bank borrowing by securities houses quickly soared to £7·6bn.

In time the 'mountain' was worked down, but not before the experience had dealt some costly blows. One group hit among many was Kleinwort, which had built an investment house from its merchant bank with the purchase of the big broker Grieveson Grant. Although, as it happened, Kleinwort fared better than many rivals by making money in the share crash of late 1987, its settlements had suffered a severe clog-up, resulting in problems which ultimately required a multi-million pound transfer from reserves. Looking back on the upset, Mr Michael Hawkes, the then Kleinwort chairman, reflected with hindsight: 'When I see St Peter, if I could play through my life again, I should know better. We should immediately have got in consultants, accountants and a head of settlements, as we did later. Everyone was surprised by the enormous increase in business Big Bang brought and within weeks the system was swamped.'[14] Well before the end of 1987, Kleinwort had mastered the problem, which was by then generally under control throughout the City.

One notable outcome of the first year after Big Bang was that total commission income, so far from falling under competitive pressure, surged up by nearly three-fifths, to £1·16bn from £0·74bn in 1985–6. This was because of the big jump in volume and the greater activity by higher-paying private investors. The expanded revenue helped make the bulk of 1987 fairly profitable, despite steep costs, for the City's stock market community. But unfortunately for it, much of the gain was offset or more than wiped out by losses in the share price crash of October.

The world stock market plunge on 'Black Monday', 19 October 1987, and afterwards, which cut around a third from previously swiftly rising British share values, severely tested the City's new trading system. Its consequences, which rippled on for months, mean the post-Big Bang period must be looked at in two distinct phases, prosperity before the crash and considerably rougher going for some time thereafter.

To the extent that London survived the October trading tornado without the failure of a firm and that the system kept going in face of an avalanche of foreign selling, the stronger revamped market was vindicated. But various complaints were heard, particularly from personal clients, about problems of getting through by telephone and about the small man's inability, at worst, to trade at all. Also, much of the vaunted depth of the market evaporated and prices spun rapidly floorwards under the weight of sales.

The plunge, which was set off in the United States and spread world-wide, was an exceptional event – and no market can cope normally with as much as was then thrown at it. Exceptional protective measures were therefore taken. For a brief time in London the SEAQ system was switched from the normal 'firm' to a 'fast' basis, meaning that market-makers could not be held to price quotes still displayed. Price spreads were sharply widened and traders started quoting in lower amounts. All these actions added up to a tough strategic defence which, with its much enlarged capital, saw the market through the crisis.

The crash hit London at an awkward moment when United Kingdom institutions were cash-scarce through having heavy underwriting commitments – including those on the government's £7bn sale of BP shares – which in the market slump they had to take up. Those institutions which were forced to do so sold shares, some foreign ones very heavily. But most big United Kingdom funds simply stopped buying to let cash build up and through dislike of the adverse spreads in the market-makers' defence tactics. Seasoned City people with memories going back to the mid-seventies share slump were unsurprised by the market's protective measures. 'The first thing any jobber worth his salt used to do was widen his prices enormously in a crisis and make them in a smaller size', one veteran of earlier crises remarked. The difficulty of dealing in size in fraught markets proved not unexpected to the experienced: 'The liquidity of a bear market is less than that of a bull market', was one institutional summing up. And the phlegmatic British affected disdain at the volatility of some overseas investors' behaviour. 'Foreigners' behaviour was extraordinary in persisting in selling after Black Monday, however far you cut your price', according to a dealer. Some holders, such as American mutual funds, felt obliged to sell as their own members cashed in. In other cases, the emotional rather than rational wish to take money home in a crisis triggered sales.

On Black Monday, 19 October, when the main force of the storm ripped through world stock markets, London's market-makers

absorbed £250m[15] of United Kingdom shares onto their books as the
'sell, sell, sell' panic proceeded. And this was at a time when they
already held the big quantities of shares they had been accustomed to
carrying during the long bullish era. Memories of that traumatic day
are seared in the minds of many City people, including investment
managers who had to make hard choices on whether to sell, hold,
hedge or even buy to do the best for the savings under their control.
One prominent fund manager, Mr Jim McCaughan, a director of
Phillips & Drew Fund Management – which had earlier made some
precautionary sales – recalls of Black Monday, with its metaphorical
deluge of punches, that 'it was like going ten rounds with Joe
Bugner'.[16]

Following Wall Street's extraordinary 23 per cent plunge a few
hours later, the City's market-makers were by the next day widely
adopting their more cautious tactics in the shape of the broader price
spreads and smaller quantities in which they would deal at quoted
prices. But the whole episode proved very costly for the market. As a
later Stock Exchange study remarked: 'Obviously, most if not all
market makers lost money, and it has been widely publicised that
some lost very large amounts.'[17] Some may have been protected to a
degree through hedging in the futures markets (see below), but the
losses sustained were extensive, as many later announcements
showed.

Although the crash of October 1987 proved a sombre affair for
large market-maker groups which took in shares whose prices then
fell further, the many who stood by their obligations to keep dealing
through good times and bad gained something for the long term in
prestige and, often, business. Here is how the chief of one of the
leading multi-part houses, Mr Richard Westmacott, chairman of
Security Pacific Hoare Govett, reflected in the market slump's
aftermath:

> If you set yourself up to be a market-maker, it is important to
> maintain continuity of service. It's inevitable in the market
> conditions of mid-October, with prices falling fast, that money is
> lost. But, having served our clients well in that period, our market
> share has gone up very sharply and we've been trading extremely
> profitably since October. So we have to take the swings and
> roundabouts in a business like ours. You can't run a business on
> the basis that you're going to have an October 19 every week,

because if you do you're never going to take a risk. The essential
ingredient is a very substantial capital base, making it possible to
take a long view and ride through difficult periods. But that's part
of the trade, and we continue to build our business for the future.[18]

As time went on, the traders' defensive measures were eased
somewhat and spreads started to contract. But some of those
investment businesses accustomed to active dealing have found the
shallower post-crash markets discouraging. Indeed, a key legacy of
the price plunge was that (after huge panic-sale October volumes)
turnover shrank ominously. Daily customer business in United
Kingdom shares was down from an earlier £1·1bn to £0·8bn for some
time. This meant falls in commission revenue, on top of the trading
losses, an adverse squeeze which prompted some houses, notably
United States ones, to cut costs through staff sackings. However, by
the early spring of 1988, share prices and business were beginning to
rally.

More than a year after Big Bang, the signs are that, in the United
Kingdom equity market, there is considerable concentration of
business in relatively few houses. As much as 80–85 per cent of
United Kingdom equity market-making is accounted for by just ten
houses.[19] The biggest single shares of it appear to be held by the two
groups built up from the former largest jobbers, Warburg Securities
and BZW, together with Smith New Court, Warburg perhaps having
slightly the largest. Others, including Hoare Govett, Phillips &
Citicorp Scrimgeour, Kleinwort and Morgan Grenfell also have
have considerable shares.

When broking activity for clients is looked at, Warburg, BZW,
Phillips & Drew, Hoare Govett and others are again prominent. But
the largest single share of this business is held by James Capel, which
chose, from Big Bang, to be an agency broker while – in contrast to
other large firms – not also acting as a registered equity
market-maker. Capel does, however, often fix up matching buying
and selling deals among its own clients, though it involves a
market-maker in such 'agency cross' business, partly in order to
'validate' the price. Thus, if such a block of shares was being bought
by Capel from one client, a minority of it would be sold to a
market-maker, while the majority was placed direct, at the same
price, with another client or clients.

Capel also sometimes acts as a principal by taking stock on to its own books, particularly when it handles large 'basket trade' deals or other disposals of big blocks of shares. However, it claims that such own-account holdings are very small proportionately to its whole business. It is often said that Capel has larger dealings with Smith New Court than with any other equity market-maker and this is so. But its transactions of varying sizes with other market-makers are substantial enough to make it the biggest single business provider to many. There are sometimes complaints that Capel is in effect a 'fair weather market-maker' but, in occasional Stock Exchange debates, it has successfully defended its unique mix of business.

Among further houses also prominent in broking is Cazenove, which is, too, an equity market-maker. Cazenove is the largest broker to industrial and commercial companies and so has a particularly significant flow of new share issues and blocks of existing shares to place.

There are naturally some differences among leading Stock Exchange people on the type of operation best suited to today's environment. One school of thought regards the integrated securities house, the classic Big Bang creation combining market-making with broking – in its facets of serving companies and investment clients, and providing research – as the optimum structure. An exponent of this approach, which his own group has followed, is Mr Peter Wilmot-Sitwell, joint chairman of Warburg Securities, which incorporates the former big broker Rowe & Pitman, of which he was chairman. 'The houses with the rounded businesses will survive', he says. 'To have a fully-fledged securities operation, you need five specific assets: corporate finance expertise, research, market-making, and distribution to investment clients. Then, finally, you need capital to finance all that activity. A shortcoming in any one of these could be very damaging.'[20]

An alternative approach, which many consider successfully exemplified by James Capel, is that there is a major role for the agency broker who uses market-makers and also matches clients' deals and on occasion acts as a principal, holding stock. The coming years will show just how far there is room in the City for both the all-rounder and the broker specialist – and in what numbers.

Foreign groups which made no Stock Exchange purchases but have built up organically in London have been less prominent so far in United Kingdom equities than British firms or foreign groups which did buy up such concerns. But many foreign houses are active in international share trading, while a number of the leaders make markets in British gilts. American groups are also busy in London dealings in the heavily-traded United States Treasury bonds, in which market Salomon Brothers, Goldman Sachs, Merrill Lynch, First Boston and Security Pacific, as well as others, are active operators.

An early impression among City people just after Big Bang was that foreign houses were 'lying in the grass', the implication being that they were not yet very active but were preparing to spring. Then later staff cuts after the October 1987 share crash were read as a lessening of interest. In fact, though, given the large numbers they still employ in London, there is little sign that the main overseas houses have lost interest in the City as the main European time-zone financial centre.

The Stock Exchange as an organisation continued to evolve rapidly after Big Bang. In 1987 a landmark in its history was reached on its link with London's Eurobond houses – briefly represented in the International Securities Regulatory Organisation – in the enlarged and renamed International Stock Exchange (ISE). The merger was partly in pursuit of the Exchange's long-term aim to have as much as possible of all securities business under its wing. But the particular occasion for the get-together was the need, under the City's new watchdog regulatory arrangements, for a single self-regulating organisation (SRO) for the securities industry. This role is now fulfilled by the ISE's alter ego, the Securities Association (TSA), whose international flavour is highlighted by its having a well-known American, Mr Stanislas Yassukovich, Merrill Lynch's European head, as its chairman. The new regulatory arrangements operative as the ISE becomes a 'recognised investment exchange' under the Financial Services Act 1986 should lead to more international equity trading now done separately by foreign houses being routed through the Exchange.

To fend off the risk of a substantial over-the-counter market springing up outside its own bounds, the Exchange, in 1980, launched its Unlisted Securities Market (USM) to give smaller, growing companies the chance of a quotation without the longer track record and other requirements applicable for a full listing. Shares of over 550 companies had been dealt in there by mid-1987 when, allowing for 'promotions' to the main market and for take-overs, 372 remained traded. These concerns include many rapidly developed entrepreneurial firms whose quotation quickly made their founders millionaires. In early 1987 a still more junior Third Market, in which thirty-seven firms traded a year later, was launched for yet smaller and newer concerns.

Ever ambitious, the Exchange has held talks aimed at joining its ten-year-old traded options sector with the separate London International Financial Futures Exchange (LIFFE – pronounced to rhyme with 'wife'), but no such link has, as yet at least, been formed. The Exchange's traded options market, now the sole occupant of the old market floor, allows clients to trade in options to buy or sell, at certain prices, the shares of some sixty leading companies as well as three gilts and the FT–SE 100 share (Footsie) index.

Formalised London trading in ADRs (American Depositary Receipts) – prominent shares 'repackaged' for trading, mainly in New York, in dollar-denominated form – began in London in 1987, the aim being to attract international business in leading United Kingdom shares in this form when New York was closed. Other planned moves include further encouragement to international share trading – recognised to have been set back by the late 1987 crash – and consolidation of information links with exchanges overseas. Another impending innovation is an arrangement for the routine trading of small share transactions through a Stock Exchange Automatic Execution Facility.

Britain's government bond – or gilt-edged – market is an outlet for funds which is rock-safe as to interest and repayment but where quoted values can swing strongly with changing interest rates and altering foreign perceptions of sterling. It is a chosen repository for investment by many big institutions and others wanting a secure home for funds providing a predictable income stream and assured return of capital at a known date. These include insurance groups and pension funds catering for long-term requirements, building societies investing shorter-term, wealthier individuals seeking tax advantages in the choice of certain stocks and foreigners wanting safe holdings denominated in sterling.

The market value of the sector is roughly a third of that in United Kingdom shares: in September 1987 it was worth £146bn (a little above its nominal value), compared with the share market capitalisation of some £500bn before the succeeding heavy crash.

However, turnover in the gilts market by the big financial and institutional groups dominating it is more hectic than that in shares, with 1987 daily customer business being often over £2bn, or double that in British equities, with more rises into 1988.

Investors wanting to be in pounds naturally weigh up the relative merits of being in gilts or shares. But in today's more open world, would-be gilts buyers, who may be in any country, also compare Britain's government bonds with the far larger pool of US Treasury bonds, now the world's biggest single international trading forum. And foreign buyers have indeed been stepping up their interest in Britain's gilts, of which they happened to be the predominant net buyers in 1987, a year in which their share of all gilts business more than doubled to about a quarter.

When the Bank of England reshaped the gilts sector onto a United States-style trading system with nearly thirty 'primary dealer' market-makers, to coincide with the other Big Bang changes, it was chiefly aiming to broaden competition and see the capital employed boosted. This aim was achieved, committed capital multiplying to at least £600m among the crowd of market-makers, including foreign houses which correctly foresaw some expansion of overseas interest in gilts. Effects of additional rivalry soon showed up strongly, with net (no commission) dealing becoming normal for big deals and total commission take from much increased business being more than halved. Spreads between buying and selling prices were also quickly squeezed, and altogether dealing costs fell especially sharply in the long gilts field, where fixed charges had in the past much irritated large investors.

Working of the revamped gilts sector is assisted by six inter-dealer broker firms (IDBs), which foster anonymous dealing between market-makers to lay off their risks. In effect the IDBs provide a screen-assisted order matching service through what has been described as 'an electronic notice board where market-makers can advertise their stock surplus or shortage'.[21]

Market-makers are also cushioned when they 'go short' in the course of their trading by being able to borrow gilts they do not currently hold – to deliver in satisfaction of orders – against subsequent repayment. This stock is lent, through any of nine Stock Exchange money brokers, by investing institutions which provide it from their portfolios and are paid at a rate of some half per cent per annum for their trouble. This is easy money, as there is virtually no risk in the operation because the gilts market is closely supervised by the Bank of England. These arrangements are comparable with the United States 'REPO' ones – by which institutions sell stock to primary dealers against arrangements to repurchase – and they have been called 'a regulated REPO system'.

Gilt price quotations differ from those in shares in that only a single indicative 'middle' price, instead of two-way prices, is put out on SEAQ, leaving a given deal's price to be individually fixed by telephone. The reason is that, in the gilts market, all stocks tend to move together, since all reflect the British government's credit and are broadly similarly influenced by interest rate factors. Thus it would not be reasonable that a market-maker should be pinned to a precise price offer, since, with such exposure, he could be overwhelmed with an order avalanche should his quote have a fractional edge over others'. The cut and thrust of price negotiation in each transaction, according to its size and timing, is therefore important and this is why it is sometimes said that the gilts market is a telephone market, while that in shares is a screen market, albeit operated to an important extent by telephone. Again in order to protect market-makers' positions, there is no deal-reporting in gilts parallel to that in top shares, though prices at which trades have been done appear in the following day's SEDOL. As the screen quotes in gilts are not fully informative, investors often watch LIFFE's futures prices for the best and most sensitive pointers to gilts trends. Gilts business in 1987, the highly-competitive first year after Big Bang, was far from lucrative. Probably about £60m was lost by the market as a whole, rather more than half of that by a few concerns and the rest widely spread across most of the other houses in the market.

As to the different traders' shares in the market, the gilts sector, like that in United Kingdom shares, is fairly heavily concentrated, despite the total number of market-makers. The ten most active houses between them have rather over two-thirds of the market. Those around the top of the size league are probably Warburg, together with Greenwell Montagu and Phillips & Drew, both groups derived from former large brokers, and BZW. Other long-standing broking houses or groups now embracing them, such as James Capel and Hoare Govett, are prominent, as are some American groups including Chase Manhattan, Citicorp and Goldman Sachs, which made a large commitment to gilts market-making. Leading discount houses are busy gilts traders, particularly with other market-makers.

Although the gilts market generally fared well as a 'defensive' investment retreat after the late 1987 share crash, the difficulty of earning profits from trading in it has led to the withdrawal of four market-makers, Lloyds Merchant Bank, Orion Royal Bank, Hill Samuel and Prudential-Bache. Poised to join the pack, though, are Japan's big Nomura and Daiwa. One London expert fears these groups will have a useful edge because their Tokyo colleagues, being up earlier, will brief them, before the start of London trading, on the previous few hours' business in Japan.

Now that markets are so international, it is worth setting Britain's gilts sector in its world size context alongside the government bond markets of three other major economies, the United States, Japan and West Germany, and the 'offshore' Eurobond market. For increasingly, as barriers between them fall in the absence of exchange control and with less discriminatory tax rules, these markets move nearer to being parts of a single whole. It is true that their denomination in different currencies of fluctuating values makes the divides still important, though Finance Ministers do have greater exchange rate stability on their agendas. In the Eurobond market, of course, issues are expressed not only in dollars but in other key currencies, and can come in the 'currency cocktail' form of the ECU (European currency unit) or even, sometimes, be convertible from one country's money to another's.

The following paragraphs sketch the relative scales of the different leading bond markets,[22] and bring out the vast size of dealings in the biggest of them, that of the United States. Turnover is given for 1986, the last full year for which figures were available at the time of writing, and outstanding debt as at the end of that year, on the basis of exchange rates at that date. The figures only cover marketable bonds and shorter bill-type paper and would be still higher if certain further state debt, like savings bonds, which is not normally traded, were included. They are given in dollar terms, which is the most suitable basis for international comparison. At the end of 1986, the pound was worth $1·4837, so that the sterling equivalent would be just over two-thirds of the dollar amounts shown.

The figures reveal some awesome quantities, particularly of market dealings. Turnover in United States government (Treasury) bonds and bills in 1986 was $24 trillion, about eight times the combined turnover in all world equity markets. This is vivid evidence of how central the United States T-bond market is to world dealing and investment – a sizeable minority of these bonds is now held abroad – and of how voluminous trade in it is in response to each rapid change in interest rate expectations.

But Japan, with its strong currency, the yen, was not so far behind, with $21 trillion turnover in its government bonds and short-term paper. By contrast, there was less than one trillion, just $630bn, of deals in British gilts (a level that was afterwards to treble). The comparable German figure was somewhat less than the British. When turnover in the international Eurobond market – of well over $3 trillion in 1986 – is set against these figures, it slots in at third place, after the United States and Japanese government bond markets, but far behind them. Eurobond activity is broadly rather above that in all equity share markets combined.

Outstanding quantities of the various nations' government bonds are in each case much less, for the bonds are many times traded each year. United States government marketable T-bonds and bills amounted to $1·6 trillion at the end of 1986, the total Federal debt being something approaching $2·3 trillion. Against this, Britain's sterling gilt and Treasury bill total was equal to $198bn, not much more than a tenth as much, and its total national debt, including National Savings and the like, around $270bn. The corresponding figure for Japan was nearly $1 trillion and that for tightly-budgeting Germany only $152bn. For comparison, there was some $650bn outstanding in Eurobonds, part of the 'offshore' Euromarket now to be considered.

In today's complex money world, business spreads far beyond traditional bounds. So while national stock exchanges trade in their own governments' bonds and in wide ranges of shares – and new cash is raised against issues of new such bonds and shares – much additional financing of various kinds goes through the so-called international capital market, or Euromarket. This is the arena where the big pool of internationally mobile 'offshore' funds is both used to cushion world banks' near-term shortages and surpluses and tapped to fund numerous medium-term lendings and the like. By contrast with earlier days when companies raised money just through share or bond issues on their own exchanges or through borrowing from their national banks, much financing has for decades now been fixed up through this truly international money forum.

Such deals may be in the form of 'syndicated' bank loans, those organised by 'lead' banks but then split among many banks, each of which normally resorts to the Euromarket reservoir to fund its portion. These loans are at adjustable (floating) interest rates, linked to LIBOR (the key London Inter Bank Offered Rate), but with a thinnish additional 'spread' for the lending bank's trouble and risk. Alternatively, the company (or government) needing cash issues a medium-term repayable Eurobond, which is placed, through an arranging investment bank and others partnering it, directly with investing institutions which put up the money. A further recent addition to the range of Euro financing has been that against short-term tradable 'paper', issued by large companies and similarly placed, through investment banks, with institutional providers of funds. Like Eurobonds themselves – on which interest may be fixed (straights) or fluctuating (floating rate notes), which come in various currencies, and which can be convertible into the issuer's shares – Eurocommercial paper – often known as Euronotes – is of various kinds. On its first use some years back, much of it was supported by a bank's agreement to finance its refunding if necessary. But now most Euronotes are on the sole credit of the issuing company which, in the case of large groups, may be stronger than that of many banks. For big-name companies, financing via programmes of Euronote facilities – which can be activated at need – is often cheaper than bank credit, while Eurobond money costs less than medium-term syndicated bank loans. Choices depend on circumstances. Sophisticated company treasurers nowadays pride themselves on fixing up, through their investment banks, the optimum mix of financing arrangements for all occasions. As Eurobonds and paper are tradable, these forms of finance are called 'securitised', meaning that they are in the form which leaves the investors with whom they end up holding a saleable asset.

In the seventies and earlier eighties, syndicated lending – much of it to the third world and financed through the 'recycling' of deposits poured to the banks from oil-surplus countries – easily topped Eurobond financing. But the tables have been turned in the eighties, when Eurobond financing has predominated. This is because the main international 'takers of funds' latterly have been, not struggling developing nations, but prosperous companies – and governments – of high credit, whose bonds are happily accepted by investors, including those in capital-exporting Japan.

While, in 1981, syndicated international bank lending was two-

and-a-half times Eurobond issues, in 1986 there were $221bn of international bond issues made, $71bn of shorter-term Euronote facilities set up, yet only $38m of syndicated loans advanced.[23] However, in turbulent times investors grow cautious of providing cash direct to companies, or at least charge more for it. This can improve the relative attractions of alternative financing by bank loan. The beginnings of a swing back to the latter were seen in 1987, following a seize-up in the perpetual (undated) part of the Eurobond floating rate note sector, even before the October share plunge imposed extra wariness.

In fact, financings by syndicated bank loan and by Eurobond or Euronote have sufficient affinity with each other to be often bracketed nowadays under the broad heading of 'international lending'. With customers able readily to opt for one method or the other, the divides between the two markets have blurred. And now that many big bank groups have both direct lending and investment bank arms, companies often fix packages (such as 'multi-option facilities') allowing them to draw cash by either route.

The Eurobond business is centred in London and is conducted by a range of big international investment banks and securities houses, the largest of which handle most new issues between them and, with a rather wider range of others, actively trade the bonds. Dealing is by telephone, profit from it is sought through bid–offer spreads and positioning – not from commission – and trade is cleared (settled) through two specialist companies, Cedel and Euroclear. Turnover spurted from $3·6 trillion in 1986 to the new record of $4·7 trillion already mentioned in 1987.

The leading houses in the market include the long-prominent Crédit Suisse–First Boston, Japan's Nomura, which has lately come to the fore, Salomon Brothers, Goldman Sachs, Morgan Stanley, Merrill Lynch, Swiss Bank Corporation, Union Bank of Switzerland, and Deutsche Bank. These and others, all with big financial muscle to absorb trading hazards, also enjoy large client networks with whom new bonds can be placed. S. G. Warburg is one of the few United Kingdom-owned houses to hold much of a place in the big-league Eurobonds rankings.

In the past year or two, cut-throat competition for market share has been so intense that, with new bond issues falling in 1987, there has been little profit and plenty of loss in the Eurobond field, which some medium-sized firms have quit wholly or partly. The houses did their best, in 1986 and 1987, to compensate by working up the growth of international equity business, in which they also specialise since they can distribute new 'global' share offers to their existing investor lists. This drive met with some success, only to be set back by the October share plunge.

A spin-off from the international capital markets which has proved a flourishing innovation in the freer eighties environment is the modern-style swap market. What this in effect offers is wide scope for bond issuers to exchange their interest rate obligations and so share the benefits each can enjoy by tapping the market where its own rating is most favourable. Swaps can be complex, and involve an arranging role by a bank, which will collect something for itself. But a typical example would be where a top-line United States group launched a fixed-rate bond issue at the low interest rate its high standing permitted, while a smaller company raised the same sum through a floating-rate note. Both would, via the bank in the middle, service each other's debt, but with adjustments. The smaller concern would add enough to leave its large counter party with something extra in hand, but would still pay a lower fixed-interest rate than it could have commanded itself. At the same time, the bigger issuer would do well enough with the extra payment it retained to finish with cheaper floating-rate money than it could have obtained directly. These transactions, which allow issuers to pick and choose their effective type and currency of debt, have become so popular that much bond issuing is undertaken in order to be fitted into a profitable swap. Issues 'swap driven' in this way are reckoned to have been worth just over a quarter of all international bond issues in the first half of 1987.[24]

There are also swaps between different currencies, one purpose of which is to allow hedging of currency positions over longer periods than the foreign exchange market normally caters for. The majority of swaps are of the interest rate kind discussed above. If all kinds are included, there are probably swaps in existence covering some $500bn of principal. American banks chiefly led the development of swap business, but around sixty to seventy banks in London (British and foreign) are active in it now.

Another long-established City market, foreign exchange dealing, has loomed larger than ever in the past fifteen years of innovation and more volatile exchange and interest rates. It has also proved itself an important profit-spinner for the banks operating in it.

In 1972–3, world currencies which – devaluations and up-valuations apart – had been closely fixed in terms of each other through the near-thirty year postwar 'Bretton Woods' period, were freed to 'float' and find their own level. This change, forced on world governments by inflationary and other strains, introduced new uncertainties and led to more hectic trading. The later launch in the United States, the United Kingdom and elsewhere, from 1979, of 'monetarist' policies based on sharp interest rate shifts tended to make for further exchange rate instability and consequently more frantic dealings. The explosion in banking, financial and investment business world wide with the ending of exchange controls in the late seventies and eighties has also greatly boosted the business flooding through the forex markets.

The London foreign exchange market, which is the world's biggest, has greatly gained in technical sophistication in recent years. Today it is a screen-based telephone forum, backed up with a web of global telecommunications links, but with no physical trading floor. It might be called the ultimate in electronic markets, given its formidable dimensions, with *daily* turnover by late 1985 of $90bn, almost double New York's total at that time.

Hundreds of banks in London take part in it, but most dealings go via some fifty of the largest. Prices in refined decimal points flicker by the second on screens in response to the sway of buying and selling. The big central banks, including the Bank of England, sometimes intervene to steady wild gyrations or, even more significantly, nudge rates though, given the market's huge throughput, their powers of influence are limited. The market has its own jargon, particularly for the most traded currencies, the United States dollar, sterling, the Japanese yen and the West German Deutschmark. The pound's spot rate against the United States dollar is, for instance, known as the 'cable', while billions of the Japanese currency (whose rates against pound and dollar run into three figures) are called 'yards' of yen, a term based on the French and Italian word '*milliard*' for 'billion'.

The market offers facilities for deals both spot – an immediate switch from one currency to another at the prevailing rate, for settlement two business days on – and forward. In a forward contract, a sale of one currency for another is arranged to take place at a given time, say three months, ahead, but at a rate fixed at the outset.

The bank doing a forward exchange deal with a client would itself be exposed to an adverse currency turn before the transaction was completed unless it protected itself against the risk. To do just that, a bank which has, say, contracted to buy dollars from a United Kingdom exporter for sterling in three months' time, may at the outset borrow dollars and use them to buy sterling, which it then puts on deposit in the money market. After three months this deposit matures and the pounds are passed to the exporter in exchange for his dollars, which are used to repay the bank's initial dollar borrowing. By acquiring the needed sterling to start with, the bank has covered itself against the danger that it might be dearer to buy later.

In an alternative and more usual, though apparently complicated, arrangement, the bank starts by purchasing sterling spot against dollars. It then immediately sells sterling spot against dollars but, in a linked transaction, agrees to take this sterling back, in exchange for dollars, on agreed terms, in three months' time. The latter two associated stages are known as 'a spot and forward swap deal' or as 'lending sterling on the swap'. The two initial spot deals have cancelled out and at the end of the three months the bank receives its sterling back from the market and passes it to the exporter, from whom it gets the dollars needed to complete its swap deal. (The forex-type swap here is different in kind from the new-style interest rate ones discussed above.) This method, too, in effect involves using the London money markets as a lending outlet during the three months. And that aspect helps explain why rates for forward exchange deals are fixed with regard both to spot rates and prevailing interest rates. A Bank of England study has spoken thus of the forex spot-and-forward type of swap deal: 'In reality the swap market is an extension of the money markets in the currencies concerned: without markets in which currencies can be borrowed and lent, there would be no swap market.'[25]

Most large banks deal direct with each other in the foreign exchange market, but brokers are also active, scouting round for the best rates on behalf of the many client banks which use them.

The scale of the total foreign exchange market now reaches dimensions which well outweigh even the US Treasury bond market, discussed above. Exact estimation is difficult. But if London's world market share is, as in 1984, around a third,[26] and given that its $90bn turnover a day in 1985[27] has gone on rising, the estimate given earlier of deals of $80 trillion ($80 000bn) as the sum total for all business days in a year looks plausible. Since this is at least thirty times the size of international exports and imports plus services like insurance, it is clear that a vast superstructure of financial activity takes place on top of the basic trade payments. This must include a great deal of short-term banking and investment activity, together with complex futures and other hedging dealing to offset risks in the present free and open but volatile markets, and outright speculation.

Given the huge turnover, it is not surprising that the banks find their foreign exchange business rewarding. All Britain's big four banks identified it in 1987 as an important profit earner, as did various merchant banks.

Often thought of alongside the foreign exchange market is London dealing in gold which, though in a sense a commodity – needed in jewellery and other manufacture – has historically had a money dimension. Though no longer in general use as coinage, gold forms part of the national reserves of many countries – bars are kept in the Bank of England and at America's Fort Knox – and is often privately hoarded in preference to any currency. This reflects the age-old mystique about gold as in some sense the ultimate store of value. However, the days of the gold standard and its aftermath when the yellow metal was formally linked to money values are over, and since 1970 gold has traded freely without any formal tie with major currencies.

London sees the world's largest trading in gold, with Zurich not far behind; outside the European time zone, the other biggest markets are in New York and Hong Kong. The major source of new supplies is South Africa, with the Soviet Union next, while the buyers are the jewellery and some other industries, investors and hoarders and, significantly too, central banks.

Dating in its present form from 1919, the London gold market has five main members, who conduct the two daily price 'fixings' with some ceremony in a stately room at the merchant bankers N. M. Rothschild, which traditionally chairs the market. The members of the fixing, in addition to Rothschild, are Mocatta & Goldsmid (owned by Standard Chartered Bank), Sharps Pixley (Kleinwort Benson), Samuel Montagu (Midland Bank) and Mase Westpac, formerly Johnson Matthey Bankers and now owned by Australia's big Westpac bank. At the fixings, the dealers, each with orders to execute, negotiate until they agree on a price, when the previously upright Union Jack flags on each of their desks are lowered. The price is at once published and is highly influential world-wide, though some market dealing during the day can be at prices other than those set at the fix.

In the early 1980s, the London gold market began to admit associate members, among them offshoots of major overseas banks active in gold trading, including Morgan Guaranty, Citibank, Crédit Suisse and Dresdner Bank. Derby & Co, now a renamed London subsidiary of Philipp Brothers (part of New York's Salomon Brothers) had then already long been a trader, outside the fixing. By the end of 1987, the number of associate members had grown from only a handful at the start of the decade to over fifty. These consisted of some twelve firms, including the fixing participants, which make markets as principals, and about forty more with just a broker role.

Organisation of the London bullion market, which also trades in silver, has lately been radically revised, partly in connection with the Bank of England's strengthened regulation of the City's 'wholesale' markets generally. All market-making firms satisfying the Bank as to their standing, management and capital adequacy will observe a London Code of Conduct and appear on a list published by the Bank (see also below) so, in effect, holding clearance to conduct business. The market-makers will be supervised by the Bank, while other operators will be subject to regulation, as appropriate, through one of the City's new self-regulating organisations (SROs) and will also abide by the Code.

A new London Bullion Market Association, to which all operating firms will belong, has recently been formed. This will give the much widened range of London bullion firms a stronger voice in the market's affairs, including development of new products and standardisation arrangements, but the fixing system will continue unchanged. The London gold market has a turnover probably of between $1bn and $2bn a day and, given the big assemblage of specialist bullion firms in London, the City is the main centre through which international trade in the yellow metal is cleared.

Another important sector of the City consists of the short-term money markets, through which large sums in pounds and other currencies are lent and borrowed for periods from as little as overnight to a year or more. The markets largely operate among London's 600 or so banks but they are constantly fed, via the banks, with big surpluses channelled in from a host of multinational companies and others wanting their cash to be put out, however briefly, at interest. The large reservoir of non-sterling deposits held in the market constitutes London's share of the world-wide Euro-market.

On the offtake side, the markets are, as earlier noted, principally used by the banks both to adjust their near-term cash surpluses and shortages and to fund their medium-term lending, domestic and international, often on a constantly revolving short-term basis. The markets are called 'wholesale' because they trade in big amounts (of six figures or more) and not in the smaller-change 'retail' sums personal bank customers handle.

The City's money markets handle huge totals and the amounts outstanding in them at any one time are very large, well over £500bn worth in foreign currency, though considerably less in sterling. For leading overseas banks, Japanese ones particularly, the London Euromarket is an important outlet for surpluses and a recruiting ground for funds with which to finance fresh business. In mid-1987, Japanese banks alone had £220bn worth of foreign currency deposits in Britain.

The markets operate mainly in deposits, cash put into a bank for, and repayable after, an agreed number of days or months, but some deposits are 'packaged' into tradable CDs (certificates of deposit). Interest rates for sterling and foreign currency deposits of different periods are published daily in such financial newspapers as the *Financial Times* under the headings of 'London money rates' and 'Euro-currency interest rates'. Specialist broker firms such as Astley & Pearce, Fulton Prebon and M. W. Marshall, actively lubricate dealings through the markets.

The sterling money market is rather more complex in its composition than its foreign currency (Euro) counterpart. Its chief part consists of its interbank market where, as on the Euro side, deposits are unsecured. Parallel and similar to this is a separate sector, through which short-term loans are available to local authorities, and which also forms an outlet for the authorities' surpluses. The former activity has in recent years produced such curiosities as Japanese banks financing part of the needs of some of Britain's biggest town councils.

Then there is also the distinct and more traditional sterling money market centring on the eight discount houses which have a key place in the mechanism through which Britain's monetary policy is oper-ated by the Bank of England. These houses take in, on a secured basis, short-term balances from the big banks – notably the British high street clearers – and invest their resources in bills (promissory notes of the government and commercial firms) and other short-term securities. They also trade in bills, standing ready to supply them to banks and other institutions wanting them for their portfolios, and two of the largest houses act as gilt market-makers.

The liquidity of the discount market – its ability to repay deposits recalled by the banks – is ensured by the Bank of England's being always able to supply them with needed cash. This is done nowadays mainly through the Bank's paying out money to buy 'eligible' bills, those 'accepted' (guaranteed) by a wide range of banks of high standing. The range of banks whose acceptances are 'eligible' was greatly widened in 1981 to include many foreign groups.

The Bank uses the discount market as its route for influencing the banking system's liquidity, purchasing bills from the houses to inject cash or selling them to mop up market cash. It is through significant changes in the rates at which these dealings are done that the Bank signals on occasion that it (and the government) want bank interest rates changed. Though more informal than the old Bank Rate and its successor Minimum Lending Rate (MLR) which were directly posted by the Bank, the modern-style informal indications are taken in the banking world as equally binding. Around the time when MLR was scrapped in the early days of the Thatcher government, the idea was that market forces would become more influential in guiding even shorter-term rates. But, in fact, today's methods leave the Bank, and behind it the Chancellor of the Exchequer, every bit as authoritative when they order rate changes as when Bank Rate and, later, MLR were announced, in former times, each Thursday morning. In the old days of Bank Rate and MLR, the current rate was shown on a board hung from a hook in the wall just off the Bank's spacious entrance hall. Later, when the system began to change, the board was put aside and a curtain was drawn over the place and later removed altogether. But the hook remains embedded in the stone, where it could again hold future notices, should another government one day revive the Bank's direct fixing of the key to all interest rates.

Big Bang has not in itself revolutionised the money markets, though it led the Bank of England to lift its ban on take-overs of discount houses, with the result that several medium-sized houses were bought up and now form part of bigger City groups. Seccombe Marshall Campion went to Citicorp, while Alexanders and Jessel Toynbee were bought by Mercantile House and merged in its

Alexanders Laing & Cruickshank, now part of Crédit Lyonnais.

The Bank of England is expected soon to admit several new discount house operations to the existing charmed circle. But although some of these may be linked with gilt market-makers, the discount market as a whole seem certain to remain as a separately functioning City sector. For one thing, the Bank of England likes conducting its cash-tightening and relieving operations through the familiar small group of the discount houses, from which their effects ripple out through the banking system, rather than dealing with banks direct for the purpose. It could in principle choose just Britain's big four groups as the conduit for such operations, but then the Bank of England and the big United Kingdom clearing banks sometimes seem like a medieval king and barons, powers eyeing each other cautiously from a distance. And if, alternatively, it were to think of casting its net wider for the purpose, the Bank would surely find it invidious to pick out just a few as the channel for its money market operations from among the numerous powerful United Kingdom and foreign banks now busy in London.

Nowadays investors and financial groups not only buy, sell and hold shares, bonds, short-term instruments and currencies but can protect themselves, through additional deals, against market swings that would adversely affect their positions. This is done via the so-called 'derivative' markets in futures and options. A future is a contract to buy or sell a quantity of a standardised entity – be it grain, cotton or a type of financial bond – on a date ahead at a set price. A futures contract of this kind to sell would obviously cover a holder against a fall in his existing asset's market price. An option gives the right, but not the obligation, to sell or buy at a pre-fixed date and price, and is similarly used to protect a portfolio against loss, or to compensate, in rising markets, for an under-invested position.

Futures have long been an essential part of commodity markets, while traditional 'tailor-made' options on shares are far from new. But what has been novel in recent years has been the extension of futures to the financial field and the creation of markets through which they and options can be traded from minute to minute, in standardised form, as conditions change. Such futures and options dealing has now become a vital adjunct to the underlying stock, money and exchange markets in many countries.

Financial futures trading got its start when it was grafted onto the traditional agricultural markets in Chicago in the early seventies. At that time, exchange and interest rates were growing more volatile and many parties welcomed the chance to safeguard themselves through the new facilities against consequently growing risks. Dealings in the new futures contracts on US Treasury bonds, Eurodollar deposits and the like soared as advantage was taken of the chance to hedge against the hazards of sharp swings in key American and Euromarket interest rates. Further contracts, including ones on currencies and stock market indices, and in the form of traded options on different shares, proliferated. Institutions, companies and others wanting to have some offset to their existing investment stances used the markets busily, as did those more concerned with outright speculation. By the early eighties, financial futures business on the Chicago Mercantile Exchange far exceeded traditional agricultural dealing, and it was buoyant also on Chicago's Board of Trade and Options Exchange, as well as in other United States centres. In the October 1987 share crash the role of stock index futures trading in the crisis was heavy enough to attract controversy.

Financial futures business came to the City with the opening in 1982 of the London International Financial Futures Exchange (LIFFE) which now trades futures in a range of short- and longer-term sterling and Eurodollar instruments and currencies. There are also contracts on US Treasury bonds and Japanese government bonds and on the stock market FT–SE 100 ('Footsie') share index. There are also certain options in futures and in other forms.

Business on LIFFE, whose hectic open-outcry system of trading by brightly-jacketed personnel echoes Chicago's with its legendary clamour, has soared afresh since Big Bang, though it is still far less than that of its American counterpart. In 1987 contracts were virtually double the previous year's. Contracts in Eurodollar deposits and US T-bonds are amongst the most popular, but the top favourite has remained that in the United Kingdom long gilt. Gilt deals through LIFFE relate to values on about the same scale as all those through the underlying gilts market itself, which shows how actively the City's markets makers, and others, use the futures market to lay off their risks. At the same time investors, too, track LIFFE trends closely. One leading institutional investor stresses that the most sensitive price indications come from LIFFE rather than from the cash market: 'We take the LIFFE long gilt contract as the purest price of long gilts.' And Mr Michael Jenkins, LIFFE's chief executive, says of the cash market and LIFFE: 'I think the two things are an integral part of running an efficient Government bond market at times of uncertainty and volatility.'[28]

LIFFE has over 370 members, including offshoots of major American and other banks and commodity houses particularly interested in trading futures for clients when their home markets are closed. Links between world futures exchanges to foster round-the-clock trading, and to ensure reasonable 'fungibility' (interchange-ability) of contracts and exchange of information, are also being actively pursued.

In today's sophisticated markets, various arrangements, linking certain techniques discussed above, are available to give any desired mix of protection against risk and chance of gain. Known as 'financial engineering', they may also involve forward rate agreements, fixing terms of a cash deposit ahead, and additional types of options.

Markets in commodities are a natural consequence of Britain's age-old role as an importer of raw materials. Many such materials have long been traded in the City, notably copper, lead, zinc, aluminium, nickel and silver through the London Metal Exchange and soft commodities, such as coffee, cocoa and sugar, via the former London Commodity Exchange, now known as the London Futures and Options Exchange, or London FOX for short. These are markets in commodities of standardised quality, with prices set at 'open outcry' market sessions. Hedging facilities are available through forward contracts, allowing prices to be fixed ahead, for metals, and through futures – special forms of such contracts which can be traded – for soft and some other commodities. The International Petroleum Exchange trades futures in gas oil and crude oil. Under the wing of the Baltic Exchange, there are dealings in ships and in carrying space in ships and aircraft. The Baltic also houses futures markets in shipping freights and in certain agricultural products, including potatoes and pigmeat. Less standardised goods like spices are dealt in through sale rooms via agents, and others, such as furs and teas, are sold through auctions after inspection by would-be purchasers.

The International Commodities Clearing House, owned by six large clearing banks, provides clearing facilities for the various markets, as well as for LIFFE. This means that clients' deals are settled with the clearing house, rather than direct with a counterparty somewhere in the system, which both smoothes completion and provides reassurance against credit risk. The London Metal Exchange has recently come within the clearing house arrangements, which have replaced the principal-to-principal settlement of earlier days, and has modernised its government, under the discreet encouragement of the Bank of England, in the wake of the tin crisis and some other upsets in the earlier eighties.

All the City's wholesale markets – foreign exchange, bullion and money – are now supervised by the Bank of England, which maintains a list of well over 200 concerns that have satisfied it as to their nature and capital. Inclusion in the list carries an obligation to observe the standards of operational behaviour required by the London Code of Conduct the Bank has promulgated. This system runs in parallel with the Bank's direct supervision of the banking system under the Banking Act 1987 and with that of the securities industry conducted through the Securities and Investments Board (SIB) and five self-regulating organisations (SROs) under the Financial Services Act 1986.

The rather more informal system for the wholesale markets was judged suitable because of their very specialist and complex nature. But although the Bank's regulation of these markets does not have the direct force of law, the sanctions behind it are powerful since only by being on the Bank's list can operators gain exemption from the 1986 Act's requirement for authorisation to conduct business in the investment field.

A look round the City's markets cannot ignore insurance, in which Britain has been active for centuries in providing cover, first for ships, and then for numerous other hazards down to aviation risks on modern-day jumbo jets. The industry, which holds huge funds in connection with its various businesses, chiefly its life insurance side, also looms prominently as an investor, with total holdings topping £210bn at the end of 1986.

Despite its very comprehensive name, insurance embraces diverse activities. The most significant distinction is between, on the one hand, its 'general' service of covering personal and company customers against the numerous risks of day-to-day existence – from burglary loss to a factory's destruction by fire – and, on the other, its long-term, or 'life' business.

In general insurance, those buying protection (policy-holders) pay regular premiums into the underwriting insurer's pool, which is then drawn on to compensate the unlucky ones who suffer actual damage, whether through blaze, storm, car accident, theft or other specified hazard.

In life insurance, the policyholder similarly pays premiums, usually to ensure a payment in the event of his early death or to accumulate savings which will accrue to him, enhanced if all goes well by skilled investment, when he reaches a given age. By contrast with general insurance, there is the important feature on the life side that, in most cases, the policy is bound to produce a payment in due course. (There are however some exceptions, as in term insurance, where the premiums only yield a pay-off if the person whose life is insured does not live to a particular age.)

Life insurance is either 'industrial', where payments are collected by an agent's regular calls on the policyholder, or 'ordinary', where premiums are paid by banker's standing order or cheque. In recent years, there has been a significant growth in a new variant, unit-linked life insurance, where life cover is linked with investment through unit trust 'pooled' funds. Often this is marketed through the operators' specialist sales forces, while much other insurance is sold via brokers.

The brokers playing an intermediary role in fixing up business between customer and insurer range from large groups to small local concerns, while part-time agents also have a function in routing business from clients.

Reinsurance, through which insurers can spread their risks, is one important segment of the industry, in which some concerns specialise.

There are over 800 companies authorised to conduct insurance business in Britain. Many are commercial or 'proprietary' – the larger quoted on the stock market – but some, such as Norwich Union and Standard Life, are 'mutual' operations without shareholders. Some companies, including many smaller ones, only do general business. Others, like such big groups as Prudential and Legal & General, are predominantly life businesses, while further familiar large groups, including Commercial Union, Royal, and Sun Alliance, are 'composites' active in both types of business.

Premium income flowing each year to the British insurance companies is very large. For general business alone, the 1986 figure was £18·9bn, of which almost half, £9·3bn, came from abroad, much of it from the United States, where British insurers have traditionally been busy. Long-term (life) premiums added up to £21·5bn, the great majority from the United Kingdom market, bringing the grand total to £40·4bn.

Insurance naturally generates large funds to be retained and invested until life policies mature or claims fall due. This makes the insurance sector, notably through its long-term life funds, an important element in share ownership and other investment, as will be seen in Chapter 9. At the close of 1986, the long-term holdings were worth £174bn, and the short-term funds £37bn, a total of £211bn, which in 1986 earned £12·6bn income. [29]

Existing separately from the companies is the unique 300-year-old Lloyd's insurance market, a society now of some 32 000 wealthy underwriters or 'Names', organised through about four hundred syndicates, who accept unlimited liability – down to the last gold cuff link, as is said – on the risks they cover. Lloyd's, where brokers and underwriting agents are also important elements, does much business in marine, aviation and other big-scale risks, but also specialises in cover tailored to particular hazards, such as damage to film stars' legs and pianists' hands. Reinsurance is a prominent activity, notably in the United States, where Lloyd's gained prestige early this century through paying out unquestioningly after the 1906 San Francisco earthquake. Lloyd's, which does no life business, has some £8bn a year of premium income, roughly half of it from abroad.

In the insurance industry as a whole, trading experience in the general business has tended to be relatively cyclical. Thus, competitive pressures, triggered by some operators' ambitions to raise their market share, have often squeezed premiums, damaging underwriting profits or producing losses. Following this, some participants may withdraw, and premiums and profits recover, so that new rivals are tempted in and the pattern is set to repeat itself. However, the flow of substantial income from invested funds built up in the course of the business – and which have themselves gained value in the buoyant markets of recent years – is consolation enough to have maintained the industry as a broad and active one world-wide.

Following the collapse of some insurance concerns in the sixties and early seventies, official regulation was stepped up and, under what is now the Insurance Companies Act 1982, the Trade and

Industry Department's authorisation is required for companies to operate in insurance. Lloyd's, which was rocked earlier in the eighties by scandals involving allegations of the disappearance of funds due to some Names and by other criticised practices is still self-regulated. But its rules and regulations have been tightened up under a fresh, more broadly-based Council, and with a new office of chief executive, in the wake of public concern about the events in question.

6 Clearing Banks: Business

Distribute your loans rather than concentrate them in a few hands. Large loans to a single individual or firm, although sometimes proper and necessary, are generally injudicious, and frequently unsafe. Large borrowers are apt to control the bank.

> From a letter of December 1863 written to United States national banks by Hugh McCulloch, then America's Comptroller of the Currency and later Secretary to the Treasury. Extracts from the letter now hang in a Bank of England waiting room.

The old saying holds. Owe your banker £1000 and you are at his mercy; owe him £1 million and the position is reversed.

Lord Keynes.[1]

The big household-name high street clearing banks – Barclays, National Westminster and others – have undergone a revolution every bit as radical as the stock market's. It is not only their altered structures, such as through their international expansion and investment in stockbroking, that makes this so. The span and composition of their whole business has also changed in the latest phase of their thirty-year evolution from aloof élitist servants of a smallish minority to financial conglomerates fighting toughly for the custom of the majority. Even philosophies have grown different and old conventions been dropped in today's more competitive atmosphere. 'When I joined the bank, I was taught it was bad form to tout for business', recalls a sixty-year-old top person. 'That seems incredible now.' Today banks see nothing amiss in wooing customers away from their rivals' books.

The recent story of Britain's large banks is the saga of how they have increasingly stepped far beyond their traditional business of basic high street banking for British individuals and companies. And throughout their expansion at home and abroad the banks have grown and grown, so that in the late eighties their tentacles not only cover many activities already discussed, including foreign exchange and Eurobonds, but also take in credit cards, unit trusts, insurance broking, and much more. The gross assets of the eight main British clearing banks multiplied five times to some £335bn in the ten years to the end of 1986, by when most had become broad-range financial supermarkets, well known on the world scene.

United Kingdom banking embraces both the activities of the City's international Euromarket financial centre, already discussed, and the domestic market. In the international sector, Britain's own banks are outranked by the many foreign-owned groups in London, but they predominate on the home front, as well as themselves having much Euromarket and overseas business. Even in the home market, though, some of the numerous foreign banks chiefly drawn by the Euromarket have muscled in to compete with the domestic bank industry for business like mortgage lending and financing of big United Kingdom companies. And if no one alone among the foreign banks has captured a big slice of sterling business, together they have considerably nibbled at the fringes of the domestic banks' market.

Britain's own banking industry centres on the big clearing banks, so called because they mainly clear, or put through, the system's myriad payments. Just how multitudinous these payments are is shown by the fact that the number of cheques put through the clearing each year would, if placed end to end, reach to the moon. The arithmetic is that, with a cheque six inches long and so six being needed to the yard and 10 560 to the mile, 2·6bn cheques would be required to span the 250 000 miles or so the moon is generally taken to be from earth. In the year to June 1987, the bulk clearing alone generated 2·2bn cheques and the clearing within banks 0·4bn more, making 2·6bn – and that excludes the paper involved in the automated transfers. In line with current competitive ideology, the clearing system, formerly the exclusive province of the big United Kingdom banks, has now been widened, in its revamped form under the Association for Payment Clearing Services (APACS), to include within its membership large foreign banks such as Citicorp and leading building societies like the Halifax and the Abbey National. The APACS clearing is in three sections: the bulk cheque clearing for ordinary branches; the same-day, big-value clearing for large payments via City branches; and automated payments via bank accounts such as firms' salary transfers to employees. In money terms, the clearing sees over £16 trillion (fifteen million million pounds) going through each year.[2]

The top eight United Kingdom clearing bank groups, best known in Britain for their 13 100 branches in high streets up and down the country, are headed by the 'big four', the National Westminster, Barclays, Lloyds and Midland. Next in size comes Standard Chartered, with its main business overseas but interests too in the United Kingdom market. TSB Group, formed from many previous savings banks and now a commercial bank, and the larger two Scottish groups, Royal Bank of Scotland and Bank of Scotland, complete the eightsome, which are all quoted on the Stock Exchange. The third Scottish clearer, Clydesdale, was a subsidiary of Midland until it was sold in 1987 to National Australia Bank, so becoming the first British clearer to pass under overseas control. Other clearing banks with a United Kingdom high street ('retail') business are the Yorkshire, owned by four larger clearers, the Co-operative, a subsidiary of the Co-operative Wholesale Society, and the State-owned National Girobank, whose business is conducted through Post Offices and which is due for privatisation by sale in 1988.

The biggest United Kingdom banks are among Britain's chief companies, the stock market value of NatWest, being, for example, in early 1988 much the same as that of such a front-line industrial concern as GEC, Britain's largest electrical group. However, in the world size league of banks (based on total assets) NatWest and Barclays ranked at the end of 1986 as only 17th and 18th, following eleven Japanese banks, headed by Dai-Ichi Kangyo, one American (Citicorp), three French (Crédit Agricole, Banque Nationale de Paris and Crédit Lyonnais) and one German (Deutsche). Midland (before it shed its Scottish and Ulster offshoots) came in at 34th, Lloyds at 44th, Standard at 73rd and TSB at 150th.[3]

Among the United Kingdom clearers there are various differences and many similarities; the former will be chiefly explored when the several banks' characteristics are reviewed later, but meanwhile it can be noted that generally the larger banks have the greatest geographical range, so that at the very big NatWest up to half the business is international, while the activities of the smaller banks are heavily UK-oriented. Even among the big four, however, the relative scale of the international lending which has loomed so prominently in the third-world debt upheaval has been far from uniform, Lloyds and Midland having proportionately higher exposure than their larger rivals. But, notwithstanding such variations, the features of their operating context and developments that the clearers have had in common in recent years are so important that they are best considered first in a look at the sector's business. One of the chief of these is the more competitive and deregulated environment which has meant that they have increasingly had to fight for market share on their traditional ground with both foreign banks, other United Kingdom institutions – and each other.

The crumbling of old barriers which has let different types of financial groups enter others' terrain has touched off accelerating incursions into the United Kingdom banking market by overseas concerns. Such American groups as Citicorp and Household International have long cultivated business in the United Kingdom consumer credit field. But more recently banks from all over the globe have broken into the British mortgage market, while American and other banks have enhanced their offers of financing deals to British companies. The result is that something approaching 25 per cent of sterling bank lending is now done by overseas-based banks.[4] Nor has the challenge been seen as a blessing by the home team. 'They have shot margins on loans to large companies to ribbons', according to Barclays Bank's former chairman, Sir Timothy Bevan.[5] And another banker notes critically, of the tendency for some foreign banks to recruit United Kingdom home-loans borrowers through insurance brokers: 'Insurance salesmen aren't necessarily the best collectors of mortgage business, which is not quite the benign affair some think. It's very easy to pick up a lot of poor borrowers.'

Falling of financial sector frontiers has also left the banks tussling for business with the building societies, another major money industry with £140bn assets at the end of 1986, compared with the clearers' £335bn, not all of it in Britain. Whereas the societies formerly dominated the home loans market, the banks – the aggressors in this context – have now moved far into it, with a 30 per cent-plus proportion of new business, while the societies' share has dropped heavily from its previous 80 per cent to 60 per cent or so. But, for their part, the societies, enjoying new legal powers, are starting to attack the banks' lucrative personal lending field. Moreover, the societies have for a number of years made large inroads into the bank-type 'retail' market by winning a major share of savings deposits, though the banks have now regained some ground with their high-interest personal accounts. As a result, the societies are following the banks into the city's wholesale money markets, where they can now fund up to 40 per cent of their borrowing needs.

Indeed, such has been the impact of the struggle between these two groups of giant institutions that the societies are currently engaged in the most radical reappraisal ever made of their roles. Some will further broaden their business, while retaining their 'mutual' (non-shareholder) status and the predominance of their home loans business. Others – particularly among the top names, including the Halifax and the Abbey National, the largest – are considering whether to exercise their right under the Building Societies Act 1986 to gain greater scope through converting themselves into commercial banks. Should any considerable number do so, the intensity of rivalry in British banking would receive a huge new boost. Whether there is room for such extra competition in a United Kingdom market of only fifty-five million must be doubtful and the top societies' decisions on 'going commercial' may depend on their view of opportunities in the whole European Community. For the present, however, the clearing banks remain Britain's primary domestic financial sector, having faced and reasonably contained the various types of new competition.

Before some of the clearers' major business developments in the eighties are considered, certain longer-term ways in which they have grown should be noted. One set of these concerns their acquisition of fresh markets through extending the range of their activities.

During the sixties and seventies, the clearers bought up the main hire-purchase companies, and then broadened them into today's finance house subsidiaries, which have the major leasing arms that, until 1984, allowed the banks large deferments of tax. Unit trust offshoots were similarly added, as were merchant banking and trustee services, which were followed, from 1966, by mass-market credit card ventures, at Barclays through Barclaycard and, at the other banks, mainly via Access. Insurance broking is another now widespread service, while Royal Bank of Scotland conducts motor insurance underwriting. Although most of the services listed above have been developed by many or all of the banks, some additional business lines are specialisations of particular banks. Lloyds Bank, for instance, has one of Britain's largest chains of estate agents under its Black Horse banner, while Midland's interests include the Thomas Cook travel agency.

In the past decade or two, the banks have also tried to widen their market through a concerted drive to extend the 'banking habit' in the poorer 'unbanked' part of the population. There were some misgivings about this policy, stemming from fears that the modest new accounts might be unprofitable to run. However, doubts were much allayed when payment of wages into workers' bank accounts was made cheaper by new technology and when the nineteenth-century Truck Acts' inhibitions on non-cash wage payments were removed. The outcome was that by 1984 65 per cent of British adults had a current (checking) account with a bank, against only 39 per cent in 1971, while 75 per cent had some form of account, including a savings one. These increases brought the proportion of Britain's population handling their financial affairs through a bank nearer to that in most advanced countries: in Canada, France, Germany, Sweden and the United States, the percentage with cheque accounts ranges from above 80 per cent to virtually 100 per cent.[6] The banks also scout for custom in ever lower age groups, not just offering incentives to students, tomorrow's promising customers, but providing gifts to school-age savers too. Alarm at the loss of university customers was one factor behind Barclays' 1986 decision to wind up its connection with South Africa, which had attracted powerful opposition from the Anti-Apartheid Movement.

Further competition has been seen in the new willingness of the clearers to poach business from each other over the past two decades. Some place the start of this more aggressive approach in 1966, when Barclays, breaking fresh ground in United Kingdom banking with its Barclaycard, offered the new credit card to non-customers and customers alike. Bankers remember Barclaycard balloons being given away outside rivals' branches in a then unfamiliarly pushy form of selling. The result was that soon a third of those signed up as Barclaycard account-holders were not on the bank's own books. One banker dates the softening of clients' lifetime faithfulness to one bank from Barclaycard's debut: 'It contributed to a breakdown of that loyalty that had always existed before.' Later the banks vied for personal customers as they moved to a free-in-credit basis of no charging for accounts kept in the black. The Midland, leading the trend, notched a gain of nearly 500 000 accounts in the early stages of the tussle. But the moment of greatest scope for fresh competition came at the beginning of the eighties when the official curbs which had for forty years been used, as part of government monetary policy, to restrict bank lending were finally dropped.

From around the start of the eighties, the big banks have remoulded their businesses in several major ways – some successful, others less so – which have radically influenced their course throughout the decade. In the first place, they have greatly expanded their personal lending in Britain, including that through the new business, for them, of mortgage finance. This development, which has posed the problems noted above for competing sectors like the building societies, has been highly successful and profitable. Significantly, it has meant a revision in the traditional pattern whereby the banks garnered deposits from a limited range of well-off personal customers and largely lent onwards to United Kingdom industry. Now, about as much is lent to individuals as is collected in 'retail' deposits from a widened personal customer base, though the banks also substantially tap the money markets to fund their bigger-scale wholesale business.

Meanwhile, the banks have had to rethink their relationships with their company (corporate) customers, now they face foreign banks' competitive pressure, and since much financing of top companies is done directly against 'securitised' tradable paper placed with institutions through arranging investment banks. The need to remould policies towards the corporate sector has been one of the big challenges facing the clearing banks in the eighties, at the start of which they also took part in a costly Bank of England-sponsored 'industrial lifeboat' operation to carry troubled industry through the pain of the then recession. Part of the main banks' strategy amidst the global rivalry for corporate business has been to climb in on the 'securitisation' act by developing their own investment bank arms through the Stock Exchange purchases described earlier.

Finally, among the prime trends of the eighties have been the international policies which led the chief clearers both to extend their own networks abroad and to channel billions of pounds in what proved disastrous loans to the third world. So heavy has been the resultant cost of building outsize nest-egg provisions against losses on this vast debt that the banks' profits have been severely hit, to the point of overall losses being incurred in some cases in 1987. In effect, lucrative profits on home consumer business have in the recent past been offset to a substantial extent by the huge sums set aside on loans to the troubled third world, so that in reality the United Kingdom man in the street has done much to finance that ill-starred overseas lending spree. The consolation now is that lessons have been learned in this disastrous episode and that, as they finally work off the loan burden, the banks will have amassed strong cushions of capital for a more cautiously planned future.

The trigger to the banks' new departure in rushing into mortgage lending was the Thatcher government's removal, in mid-1980, of the previous 'corset' control which had for long curbed the banks' freedom to expand their loans. But the decision then to invade the home loans market, taken separately by the banks, yet with some awareness of others' thinking, was no mere sudden impulse.

Bankers had long felt angered that the rival building societies had so successfully wooed the public's savings – as a means of financing their surging home loans business – that they held a substantially greater share of these than did the banks themselves. This development had been encouraged by the high rates paid by the societies, but there was also the factor that intending home buyers knew they would more easily get a mortgage in the seventies days of home loans rationing if they already saved with a society. In remarks highlighting the jealousy between the two financial sectors, one bank chief recalls:

> We'd been watching for years the societies building up their share of deposits, because they had not only the house lending but the deposit-taking. It was very easy for them to say to people: 'This is the big thing in your life, when you come to buy a house, and you'd better get your savings going with us.' That's a marvellous way of attracting deposits. So we got to the point in mid-1980 when the building societies' deposits had got bigger than the clearing banks'.

Part of the banks' complaint at the time was that the societies had the edge in winning deposits through their below-average 'composite' tax rate. 'There was a longish debate in the clearing banks', the same banker remembers, 'on whether we should compete with the societies or whether we should go to the Government and say: "The building societies have all sorts of tax advantages and that kind of thing: pull them out of banking." And rightly, in the end, it was seen that that course was not viable and it was decided to compete. And really for the fear of [the societies] getting too big on both sides of the balance sheet – but particularly on the deposits side.'

The clearers' first big drive into the mortgage market, in which their publicity stressed the availability of quick decisions, was remarkably successful. The banks' share of mortgage lending leapt from very little to 26 per cent of all net new home loans in 1981 and to 36 per cent of a greatly enlarged total in 1982.[7] When the banks decided to step strongly into the mortgage market – and also to woo the public's deposits with higher rates – they were astonished at the ease with which they carved out a major new market. 'When we did go in', the banker quoted above relates, 'we found their [the societies'] underbelly was much softer than we'd expected. They *had* been very popular, we [the banks] had been unpopular; they'd been small-scale, we'd been big-scale. And we just literally went in when popularity was shifting, when they were rather ... not very efficient because they had a monopoly ... and we captured much too big a share of the market too quickly.'

Thus, by late 1982, it was time for a pause and reappraisal as to whether the trend was not going too far and bidding fair to transform the whole nature of banking. At this stage one big bank reckoned its home loans operation would, if split off, rank as equal to Britain's fourteenth largest building society. 'We had to stop and think whether we wanted to become a mortgage bank', a top director recalls.

The result of the rethink was some application of the brakes before the banks settled down to conducting, as an important permanent part of their activities, a mortgage loan business which has the merit of being well secured and of useful, if varying, profitability. The banks, of course, started with the advantage of established acquaintance with those of their mortgage borrowers who were existing customers and so were well placed to judge their creditworthiness. By late 1987, the banks accounted for rather more than a fifth of net new home loans, while their outstanding mortgage loans totalled over £32bn–£30bn of it from the clearers, of whose sterling loan portfolios it made up nearly a quarter.

While the fresh competition has widened most borrowers' choice, the banks have paid special attention to the more affluent home buyers and not infrequently provide six-figure loans. This has effectively broadened the market since the societies' maxima in former days were far lower, even allowing for price changes. As recently as 1979, a bank director confided to the author that although his group offered £100 000 home loans he would not like the fact publicised.

The clearers have also much expanded their even more profitable unsecured lending to individuals and so led in fostering the consumer credit boom which has been a big feature of the eighties. Doubts have at times been voiced by the Bank of England as to whether this borrowing spree was not going too far. But on the whole the authorities have (with occasional tightening of interest rates) tolerated the banks' soaring consumer lending on the ground that many creditworthy United Kingdom families were previously underborrowed. One irony is that the assumed backing for much unsecured borrowing is the rising equity value many debtors have had in their own homes, as house prices have soared, fuelled by the very mortgage boom the banks have stoked. In taking their permissive view, the Bank and the government are no doubt conscious too of how useful the personal lending profits are to the banks at a time when they are carrying big third-world loan burdens.

There is no doubt that profit margins on the banks' various lendings to the personal sector are large. Mortgage loans, the safest, typically cost 1½ per cent to 2 per cent over the banks' base lending rates, overdrafts are 3 per cent – 7 per cent above – and unsecured personal loans may be at least 10 per cent above – while instalment and credit card finance can be up to 15 per cent or more over base rate. The fact that rates on finance via the leading mass-market credit cards were so high (though the card companies argue the average is lowered by quick payers being charged no interest) led in 1987 to the Barclaycard and Access arrangements being referred to the Monopolies Commission. The banks sometimes argue that high interest rates are needed to allow for the risk of bad debts, an approach that hardly seems fair to the vast majority of good payers. Nor has this attitude gone without justified criticism. Mr Brian Quinn, an executive director of the Bank of England, said in July 1987: 'I feel a degree of discomfort when bankers tell me that rising delinquencies (non-payment of debts) do not worry them so long as margins compensate for the growing incidence of loss.'[8]

The loans to individuals, mortgage and otherwise, by all banks in Britain account for over a quarter of all their sterling lending. They amount to as much as over two-fifths of that by the clearing banks, whose mortgage loans have multiplied ten times since 1981 and whose personal lending is approaching four times its size in that year. These changes represent major shifts in the balance of the clearers' business, since loans to commerce and industry have grown much more slowly, as have international loans in recent years.

There is no doubt that the larger prominence of the lucrative personal business explains why profit margins on the clearers' United Kingdom business as a whole are more than twice as large as on their stiffly competitive international business. In 1986 margins (the difference between interest funding cost and interest received) on domestic business ranged between 5·3 per cent and 5·7 per cent among the big four, while those on international lending showed a far slimmer 1·9 per cent–2·1 per cent, and the pattern was little changed in 1987. These facts underline how far the total profits the banks have made in recent years derive from their home business and, within it, from their lending to individuals.

Suiting their services to the changing needs of corporate clients has been one of the main tasks for the big banks in the 1980s. Lending to companies, from industrial giants and traders to the smallest family firms, has been traditional for the banks, both by overdraft for working capital and, in recent decades, through medium-term loans. But the latest years have brought great changes. Deregulation, the more global nature of competition between banks, swaps and other modern devices mean that large companies are no longer bound to one country but can pick and choose the best money-raising bargains in any currency. Equally – and important since many groups, having streamlined, are now cash-rich with funds to invest – they can also select the most favourable outlet for their surplus cash, no matter where geographically. A banker skilled in working out the right deals for large corporates says:

> The customer can choose: he can organise his financing in such a way as to get the best rate that's available in any market for any period he wants. And he can now lend money for any time at any rate, because it's possible to transpose savings all over the world into markets that show the highest return.'

At the same time, large industrial and commercial companies now often opt for Eurocommercial paper programmes allowing them to call up funds, as they wish, against issues of the paper to institutions through investment banks. For them this tends to be cheaper than bank finance, just as cash raising against bonds costs less than medium-term bank borrowing. All this has, in recent years, restricted the growth of bank lending – and driven the banks to reshape the nature of their services to their larger company customers.

But the evolution in conditions is far from having downgraded the corporate role of the banks. For one thing, even the biggest companies rely heavily on banks for a range of needs quite apart from borrowing. There is the transmission of payments (multitudinous for groups like those in stores and insurance), foreign exchange, arrangement of overseas transactions and much else besides. These many services generate the commissions and fees which have in recent years assumed sizeable importance for the large banks' revenues. Foreign exchange alone earned the big four £400m of profit in 1986.

Then again, on any adverse shift in markets that relays uncertainty or slashes share prices, as in late 1987, the new-fangled financing through paper may grow dearer or harder to fix and bank finance again look more attractive. For all these reasons, there are few big groups which do not want well-tended relationships with banks which can, in time of need, be readily activated to produce funds. Many large companies anyway retain stand-by overdraft drawing rights from their best-known banks, while the multi-option facilities already mentioned, which allow financing via paper or bank loan, are often provided by large bank groups with investment bank arms.

While direct medium-term lending by means of syndicated loans to large firms has declined over the past decade – though it has revived somewhat lately – the banks have made great efforts to nourish particular sectors where extensive loans are still needed. One is the area of 'project' funding required over spells of years to finance big investments in aircraft replacement, oil rigs, large international trade deals and the like. Barclays is a bank which has departments studying developments in such sectors with an eye to spotting scope for new business. Other fields where the banks have lately developed substantial – sometimes shorter-term – lending are the financing of major take-over bids and of buy-outs by entrepreneurial managements of businesses from larger groups. The City's securities industry has also, as recorded earlier, been a heavy borrower from the banks.

In the wider world context, the large United Kingdom banks also cast their net over foreign as well as British customers, which is one reason why they have broadened their overseas representation. As the National Westminster's former chief executive, and a present deputy chairman, Sir Philip Wilkinson, told shareholders in 1987: 'NatWest has a relationship with over three quarters of the largest 500 companies in the United Kingdom ... As a major international bank we have strong links with many of the world's leading corporate institutions.'[9]

If there is one term which encapsulates the aims of the banks *vis-à-vis* corporate customers it is 'relationship banking'. What the expression represents is the maintenance of persisting links between a company and its chief banks so that the banks know the customer, are able to assess its creditworthiness and can rely on a reasonable flow of continuing business coming their way. This would exclude complete chopping and changing by companies between banks in quest of the last saving in charges, tactics which could make for a less than warm welcome when a former corporate customer returned for a bank's help in time of trouble. Like those other long-lived creatures, elephants, banks never forget. Yet, at the same time, they themselves have obligations to their customers, whose business they cannot hope to retain unless they are competitive.

'We aim to be a long-term continuous supplier of financial services', a leading corporate banker at one of the big four sums up. He is one of those who acknowledge that banks do not lose even on slim-margin loans to big companies if the finance is provided as part of an all-in package of dealings with a major corporate which, overall, is profitable.

Below the level of the top companies, bank borrowing is relatively more important since 'securitised' finance is often dear or unavailable. Thus numerous sizeable medium-scale industrial and commercial companies look chiefly to the banks for funds. In recent years, however, borrowing demand from manufacturing industry has been somewhat sluggish following the contraction in this sector's size, after the acute earlier recession, when exceptional bank help was, as will later be explained, provided.

The smaller the company the higher is likely to be its reliance on bank finance, particularly in initial and growth phases. Many banks therefore give great attention to the littlest businesses, offering various special loan schemes. The NatWest alone has £7bn out in advances to small firms, and other banks substantial amounts.

The fact that the Thatcher government has placed great stress on growing infant businesses for revivifying the economy, and has backed that policy with plans like the Small Firm Loan Guarantee Scheme (SFLG), has often led the banks to stretch their normal rules to accommodate the needs for such borrowers. This has somewhat modified their traditional reputation for being tight-fisted in lending to the needy. It is a striking fact that at one stage over a third of little businesses helped through the SFLG were collapsing and, though most of the resultant loss has fallen on the government, the situation has added substantially to the small-scale bad debts of the banks. This is a significant aspect of the heightened climate of risk in which, in various contexts, the UK banks groups have operated in the eighties.

Evolving from inward-looking United Kingdom high street operations into groups with a global reach has been a key part of the biggest British banks' strategies over the past fifteen years. This internationalisation policy was aimed at seeking new markets, keeping pace with foreign rivals and serving the overseas needs of growingly multinational United Kingdom companies. As a former bank chief who had a hand in planning tactics overseas remarks: 'The world is one world and if you're lending to ICI, why limit your lending to that bit that happens to be on your doorstep in the UK?' The whole expansion process was quickened by the ending of the exchange control in 1979.

The relatively trouble-free part of the expansion has been that through the building up of direct representation in the main centres throughout the continents, either by opening branches or by the purchase of small local banks as a base. Broadly speaking, the top banks, the big four and Standard Chartered, now have the footholds in key financial markets necessary to service large clients and, as desired, to pick up wholesale financing business there too. None of these moves to create world-wide networks of representation has created great problems.

The more difficult issues have revolved round the question of whether the United Kingdom clearers should go further and buy existing banks with retail branch chains in other countries. The case often made for doing this cites the desirability of enlarging business beyond the limited United Kingdom market and of participating in the growth of a flourishing economy, like that of the United States. However, expansion of this kind overseas may be no smooth path, as banks have found to their cost, since it can be hard to make headway into markets dominated by established local competition. In any event, purchases of retail banks are costly, so that at best only a selected few were possible even for Britain's largest groups.

The United Kingdom banks have handled the retail aspect of their foreign expansion in different ways and with varied success, their approaches being partly conditioned by their disparate existing situations when new global patterns came to be reshaped from the 1970s. Barclays, for instance, had already long owned the biggest banking chain in South Africa, together with banking operations in other parts of the African continent. Standard Chartered ran South Africa's second largest bank, as well as big Asian operations, and Lloyds owned sizeable retail banks in Latin America, Australasia and Spain. But past patterns were to be no necessary guide to the future and the decisions by Barclays in 1986 and Standard in 1987 to sell out of South Africa show how radically the United Kingdom banks have remoulded their scope abroad.

By contrast, the NatWest had little in the way of links abroad two decades ago. This bank's international build-up thus forms a classic case of expansion in the recent era from a situation where, in 1970 – when it was created by the merger of the old National Provincial and the Westminster – the group had just a few branches across the Channel and some representatives in New York. As one of the biggest of the United Kingdom banks, it knew global ambitions were essential if it was to compete in the increasingly international world bank league. Opportunities were steadily taken in the seventies to buy control of, or stakes in, Swiss, German and Dutch banks to obtain appropriate overseas representation, while extensive expansion occurred further afield in the East and Australia. More major moves also took place in the United States and elsewhere.

Sir Philip Wilkinson, NatWest's former chief executive who presided, in the mid-eighties, over the group's growth to being the largest United Kingdom bank, recalls of the mid-seventies: 'There was a determined strategy to move into the financial centres of the world and to go for the business of the top multinationals, the 1000 list – to seek the wholesale business. And so we were putting in place a network of operations to deal with wholesale banking [that for large corporate and other customers].'[10] Apart from building up offices in many world centres to service sizeable clients and tap local lending opportunities, the bank decided on a move into retail banking in the United States and, in a smaller way, in Spain.

It was in 1979 that NatWest purchased the New York concern National Bank of North America. Despite its high-sounding title, the bank was no household name and indeed was well down the size league compared with the New York bank giants. Just before the deal was announced, NatWest's then chairman, Mr Robin Leigh-Pemberton (now Governor of the Bank of England) telephoned a well-known international banker in an associate company of the group to tell him of the purchase and of how pleased his board was with the acquisition. 'Yes, but what is it?' the banker impatiently enquired. 'The National Bank of North America' the chairman spelled out proudly. 'Never heard of it', the other answered dampeningly. The NatWest sent one of its top men, Mr Tom Frost, the present chief executive, across the Atlantic to oversee the revamping of NBNA which, as National Westminster Bank USA, has proved a good earner with a business largely to personal customers and middle-market companies. In 1987 the group bought another retail bank, First Jersey National, in a neighbouring state.

Other big United Kingdom banks were meanwhile extending their overseas representation and business. Barclays followed up an earlier purchase (Barclays of California) by acquiring a sizeable finance house, renamed BarclaysAmericanCorporation, in the United States in 1979, and Lloyds took over the concern it retitled Lloyds Bank California. Standard Chartered broadened its geographical span by acquiring Union Bank in California in 1979 and later adding United Bancorp of Arizona. Purchases of banks were also sometimes topped up by the take-over of chunks of loan portfolios or strings of branches from neighbouring United States banks.

Just how uphill retail banking abroad can be was highlighted, however, when both Lloyds and Barclays sold their California banks in 1986 and 1988 respectively, while Standard Chartered put its two United States banks up for sale and disposed of, first, the Arizona, and then the Californian one. But, while quitting retail banking in toughly competitive and recession-vexed California, Barclays retained its larger BarclaysAmerican finance operation, while Lloyds, in 1986, invested afresh in North America through buying the sizeable Continental Bank of Canada. The Scottish clearers and other smaller United Kingdom groups steered cautiously away from any attempt at expansion abroad on the retail side, though the Scots and the TSB have some representation abroad. Early in 1988, however, Royal Bank of Scotland arranged to buy Citizens Financial Group, of Rhode Island in the United States.

The drive by the fourth big clearer, Midland, into North America was the latest and largest move in the British banks' seventies-to-eighties $6bn-plus invasion of the United States. Midland's $1bn purchase in 1980–1 of California's Crocker National, then America's fourteenth largest bank, proved disastrous through the later losses which heavily burdened and, for years, weakened the group. What mixture of ill-luck and miscalculation surrounded Midland's decision to buy control of the West Coast bank is debatable, but of the horrors of the sequel there can be no doubt. The Californian property and agricultural markets turned sour, rapidly enlarged third-world lending brought further troubles, and the outcome was a huge harvest of bad loans. The main Crocker business was later, in 1986, sold off to the neighbouring Californian bank Wells Fargo, but Crocker's big Latin-American loans remained with Midland and necessitated further major debt provisions. Although the sale broadly recouped the first outlay, the cost of the Crocker catastrophe, which scarred Midland's image, may be put at up to about £1bn, allowing for loss provisions on the loans retained and income forgone on the sums invested.

The episode was one of the roughest in recent banking history. The choice of then-booming California looked fair in 1980, but there is little doubt the Midland, which did not fully own Crocker until a late stage, should have taken a firmer management grip on it sooner, however much it had to allow for local susceptibilities. With hindsight, it should perhaps also have longer considered the initial deal: at least one other United Kingdom clearer believed around 1980 that Crocker could be available, but was not tempted to pursue it, which suggests some problems might have been more foreseen. Perhaps the chief lesson of the affair which is worth pondering concerns the very real difficulty a new foreign owner can have in imposing its will on a freshly acquired bank. This merits deep reflection by would-be buyers, considering that banks which can be bought do, on occasion, contain some problem business.

In 1987, Midland, under its new chairman, Sir Kit McMahon, formerly Deputy Governor of the Bank of England, forged a major alliance with the large Hongkong and Shanghai Banking Corporation (owner of the big Marine Midland Banks in the United States), which took a 14·9 per cent stake in Midland in return for a cash investment of £383m. Midland, which has over recent years built up representation in many countries, is now co-operating with Hongkong Bank in several continents and it is widely thought that the two groups could in time get closer together.

A move which would, if successful, have extended the international range of another of the big four came in 1986, when Lloyds Bank made an abortive attempt to buy Standard Chartered, which had been pushing into Europe as well as America to balance its Eastern and African interests. The stiffly opposed £1·3bn bid, which, had it gone through, would have made Lloyds Britain's biggest bank, was beaten off with the help of several 'white knight' rescue shareholders, who bought Standard shares heavily, backing the board's defence. The chief two among these holders were the Hong Kong tycoon Sir Y. K. Pao and the Australian financier Mr Robert Holmes à Court, both of whom built a near-15 per cent share stake and each of whom became a deputy chairman of Standard.

Altogether by early 1988 it can be said that the British banks' moves in branch banking (retail) expansion, as distinct from wholesale business representation, abroad have had at best a patchy record. And increasing caution over fresh initiatives has been imposed as the full harvest is garnered of their – and other world banks' – costliest-ever venture, the earlier disastrous multi-billion dollar financing festivity with the third world. So expensive has this loan spree proved in the need to put aside huge sums to cater for losses that a sombre prudence now characterises big banks' planning all over the globe.

In retrospect, the money tide through which, in 1979–82, the world's banks channelled to developing countries hundreds of billions of dollars of loans, much of which may now never be repaid, is easy to understand. The second big boost in oil prices in 1979 left the 'petro-nations' with huge surpluses that were prudently placed by their owners with Western banks, which in their turn thus needed large lending outlets. The borrowing needs of hungry new economies in Latin America and elsewhere provided just that market and the globe's banks competed happily for the business, which was through loans syndicated, or split up, by the lead banks arranging them among numerous banks, large and small. Much of the lending was to the borrowing nations' governments or on their credit and any worry on credit risk seemed stilled by the reflection, voiced in the dictum attributed to Citicorp's then chairman, Mr Walt Wriston, that 'countries do not go bust'. Banks throughout the world gloried in gaining this business, which seemed safe and profitable, while many bank loan officers – American rather than British – were personally rewarded for obtaining what seemed profitable additions to balance sheets. Annual meetings like the International Monetary Fund's autumn sessions even took on the character of bankers' fairs, where new loan deals were fostered and celebrated with champagne, even though the binge later brought an outsize headache.

The movement also had the blessing of leading Western governments, which saw the 'recycling' trend as the right means of adjusting the oil price-induced imbalances. The communiqué after the top seven nations' Tokyo summit in 1979 said, for example: 'We recognise in particular the need for the flow of financial resources to developing countries to increase', while that after the following year's Venice gathering 'emphasised that the international capital market should continue to play the primary role in rechannelling surplus oil funds on the basis of sound lending standards'.[11] That last qualifying clause came across less emphatically than the preceding words.

The result was the piling up of a huge new mountain of third-world debt to the advanced world's commercial banks, much of it owed by, or with the backing of, many developing states' governments from Mexico to Brazil and from Argentina to the Philippines. One factor that helped mask the dangers was that some of the borrowers, such as Mexico, enjoyed a high credit rating at the start of the eighties because they were oil producers.

As the world now knows, all this lending subsequently posed huge problems for the banks, including Britain's, after the third-world debt crisis exploded, following Mexico's near-collapse in August 1982, and left question marks over hundreds of billions of dollars on the banks' loan books. Had the whole exercise been a monumental blunder or was it inevitable?

One overwhelming fact is that the oil rich states' surpluses of $350bn–$400bn[12] from the two petroleum price hikes very closely matched the debt quickly piled up by the thirty or so later troubled third-world debtor nations to the banks. And these two similar quantities were without doubt to be regarded as linked by deliberate 'recycling'. It can persuasively be argued that there was nowhere else where such vast sums, drawn from oil users around the world, could have been channelled on, except to willing new final borrowers. This view has been powerfully advanced by a senior United States banker, Mr Hans Angermueller, vice chairman of Citicorp, in a speech in 1983:

In the wake of the first 'oil shock', after OPEC increased the price of oil to more than 400 per cent of its 1973 level, they accumulated a surplus of almost $200bn. Another $200bn or so flowed from the oil importing countries to OPEC after the second 'oil shock' in 1979 when the price rose to more than 1300 per cent. In recycling some of these and other funds to the developing countries that didn't have oil to export, the banks that make up the Euromarket performed an invaluable service – cushioning the impact of the two oil shocks and providing time for the world to make an orderly transition . . . . As a practical matter, *there did not exist any real method to prevent OPEC's approximately $400bn of proceeds from the two oil shocks from flowing into the international credit markets.* Once there . . . the industrialised country governments *could* have prohibited their banks from making any cross-border loans to the oil importing LDCs [less developed countries]. Such a move could have reduced industrial country interest rates or increased the inflation rate, depending on your economic background. But it would *surely* have caused the economic collapse of the LDCs: hardly a desirable outcome.[13] (Italics added by present author, except that for the word 'surely'.)

The thunderstorms with which the loan saturnalia climaxed duly broke in August 1982 with the troubles of Mexico, which owed $80bn, much in short-term loans, and found itself unable to meet due payments. The emergency, heightened for the United States because numerous of its 14 000 banks held Mexican loans, made urgent demands on the world's financial chiefs. The response to it broke fresh ground in crisis control internationally. By contrast with the position at the time of the 1930s' world financial crisis, in which chaos spread unrestrained, leading countries got together to stave off the threat of repercussive catastrophe. The United States provided some first-aid help to Mexico, then key central bank chiefs combined to urge the very large number of banks with loans to Mexico to hold back their claims in order to give that hard-pressed nation time to sort out its affairs.

Different lenders in different circumstances tackle the problem of getting debts paid in their various ways. The story goes of an Indian banker who, true to his country's traditions, went on hunger strike outside the gate of a laggardly payer until the debtor saw the light. In the vast third-world debt crisis from mid-1982, which spread to Brazil, Argentina, Peru and many more states, the debtors could not pay sums falling due. So the idea was worked out by the Western central bank chiefs that suitable belt-tightening economic plans should be negotiated by the world's supra bank, the International Monetary Fund (IMF) with the countries up against payments difficulties. Conditional on their adopting these 'adjustment' programmes, the IMF would then make a modest loan and the lender commercial banks of the world would 'reschedule' (lengthen out) their much larger loans, while still requiring interest payments. With greater or less willingness, the numerous banks involved, including virtually all the world's largest, fell into line and sometimes provided additional loans. This approach held the situation in check, the more so since the United States in August 1982 engineered a cut in interest rates which eased the burden of the third world's interest bills and incidentally helped stoke up an unprecedented five-year boom in the world's stock markets.

The crisis-fighting approach of central bank-sponsored aid action by the big lender banks had a precedent in Britain's secondary banking crisis of the mid-seventies, but was new for the United States. Here is how a leading British banker of long experience, Sir Jeremy Morse, chairman of Lloyds Bank and a former Bank of England executive director, remembers the 'lifeboat' action of the late summer of 1982 and the roles in it of Mr Paul Volcker, then and until 1987 head of the United States central bank, the Federal Reserve, Lord Richardson, at that time Governor of the Bank of England, Mr Jacques de Larosière, then the IMF managing director, and Dr Fritz Leutwiler, then president of the central bankers' club, the Bank of International Settlements (BIS):

> The four heroes were Paul Volcker, Gordon Richardson, Jacques de Larosière and Leutwiler. The whole idea was of co-operative reschedulings and the banks going further [providing new money] in order to improve the quality of their existing exposure. Gordon Richardson played a very big part originally and that was in a totally British tradition. It was consciously modelled on the [nineteenth century] Baring crisis and the [1973–5] secondary banking crisis – the idea that, when you have widespread debt, the central bank organises a lifeboat. That was *the* model, transferred to the international stage. Larosière is, I think, the real long-term hero of this story, because he assumed internationally the job that the Governor of the Bank of England would take in a domestic crisis. And Volcker deserves very great credit, not only for putting his authority behind it, but because it was quite against the US tradition for the Fed to get so involved and to order banks to do things. So he really has been very tremendous. For him to go to bankers' meetings and to lecture them about contributing to arrangements was a totally new thing. Then, again, to the American banks, we have to say 'Well done for accepting this, not standing on your high horse' – though maybe they didn't have much scope to do that – 'and also operating together.' And

Leutwiler was very helpful and the BIS made quite a number of bridging loans in the early stages.[14]

The rescheduling agreements, covering debt mounting up to hundreds of billions of dollars as over thirty countries eventually faced payments problems, were just sufficient band-aid for the problem, for some years at least. Even under fresh reschedulings, further postponing capital payments, the debtors mainly continued to pay interest, being helped to do so by lower rates and soon by healthier earnings generated by a United States import boom. The fiction was preserved that, so long as debt was serviced with interest, it would still one day be repaid.

But bankers knew in their hearts that this was not so and started to build fresh reserves against trouble by setting aside unprecedentedly large bad-debt provisions, charged against their profits. Nudged by their official supervisors, they also enlarged their cushions of capital in relation to assets, both by raising more capital through share and loan stock issues and through slowing the growth of their businesses. Another turning-point came when, in mid-1987, Brazil, the biggest debtor with by then over $100bn owing, declared a stop on interest payments. This was seen as a major deterioration by the banks which, led by America's biggest, Citicorp, embarked on major new provisioning which brought their nest-eggs against third-world loan losses to at least around 30 per cent of the sums owing.

From this time, more radical schemes for shaky debt disposal – including plans for cut-price sales of third-world loans or their swapping into share stakes in borrower country enterprises – gained some favour with the banks. Formidable discounts, of 48 per cent below the face value of loans to Brazil and Mexico and more on certain ones elsewhere were quoted in 1987, but some saw these as unduly magnified by debtor states' interest in seeing their obligations disposed of as cheaply as possible.

One little discussed aspect of the third-world loan crisis is the question of capital flight, the suspicion that much cash borrowed in the 1979–82 spree found its way to bolt-holes abroad and was not kept for use in the developing countries. An IMF study has suggested that $150bn–$200bn, between a fifth and a quarter of debt built up by capital-importing countries in the eleven years to 1985, went out in capital flight, chiefly from Latin America.[15] If this estimate is anything like right, the poor of the developing nations who have been subjected to belt-tightening might complain against some among their own privileged classes, not just against hard-hearted banks. Indeed the banks have probably been made more reluctant by the phenomenon of secretly fleeing capital to put new cash into countries from which it might soon be syphoned away.

Britain's main banks provided large loans to Latin America and elsewhere in the third world during the big recycling, most of them being arranged out of London, just as foreign rivals' financing was often fixed from their own money centres. But their lending was proportionately lower in relation to their size than that of many big United States banks which had closer links with Western Hemisphere borrowers.

All told, by mid-1987, the United Kingdom big four had a total of £13·7bn outstanding in loans to thirty or more troubled third-world countries which were having problems paying their debts. In the first half of 1987 they kept step with other leading world banks in drastically hoisting their provisions against loss risks on these loans. In this way they put aside an extra £3bn between them, raising their total sum earmarked against the shaky advances to just over £4bn, or some 30 per cent of the suspect debt. These big charges were to cause the smaller two of the big four – Lloyds and Midland, which had lent especially heavily to Latin America – exceptionally to report big overall losses for the whole of 1987. Standard Chartered, which likewise made large provisions, also ended in the red for 1987. At the start of 1988, however, there were signs that the Bank of England felt nearly enough had been set aside against the debt danger and that no more big charges appeared to be needed. The hope evidently was that, either through eventual repayment or disposal, at least the remaining 70 per cent or so of the debt owing would in time be recouped.

It is a remarkable fact that the £4bn-plus built up by the big four against the third-world debt hazards was equal to all earnings from their profitable United Kingdom business for well over a year. Thus, in a very real sense, home customers – and chiefly high-interest personal borrowers – have met the third-world toll. Put another way, without the feared third-world losses, British bank profits would have been much higher than they have been in recent years. At the same time, without their profitable domestic business and lucrative personal lending, the banks would have been much less well placed than they have proved to be to withstand the third-world shocks.

While it is true to say that British banking is notably profitable in normal times, recent years have often been far from normal. In fact, the eighties have been a decade strewn with costly problems for the large clearers. It says much for their formidable power to generate profits at home that they have still, despite the major hiccup of 1987 and some earlier setbacks, kept their profits on at least a slowly rising trend over time. Yet a glance back over the present decade quickly spotlights how recurrent difficulties have been.

In 1981 the big four made combined profits (before tax) of £1·7bn, having first set £394m aside against losses on shaky loans. But in the following year, as recession gripped at home and the international debt crisis broke, loss provisions soared to £972m, leaving profits after this charge down at £1·5bn. Despite still higher debt charges in the next two years, in the second of which Midland absorbed body-blow losses at its Crocker offshoot, the clearers' total profits edged up, reaching £1·9bn in 1984. Following that there were further rises (after flatter provisions) to £2·6bn and £3·0bn in 1985 and 1986. The leap in third-world debt charges which then made 1987 a horror year profit-wise will, bankers hope, stand out as quite exceptional on a long view.

On one further front the banks have faced special blows in the eighties. Government tax moves, through a special levy costing them £400m in 1981 and wider changes requiring £2bn set-asides in 1981, hit their net profits hard in those years, as will be further discussed in the next chapter. As a brief reminder of the relevant figures, the following tables set out first the total assets and profits – before and after tax – of each of the top eight in the latest 'normal' year, 1986, and then the combined pre-tax and net profits of the eight over a longer span from 1982 to 1986.

Table 6.1   Eight largest British clearing banks: 1986[1]

| | Group figures: £m | | |
	Total assets	Pre-tax profits	Post-tax profits
Barclays	76 952	895	618
Lloyds	47 829	700	470
Midland[2]	53 169	434	262
NatWest	83 325	1 011	621
TSB[3]	14 304	206	132
Bank of Scotland[4]	9 343	119	72
Royal Bank of Scotland[5]	16 597	185	119
Standard Chartered	32 225	254	158
Total	333 744	3 804	2 452

Notes:
1 End-year for assets.
2 Before sale of Clydesdale and Northern Bank subsidiaries.
3 Year to 20 November 1986.
4 Year to 28 February 1987.
5 Year to 30 September 1986.
Source: *Clearing Bank Fact Book* 1987: *Facts and Figures 1981–86* (Alexanders Laing & Cruickshank). Based on individual banks' reports and accounts.

Table 6.2   Eight largest British clearing banks, 1982–6, combined profit figures (£bns)

	1986	1985	1984	1983	1982
Pre-tax profits	3.80	3.25	2.48	2.22	1.98
Post-tax profits	2.45	1.76	1.11	1.42	1.45

Source: Bank of England, Report and Accounts 1987, p. 38.

7 Clearing Banks: Organisation

I was asked to help ease the bank forward from the nineteenth century, but the actual transition was more like one from the eighteenth to the twentieth century.

A former bank deputy-chairman.

The capital of a bank should be a reality, not a fiction.[1]

Britain's big banks today differ much, though not wholly, from their old selves twenty years ago. They have become multinationals, with their chiefs highly rewarded in line with trends in modern United Kingdom industry. They have fallen in with the march of technology, so crucial to today's financial world and have spent billions on electronic gadgetry from hole-in-the-wall cash dispensers to the most complex equipment for international and stock market operations.

But all this diversification and modernisation has brought key change in relationships with customers and consequent need for reshaping of services. Now that nearly two-fifths of money withdrawals are by cash machine, individuals feel more impersonally towards their bank branch. Thus, the public's needs can often be catered for, with the aid of plastic cards, at any branch, while services like insurance, loans and cards may be offered by mail shot and arrangements fixed direct with the bank's specialist centres. At the same time, the requirements of corporate customers have grown increasingly differentiated according to their size. All this is steadily outmoding the former network of all-purpose branches headed by managers with similar skills.

Big banks are thus nowadays 'segmenting' their services, with chains of 'retail' branches for personal and small business customers, while specialist centres minister to more sizeable companies and the largest corporates are perhaps handled from head office. Barclays is separating its United Kingdom retail and corporate branch network, planning around 325 business centres for corporates up and down the country, while its remaining 2400 branches will serve individuals and small firms. Others have their own organisational structures to match

149

their particular pattern of business both at home and internationally. For instance, Midland divides its total business into retail, corporate, international and investment banking.

Segmentation, like other intended improvement, could carry risks for the banks, particularly if retail management posts were seen as unglamorous, with little pulling power for top talents. For there are job fashions in clearing banking as elsewhere. 'When I entered banking', a clearer's former chief says, 'being in the inspectorate would have been a top choice. Now the corporate side is a favourite.' However, the banks, knowing their retail consumer business is not just the bread and butter, but the jam and icing of their profits, seem resolved to man it well, just as they have spent heavily on smartening up branches and on staff training.

Apart from the calls on staffs redeployed throughout the reshaped organisations, the demands on top management of running the large and sophisticated groups which are Britain's main banks have grown dramatically in the past two decades. Major strategies have had to be formed on the designs for overseas expansion, the scope of much larger lending to a greatly widened United Kingdom banking public, and the new shape of branch networks. Crucial decisions have had to be reached, too, on the degree of commitment to be made to the stock market and investment banking. And beyond these issues have loomed the massive problems of the third-world debt crisis, delicate questions over tax and relations with the Bank of England and the government, as well, on occasion, as central issues concerning mergers and take-overs.

Handling such major matters has presented big challenges to even highly experienced traditional bankers, who, some years back, had operated chiefly on their flair and instincts for judging United Kingdom loan risks. For, from the seventies onwards, the banks' senior managers have had to take on the character of top administrators, planning and executing hosts of policy decisions of international scope, as at other multinationals. According to some former bank bosses, the required transformation and evolution of style have not always been easily brought about nor achieved without considerable cultural shake-up.

To meet today's broader needs, some banks have resorted to additional high-level recruitment to reinforce their cadres. The Midland is notable here for having brought in as its first-ever executive chairman Sir Kit McMahon, the economist who was formerly Deputy Governor of the Bank of England, and for having appointed finance directors and some other senior people from outside. Other banks have kept mainly to traditional career structures. But most have for long been widening their main entry to include graduates as well as the traditional bright school-leavers. Clearing banking today has the attraction of offering young recruits not only a wide span of different roles but lucrative top jobs as eventual goals.

One contrast with a quarter of a century ago is that the clearers' top managers (now frequently known as senior executives) are today customarily on their groups' boards. This is a marked change from the traditional position under which, before the sixties, there was a virtually total split between boards as overseeing supervisors and the management as the supervised – a sort of gentlemen and players divide, with not even the chief general manager being on the board. In the eighties, not only are the chief executive and at least a few of his colleagues directors of the bank, but, on their retirement from full duties, chief executives usually serve a spell as deputy or vice chairmen. 'That way', a former outside board member remarks with a dash of cynicism, 'the new top management can't get anything unsuitable past the chairmen's room.'

Nowadays the executive top managements of the clearers are groups of powerful and highly influential men, well rewarded in salary and other benefits on a par with those in many top industrial and commercial posts. If their pay is not quite as high as that in the volatile world of investment banking, at least their job security is greater. As elsewhere in the City, six-figure pay (exclusive of pension contributions, share options and other perks) is now common in the upper reaches of the clearing banks. Within the big four banks (excluding their investment bank arms), thirty-six directors and others in the United Kingdom alone had pay of over £100 000 in 1986 and the number is certainly now greater.

There have been significant changes too in recent years in the composition of bank boards, whose large complements of non-executive directors were sometimes in the past seen as of little influence. Traditionally, when banks were amalgamations of small regional concerns, clearers' boards were, according to one former member of a 'chairmen's room', 'drawn together to supervise the work of the chief, and more particularly that of the regional general managers'. For this purpose, peers and other county bigwigs, with knowledge of, and influence in, their areas, were fitting choices as directors. But as the banks have evolved into sophisticated groups ranging far beyond

United Kingdom high street banking, leading industrialists, able to advise banks on the complexities of world-wide operation, have increasingly dominated among outside bank directors. And some of these non-executives, particularly those committing large time as deputy or vice chairmen, have played important roles, with management and chairmen, in guiding the banks' key transitions over recent years to their present multinational status.

Just how significant have the changes in the role and contributions of bank boards been? Many top bankers are positive about the reality of the change and modernisation. 'The board is no longer a rubber stamp: it is a debating society', says one who has seen big change at his own bank and thinks it general. 'Some of the old-style managers had been brought up on the banker's duty of secrecy – and the best way of ensuring this is to make sure that nobody knows anything they don't need to know. I'm afraid there was a time when they regarded directors as not needing to know much. Now that has changed.'

Sir Timothy Bevan, chairman of Barclays for six years until 1987, highlights the change in this way:

> I think boards have become much, much more active and directors feel a much greater sense of responsibility. I remember being told after I'd been on the board for nine months that I'd been very helpful, which surprised me as I hadn't uttered. 'Ah' they said 'you nodded once to support the chairman.' Now that sort of remark is absolutely inconceivable today.

Sir Timothy also comments:

> I've always believed that the use that can be got from a board depends enormously on how they're consulted and how far they're informed. And so I made it a policy to try and ask them more, because that way you get more. And I think the outside directors are now much more a force to be reckoned with.[2]

One director with a long memory dates the relatively greater assertiveness of bank non-executive directors from the 1973 secondary banking crisis. At that time, the clearer's chairmen agreed, at very short notice, to take part in the Bank of England's 'lifeboat' rescue mission, but outside directors pressed questions, as time went on, about how far the commitment should extend.

Directors' expertise appears to be particularly drawn on where their own fields of knowledge are concerned, often through specialist board committees. But it may not always be easy for a director to get his oar in with a question outside his own area. Loan schedules are, for example, handed round and swiftly scanned at occasional board meetings, then collected up again at their conclusion. This is a context in which, as one board member remarks, it would be a bold director who would venture an off-the-cuff query.

The trend towards change affecting bank boards has also reached into more social aspects. The story goes of a big bank where the lunch served after the directors' monthly board meeting had been of an unchanging content down the years: oysters (small lobsters in summer), smoked salmon, capon, lamb cutlets, fish, apple pie, rice pudding, Stilton and such delicacies. However, one day a high-ranking part-time director was entertained in the separate general managers' Mess and found the meal there more interesting. But on its being put to the chief general manager that the directors' list of dishes might be varied, horror of reformism was expressed: 'You can't do that: the menu hasn't changed since nineteen-oh-six.' Nevertheless, the matter was persisted with and eventually the board's range of choice was somewhat widened.

All change is relative, though, and to some the style and formality in the top reaches of the big banks, perhaps encouraged by the still ubiquitous marble halls atmosphere, is more notable for what remains the same than for what has changed. One younger chief, acknowledging how hierarchical and deferential bank styles remain, says: 'We still have a significant way to go, in common with other banks, to change the culture of the bank into a much more open organisation.' And he accepts that, while he says 'anybody can come in through my door', most would think long and hard before doing so.

An eminent outside businessman and one-time bank deputy chairman recalls how important matters of protocol and precedence were in his experience. The chairman and his deputies were viewed as a class apart, as God-like as the legendary heaven-born Indian Civil Service of old. This observer relates: 'X [heading the management] and I had been at comparable public schools and Oxbridge colleges, so in the educational hierarchy there wasn't a feather between us. Yet never once could I get him to walk into a room ahead of, or even beside me.'

Considerations of social minutiae may indeed persist longer in the clearing banks' traditionalist structure than seems fitting in the increasingly Americanised and 'democratised' City. For instance, lunching arrangements, even for various gradations of top people, are not yet fully integrated at all banks. A few years back one chairman of one of the big four sighed in feigned despair: 'The most difficult decision you ever had to make is where somebody has lunch.'

One situation which seems surprising when female influence is strong in public life and when there are many youngish women executives in the City is the almost exclusively male character of clearing bank boards. Of the 106 main board directors of the big four at the end of 1986, 105 were men, the only woman being a Midland director, Ms Detta O'Cathain of the Milk Marketing Board. More recently the NatWest has appointed Lady Young, a former Foreign Office Minister, as a director, while Mrs Mary Baker, wife of the Education Secretary, Mr Kenneth Baker, has joined Barclays' board.

Central as the banks are to the economy, they are inevitably of interest to those charged with guiding the nation's affairs and recent experience has shown that their standing in relation to the government of the day can have a considerable impact on their affairs. The continuous effect on them of monetary policy, operated through the Bank of England, is a persistent reality, of the kind taken for granted by banks world-wide. But beyond that there have been individual episodes where the banks have been, or have come near to being, touched by politics or special governmental action in ways that stand out as curiosities of the recent story of British banking. One example arose from the demand in the Labour Party in the late seventies for the banks, or some of them, to be nationalised. The banks mounted a vigorous campaign of resistance to the threat, which in the event came to nothing. The Wilson committee, appointed in Labour's time, came down firmly against the idea and anyway reported after the triumph of a fresh government to which the very idea of nationalisation was anathema.

None the less, the banks were far from getting any special favours from Mrs Thatcher's new Cabinet, which in 1981 slapped on the so-called 'one-off' levy, costing the clearers £400m. The full reasons for this action have been exstensively debated. Part of the background is that the banks had, in early 1981, revealed buoyant profits for the previous year at a time when much of industry was groaning in recession. The total pre-tax profits reported by the big four, a then record near-£1·5bn, were seen by some as provocative in the prevailing sombre climate, however much at odds such a view may have been with free-market principles.

Another possible factor leading to the tax action was government annoyance that the banks were paying highish wage rises from their then buoyant earnings. Although no overt incomes policy was in operation – earlier such strategies had been discarded by the Tories – Ministers felt the banks would have acted more helpfully had they cut back their wage rises at a time when fighting inflation was a top government priority. Strong increases in bank lending, boosting money supply had – although partly made to ease industry's parlous state – also angered the government in the context of its drive to force down the rate of price rises. When Mrs Thatcher, the Prime Minister, lunched with the top banks' chairmen in early 1981, she left them in no doubt of her strong views on these matters.

The 'one-off tax' was soon afterwards introduced in the spring of 1981 by the Chancellor of the Exchequer, Sir Geoffrey Howe. Being geared to deposits, it fell essentially on the high street clearers. Efforts to persuade the government that the levy was unjustifiably discriminatory against the banking industry and should be dropped proved unavailing. One banker recalls of this special bank tax:

> It was a direct attack. I remember we felt very hardly about it. We weren't absolutely sure of the reason, except a certain animus, I think, against the banks. Part of that was related to pay, though we were already curbing the pay by then. But it was linked up with a feeling on the other side that somehow bank pay was like Civil Service pay. We had difficulty persuading either Geoffrey Howe, or through him the Prime Minister, that the banks were market companies, not sort of Civil Service organisations.

Then, in 1984, the banks suffered a heavier, though not discriminatory, fiscal blow. Most had for long enjoyed big tax breaks because the heavy equipment outlays of their leasing arms could be set against tax liability under 100 per cent first year capital write-off rules. True, the effect of this system had been only to defer tax bills, but since deferment seemed likely to roll on indefinitely as leasing expenditures escalated, the banks had grown accustomed to paying below-average tax bills and were not fully provided against all the liabilities. The 1984 Budget, launched by the new Chancellor, Mr Nigel Lawson, introduced a gradual switch to a phased capital write-off system, a change which in time slowed the leasing boom. Immediately, though, it created the need for the banks to provide against major, catching-up payments of previously deferred tax bills, to the tune of some £2bn in all. In effect the groups faced the need to replenish their capital reserves, already pressured by the other adverse factors of the time, by this enormous amount. The required extra capital was obtained through curbs on dividends, leaving more profit to be ploughed back, together with large share and loan stock issues.

A bizarre aspect of the 1984 tax affair was that it necessitated huge and unexpected new capital-raising by the banks, just as they were already under persistent pressure from the Bank of England, as supervisor, to build their capital in face of the pressures from the third-world debt crisis. Thus a tax move that was not unreasonable in itself seemed astonishingly clumsily timed. Some top bankers felt anger that the Bank of England had not fought their corner with the Treasury in resisting the tax change in pre-Budget consultations. There were also doubts as to how far the Treasury had, in advance, fully understood the implications of the change for the capital strength of the banks at a time when the third-world debt crisis was casting a long shadow.

One bank chief, looking back on the years of recurrent tax blows, says:

The tax measures were very worrying to us in relation to our share price. Bank shares for a long time stood at a big discount to their net assets values. There was a widespread feeling that, unlike other companies – and we were very much contrasted with the favoured retail companies, which were having a pretty good time – the banks would somehow never be allowed by the government to get away. If they did badly, they did badly, and if they did well, they'd have some of it taken away from them. It made it very difficult to get the banks' shares better.

Among the biggest strategic decisions banks can take are those in which they either seek to take over other banks or respond to bid approaches for themselves from would-be buyers. A number of such issues have arisen in the past decade and have, again, attracted the attention of the government which, like the Bank of England, has throughout this century kept a watch on the banking industry's structure. The course of recent events has indicated that the Thatcher government is rather more receptive than its predecessors to the idea of at least some take-overs of banks, on the general principle of not unduly inhibiting freedom of action. This is in contrast to the view of previous administrations which for decades – with the exception of the approval given to some clearing bank link-ups in the late sixties – had been notably cool about any moves to acquire United Kingdom banks, most of all ones from overseas.

The bid battle for Royal Bank of Scotland Group in 1981 proved a significant landmark in United Kingdom banking because, although no take-over occurred, the affair seemed to open up a previously set scene. Standard Chartered Bank first made an agreed offer, with the Bank of England's blessing, to buy Royal Bank of Scotland, the largest bank north of the border, and so create a geographically wide combined group. But then the big Hongkong and Shanghai Banking Corporation stepped in with a rival offer, the sequel being that both £500m bids were referred to the Monopolies Commission. The situation was complicated because Hongkong Bank entered the fray in defiance of the Bank of England's wish that it should keep off, so that the Bank's authority came to be on the line. The Monopolies Commission's decision to block both offers was reached partly through regard for Scottish feelings against a take-over. But the Commission was also moved by the arguments that an overseas-owned large United Kingdom bank might be less ready to be 'leant on' in the national interest than a 'native' one, or might feel a conflict between public demands – say, to help out in a troubled situation – and its owner's interests. 'We find', the Commission reported 'that the transfer of ultimate control of a significant part of the clearing bank system outside the United Kingdom would have the adverse effect of opening up possibilities of divergence of interest which would not otherwise arise.'[3]

Despite the blocking of both bids, the Royal Bank affair left unresolved long-term questions on whether any future clearing bank take-over from abroad would necessarily be ruled out. For Hongkong Bank had enjoyed considerable sympathy within the government, while a willingness at least to question long-established assumptions on all-British clearing bank ownership was evident in the Treasury.

When the Banking Act 1987 was later going through Parliament, the banking industry lobbied strongly for the inclusion in it of a provision giving the government, or the Bank of England, power to bar any proposed overseas bid for a British bank that was held to be against the national interest. The Bank of England also favoured this idea, but the free market-minded Thatcher government turned it down. None the less the Bank has gained new powers to disallow the buying of any stake of 15 per cent upwards in a United Kingdom bank by any party it does not view as 'fit and proper' for the purpose.

There have now been some further recent signs of a more liberal, though not free-for-all, official attitude to at least certain bank take-overs. No effort, for instance, was made to block the ultimately abortive offer by one big United Kingdom bank, Lloyds, for another, Standard Chartered, in 1986, although the latter hotly opposed the deal. And no impediment was put in the way of National Australia Bank's buying Clydesdale Bank from Midland when the latter, in 1987, decided on the sale to replenish its capital. Also, the Bank (and the government) clearly smiled on Midland's sale of a 14·9 per cent stake in itself against a large cash injection from Hongkong Bank, though its consent for that modest holding was not formally required. However, when earlier in 1987 the Saatchi & Saatchi advertising group had made an unwelcome informal take-over approach to Midland, it was also politely but firmly waved away by the Bank of England. As the Governor, Mr Robin Leigh-Pemberton, explained in general terms, the Bank was wary over industrial and commercial firms seeking to take over banks.[4] The real test of policy will come, however, if foreign banks seek a major incursion into the United Kingdom banking field.

Even over the procedures by which the big banks seek to get their views across to the government, time has recently brought changes. Just how much matters have altered in this respect is highlighted by comparison of present practice with the earlier unbreakable convention under which communication from the banks to the government was via the Bank of England only. As Mr Andrew Boyle has written of the inter-war period of Montagu Norman's dominating Governorship: 'Being a completely closed system, the City spoke out rarely – and then *ex cathedra* through its appointed high priest, the governor of the Bank [of England].[5] Much the same situation of City representations only through the Bank persisted broadly for decades afterwards, under such powerful later Governors as Lord Cobbold (1949–61) and others.

But several influences have now broken down old barriers to clearing bank–Whitehall communication. The Treasury itself, which has gained power in the Thatcher era, has made a determined drive to know and be known in the City. The Bank is still the routine channel for the banks' joint representations to the government on budget and other subjects of general public policy, and remains the normal, available route, through which the banking industry claims the government's attention to any requests or complaints. Yet in recent years the old rule barring direct contact between the banks on the one hand, and the government and Civil Service on the other, has clearly become eroded. This is not least because of some bankers' disenchantment at the Bank of England's seeming inability on occasion – as over opposition to the 'one-off' tax – to get their, and its, views sufficiently heeded.

At any rate, the banks now do, on occasion, talk more directly to the 'West End of town', as Whitehall and Westminster are colloquially known. Of earlier days, one top banker recalls: 'The Bank would give you the most appalling rocket if you ever went outside it to Whitehall direct. Now I think the banks have learned better and *do* go to Whitehall direct.' But this may at least partly refer to informal communication via the greater social and informal links now existing. Another top banker says: 'If we can operate through the Bank of England – the Governor – I think that is the best way to do it.'

Two years from the end of the eighties, Britain's clearing banks are far from being uniform monoliths but display many differing characteristics of business balance and style. Moreover, with the third-world debt crisis now worked through to a major extent, they are poised for a period in which fresh developments, and even some changes in ownership patterns, could be in prospect.

Among the banks, the National Westminster and Barclays stand out as both substantially the largest groups and those which have shown the most sustained ambitions to be comprehensive. Both, in tune with their front-line size status, have not only been active in overseas expansion, but have moved importantly into securities trading and investment banking. The routes they have followed in the latter diversification have, however, been diverse, Barclays having made major £130m purchases, while the NatWest opted for only £30m of initial buys. But NatWest, though proceeding so much more economically at the outset, has committed no less total capital than its main rival to its investment bank enterprise, though it has faced greater complexities and difficulties through building from a small starting base. Latterly it has filled out its operation through buying the broker Wood Mackenzie and fitting it into the County NatWest arm of its NatWest Investment Bank.

Both these two large clearers' investment bank ventures also suffered in the October 1987 share crash. Barclays' BZW incurred losses of £50m–£60m at that time – though its overall 1987 loss was only £11m – and the parent group channelled £95m in to top up the resources of this subsidiary, which was previously capitalised at £250m. Following County NatWest's much larger 1987 loss of £116m, £80m more was put in by NatWest to offset the depredations to its previous £300m capital. But despite these setbacks, both groups retain important long-term ambitions in securities trading in London and abroad. And BZW already enjoys a major share of the City's stock markets.

For the Barclays group as a whole, being overtaken in size and profits in the mid-eighties by NatWest, and so yielding the top of the league place in United Kingdom banking, was a wounding blow. The switch of positions was partly due to some slowing down for a year or two in Barclays' pursuit of new loan business after strong expansion and partly to the contraction in its balance sheet with the sale of its South African interests.

Now Barclays, under its new chairman, Mr John Quinton, has a drive on to regain its lead, with the deployment of substantial new capital. The reshaping of its branch pattern and a tightening of its command structure is aimed not just at improving services but at the streamlining of costs now sought by most banks in the currently competitive climate. Like NatWest, Barclays now has its shares quoted in New York and Tokyo, an arrangement which is designed to get its name widely known internationally. By the end of 1987, Barclays' total assets were just ahead of those of the NatWest, at £87·8bn, against £87·0bn, though in profits it was still the smaller of the two banks. In 1988, Barclays boosted its capital through a major £921m rights issue.

One long-run Barclays tradition was broken in the appointment to the chairmanship of Mr Quinton, who had guided much of the bank's previous United Kingdom developments, including its pioneering of the trend to Saturday opening. For, over the ninety-one years after its formation from as many as twenty local banks in 1986, the group had been chaired almost exclusively by members of the Barclays founding families, including Sir Timothy Bevan, a descendant of the first chairman, who steered the bank through the eventful 1981–7 period. But by the late twentieth century it was felt that the field for chairman should range beyond the old dynasties, particularly as the Barclays families' shareholdings in the bank were by then minimal. Mr Quinton, a banker well known in the City and in industry, and who once did a spell of secondment in the Civil Service, was unanimously picked by the board as Sir Timothy's successor. The appointment was welcomed as confirming that competition for the top job had been opened up. Then, early in 1988, it was announced that Mr Andrew Buxton, who is from one of the 'Barclays families', would become the bank's managing director, a move that many people have interpreted as pointing to his probable eventual succession to the chairmanship.

Lloyds Bank, now the third in size among the big four, has confronted as many major strategic decisions in recent years as any of its rivals and indeed still faces them. With a reputation as the most conservatively-run group, with the most up-market United Kingdom personal business among the top banks, Lloyds has been strongly motivated by profitability standards, notably under its present chief executive, Mr Brian Pitman, who likes to see a 15 per cent return on equity. Lloyds has also had, for over ten years, one of the City's most distinguished bankers, Sir Jeremy Morse, a former executive director of the Bank of England who is still aged under sixty, as its chairman.

One illustration of the cautious aspect of Lloyds' approach was its sale in 1986 of its thinly-profitable Californian bank, followed, however, by its purchase of a Canadian bank. Another was its decision in 1987 to withdraw as a gilt-edged market-maker – a move first closely debated – and from Eurobond trading. The latter moves allowed Lloyds to avoid securities market losses in late 1987 on the scale suffered by its two larger competitors, but have left it without a substantial investment bank business. At the same time, the group's £1·3bn bid for Standard Chartered in 1986 evidenced the far-ranging nature of some of its ambitions. The burden of its large third-world debt, shouldered notably in a £1bn-plus special loss provision in 1987, has lately slowed Lloyd's growth, but questions as to the renewal of its play for Standard or other developments may well arise in future, perhaps after a capital-strengthening rights issue.

To outside observers, it seem clear that Lloyds faces the need to make some important policy decisions in the coming years. Unless the bank proceeds by major take-over of the kind attempted in 1986, its size must impose some limit on its breadth of operations. So, in the absence of a tie-up with another big group, a selective rather than an all-purpose development strategy may be its necessary course. Yet, in a world where the biggest banks span ever-wider ranges, an accent on limiting ambitions may not be comfortable. Altogether, the general direction of Lloyd's future course is among the more interesting topics in banking today. Sir Jeremy Morse, one of the country's top brains as a Fellow of All Souls College, Oxford, and a chess problemist – skilled in the final difficult moves – will find his judgment and that of the chief executive, Mr Pitman, fully tested in facing up to the choices involved.

For Midland, once Britain's largest clearing bank and now the third among the big four, the mid-eighties were clouded by the troubles from its ill-starred United States purchase of Crocker. But a major new chapter has opened for the bank with Sir Kit McMahon's taking over in 1987 as chairman, subsequent moves through a £700m rights issue and £400m of disposals to reinforce capital and, above all, the link with Hongkong Bank. The latter connection has all the hall-marks of being a very serious partnership, as it involves the dovetailing of many of the two bank's international businesses and top-level representation on each others' boards. The agreement on the deal provides that Hongkong Bank will not step up its 14·9 per cent holding in Midland before November 1990, unless Midland consents or a new bidder pursues the British bank. Equally the Eastern bank will not cut back its stake before late 1990 against Midland's wishes. It is widely thought that the current co-operation between the banks could, if successful, lead to a fuller get-together: if not a trial marriage, the present arrangement at least looks like a friendship with a view to something closer. Were the two banks to merge fully, the combined group would rank as one of the world's largest banks. Whether to permit such an outcome when the Eastern bank's base is due to change in 1997 from a British colony to part of the People's Republic of China could prove a key decision for the United Kingdom authorities who, as already noted, have been content with the limited tie so far formed.

Meanwhile, the partnership avoids the need for big expansion outlays abroad by Midland, which at home is questing for economies while seeking, with innovations, to develop its retail business alongside its traditionally prominent industrial clientèle. As to securities business, the bank has, after incurring losses, closed the equities side of its Greenwell stock market arm, but continues the latter's successful gilts side, along with the also prospering Samuel Montagu merchant bank and some other investment banking. Co-operation with Hongkong Bank's London stockbroking subsidiary, James Capel, is looked to to help fill the equity gap.

Of the big four, the National Westminster has had the most obviously successful record in recent years, having not only overtaken Barclays in the mid eighties to become Britain's top bank in scale and earnings, but been the first to make (in 1986) £1bn of profit. This good trend has come after a bumpier experience in the seventies and despite some problems building its County NatWest securities arm. The group has also successfully handled a retail banking move in the United States and has benefited from having relatively less third-world debt exposure than its main rivals. Particular interest thus attaches to its management arrangements.

The NatWest, under a succession of distinguished chairmen – the present incumbent being Lord Boardman, who followed Mr Robin Leigh-Pemberton, now the Bank of England's Governor – is probably the one among the big four where the running of the bank is most decisively concentrated in the hands of the executive.

Its management is conducted by a tightly-knit band of top full-timers, led by the chief executive and including two deputy chief executives and nine general managers. Virtually all have spent their whole careers with the bank. Sir Philip Wilkinson presided over the management as the group's chief executive in the four and a half years (1983–7) during which his bank pulled into the lead spot. Before handing over to his successor, Mr Tom Frost, in 1987 and becoming a deputy chairman, Sir Philip talked[6] of the particular style of his bank, and of the way in which the executive manages this now wide-ranging international group and interlinks with the chairman, deputy chairmen and board.

The key to the system is that the holder of the post he occupied is, as he said, the group's 'chief executive in title and in fact', with the reins of control very much in his hands. Sir Philip also stressed the importance of the concept he nicknames 'groupiness'. 'There is a very strong group relationship and I believe that is something that marks us out', he said. 'In the management, we are very supportive one of another. We have absolute confidence in each other and we do take great pride in working as team.'

Functionally, these principles are translated into an active system for communication and consultation, partly formalised, partly not, so that management co-ordination is achieved in several ways. To an extent the chief executive and his two deputies split between them the regular oversight of the four 'line' divisions (domestic, international, and related services business, and NWIB, the investment bank) and five 'support' divisions (business development, financial control, management services, personnel, and premises), all headed by general managers, taking three apiece. But the top three executives take pains to keep each other posted about what is of interest in his own bailiwick, so that when each of the three groups meets, a note of significant points goes to chiefs of the other two. (Sir Philip personally supervised business development, financial control and personnel, as does his successor, Mr Frost.)

The chief executive presides each month over what Sir Philip calls a formal structured meeting with the two deputy chiefs and all the general managers, a session which is clearly an important element in the bank's decision-making. But, beyond this, an environment is maintained to foster continuous informal exchanges: for instance, coffee is served each morning in the chief executive's lounge for half an hour, when all others of the twelve-man top executive are welcome. On Monday mornings this gathering becomes a more important forum for a comprehensive exchange of views and information which is a 'must attend' occasion. Colleagues recall that Sir Philip would good-humouredly tease them by saying, of this slot in their diaries, 'only death is your excuse'.

A further aspect of procedure is the weekly meeting, later the same day, of the chairman's committee to process papers ahead of the monthly full board meeting. Lord Boardman and the chief executive attend this, along with as many of the deputy chairmen and top management team as are to hand. The board itself contains three committees – home, overseas and establishments – through whose own meetings part-time directors' views can be garnered on their special subjects. These committees' minutes are available, not just to their own members, but, at the main board meetings, to any other interested directors.

This apparatus of formalised consultation and informal communication, developed further under Sir Philip, amounts to an extensive co-ordinated management system, which looks fitted to work successfully, given the right direction at the top. That it has acquitted itself well is evident from NatWest's impressive showing in recent years. While each top executive has his own style, Mr Frost, the present incumbent, seems likely to retain the well-tested system. 'We have twelve of us in the general management', he has said. 'We operate together and we regard the chief as the leader of the pack. If I am so regarded I shall be delighted.'[7]

Another aspect of what can be seen as the NatWest's management formula is that generally it eschews senior outside recruitment,

except of occasional specialists, a policy Sir Philip believes importantly fosters team spirit.

Standard Chartered, the next in size among the big banks, faces,
like its rivals, the need continuingly to update its strategic policies.
Having widened its international range beyond its traditional Asian
and African interests by branching out into the United States and
Europe, it has been obliged to sell its American banks to rebuild
capital in the wake of the third-world debt crisis. The South African
business has also now been disposed of. The group's key move to
expand in the United Kingdom retail banking through buying Royal
Bank of Scotland was, to its deep disappointment, frustrated by the
Monopolies Commission's block in 1981, but it has a sizeable United
Kingdom finance house business, as well as bullion (Mocatta &
Goldsmid) and other activities.

In recent years, Standard has fought doughtily for its independence. It successfully fended off Lloyds Bank's bid in 1986, with the
support of its new 'white knight' shareholders from the East,
Australia and elsewhere. However, loyal to it as these investors have
been, there must be some question mark over the group's long-term
independence, since over 40 per cent of its shares are in the hands of
the several significant new 1986 buyers whose holdings, in early 1988,
still showed a loss compared with their purchase cost. In principle, if
a new take-over offer were made, some of the 'white knight' stakes
could be sold. Meanwhile, Standard has continued to shape its
policies as an international bank, though with a rather narrower
geographical span than a few years back. In the spring of 1988, Mr
Rodney Galpin, an executive director of the Bank of England, was
named as the future executive chairman of Standard after the
resignation of the managing director, Mr Michael McWilliam, and
ahead of the retirement of the chairman, Sir Peter Graham. Mr
McWilliam is to be the Director of London University's School of
Oriental and African Studies.

Among the other larger clearers, TSB is still in the early stages of
its life as a quoted commercial bank. Since its predecessor savings
banks had a high proportion of their assets in gilts, a key policy of the
bank in its new form has been to build up the previously below-
average scale of its loan book. The bank, under its first chairman, Sir
John Read, has also been diversifying its activities, with the aid of
purchases financed from the large cash inflow its stock market
flotation brought. A major move was its purchase of the Hill Samuel
merchant bank in a deal clinched at what proved a somewhat

controversially high price of £777m not long before the October 1987 share market collapse. TSB is largely protected from any risk of itself becoming a take-over target by the restrictions on large shareholdings in its first few years which were built into its commercial constitution. Sir Nicholas Goodison is to become the TSB's new chairman after twelve years as head of the Stock Exchange.

By contrast with their big four rivals, the Scottish clearers, with their business principally in the United Kingdom, have suffered relatively little from third-world debt problems, though they have limited exposure of this kind which has been specially provided against. Royal Bank of Scotland Group, having survived the attentions of two suitors to stay independent in 1982, has recurrently been thought still a take-over target, though Hongkong Bank's deal with Midland has probably removed the chance of a renewed bid from that source. Scottish opposition could once more be a potent factor were a fresh would-be purchaser to declare itself, but it cannot be quite ruled out that the 14·4 per cent stake held by that big investor the Kuwait Investment Office might one day pass to a serious bidder.

Bank of Scotland, sometimes thought of as an alternative take-over target to Royal Bank, has been considered fairly bid-proof since Barclays' 34 per cent stake in it passed in 1984 to the large Scottish mutual life insurance group Standard Life. This bank, the middle-sized of Scotland's clearers, has been a pioneer of the screen-based 'home banking' services via TV and telephone links, angled at small business and personal customers.

A further clearer is Yorkshire Bank, which now stretches far beyond its native county and which is owned jointly by Barclays, Lloyds, NatWest and Royal Bank of Scotland. With its accent on banking for personal customers and small and medium-sized business – and with virtually no overseas exposure – Yorkshire is Britain's most profitable bank, a fact that leads its shareholder banks to leave its management, led by Mr Graham Sunderland, very free to run the bank. Yorkshire has on occasion attracted take-over interest, notably in the early eighties from Standard Chartered,[8] which was then actively seeking United Kingdom retail interests. But the owners have shown no wish to part with their lucrative investment, least of all to a buyer who might pose new competition to themselves by going further up-market. Also concentrating on the personal retail market is Co-operative Bank, which challenges its commercial rivals with its 'caring, sharing' slogan.

One important question for all these clearing banks, and the soon-to-be-privatised National Girobank, in the years ahead will be whether their sector will be joined by large building societies in a new guise as banks and what such a development might mean in owner-ship restructuring, as well as in competition. Yet a further vital issue is how the British groups will mould their strategies for the best advantage at home and on the Continent in the more open European Community forum from 1992.

8 Other Banks: Merchant, Investment and Foreign

> Merchant banks today are short of capital and need to do as much of their activities as possible in ways not needing large capital.
>
> A banker.

> The Japanese are carving a huge share of the Eurobond market – it's the car manufacturing story all over again.
>
> A banker.

Merchant banks live on their wits and clearing banks on their deposits, according to an old saw which both captures the size split between the two sectors and pleases the former's self-esteem. Certainly the two fraternities have long been different and not just by reason of the merchant banks' smaller scale. Traditionally merchant bankers have tended to hail from wealthier and more privileged social backgrounds than clearing bank officials, while some, like the Rothschilds and the Barings, are centuries-old banking dynasties. The Rothschilds gained a famous market advantage when their carrier pigeons brought the first news of the victory at Waterloo. And so high was the standing of the other house that in 1818 the Duc de Richelieu, France's first minister, named the six great powers of Europe as England, France, Russia, Austria, Prussia and Baring Brothers.[1]

Another, less kindly, maxim credits merchant banks with living on their reputations, which at least reflects the fact that some of these businesses are so rooted in the past that their names, their experience and perhaps the banking in the blood of their executives count strongly among their assets.

In recent times, the divergence in size between the merchant and clearing banks, and among the former, has been growing, with implications for the nature of their activities. Kleinwort Benson, one of the largest merchant banks, is, in terms of gross assets, a tenth as big as the National Westminster, though itself many times the size of its small fellow-merchant bank Rea Brothers. This discrepancy in resources has necessarily dictated the strategies of the merchant banks, leading them to go easily on lending, which needs large capital backing, and to emphasise advisory services to companies and investors, which do not.

More recently, though, a fresh challenge has arisen as Big Bang has made it possible for banks of all kinds to enter the field of stock market trading, which requires large capital. This has faced the British merchant banks with critical fresh choices as to how ambitious, or more cautiously specialist, they should be in the newly available area or whether they should altogether avoid it.

At the same time as they have wrestled with difficult decisions on this front, the merchant banks have also been up against growing competition in what are now their mainstream businesses. American and other big commercial banks are nibbling, if tentatively, at their corporate finance market and specialist groups at the fund management field. More traditional lending and short-term financing have also become areas of new competition. With often powerful new entrants thus looming large in terrain they view as their own backyard, Britain's merchant bankers have increasingly faced the need to select strategically among the business options open to them.

Some, such as the big Warburg and Kleinwort, aim for a position as wide-range independent entities in the global market, with their size and strength reinforced by capital injections. But for groups of lesser size capital restraints rule out all-purpose ambitions. Some, like the still private Barings and Rothschilds as well as Lazard – in the Pearson group – have chosen to concentrate on areas such as corporate finance and investment management, with at most restricted securities activities. Still smaller banks must specialise yet further. Naturally, all those eschewing securities involvement make a virtue of necessity – or choice – by stressing how free they are of the conflicts of interest inseparable from combining market-making with supplying unbiased advice to clients. The wide-range houses, for their part, control such conflicts through segregating different departments behind 'Chinese walls', an expression meant to signify an impregnable barrier, not a permeable bamboo curtain.

Merchant banks in the second-size tier below the leaders face some of the hardest choices as the City becomes more polarised between broad-service groups and smaller-scale 'niche' specialists. One middle-sized bank, Hill Samuel, has already found its capital inadequate for a widened role and has yielded up its independence, accepting a generous bid from the TSB clearing bank and shedding its gilts and equity securities sides. And the possibility of further such take-overs continues to hover over merchant banks whose size falls well short of that of the rival American, Japanese and other securities houses which are now active in London.

However, between the smaller of the latter and Britain's top merchant banks, there is not so much size difference, as is shown by the fact that Kleinwort Benson is similar in scale to the well-known American investment bank Morgan Stanley. So it is fair to look for an increasing convergence between Britain's broad-span big merchant banks and a range of competing investment banks, some foreign and others controlled by British clearing banks. Yet the traditional British merchant banks are still often seen as an identifiable sector, with their own characteristics, although their club, the Accepting Houses Committee, is now evolving into a wider grouping. Many, unlike the clearing banks, pay contributions to the Tory Party.

Even before Big Bang gave them the new option of entrée to the stock market, the merchant banks had been shifting the balance of their businesses in response to changing conditions and fresh competition. They had long shied off from all-out loan rivalry with the big United Kingdom and foreign banks, often preferring to link their lending with their advisory and other work. Then, from the early seventies, their traditional acceptance business of guaranteeing short-term financing 'bills' on the strength of their wide contact networks came under competitive challenge. The numerous foreign banks by then in the City had their own good information channels, on the basis of which many developed an acceptance business at keen prices. By 1981 the acceptances of many such newcomer banks were well-regarded and the Bank of England extended far beyond the range of the old merchant bank 'accepting houses' the list of banks whose acceptances made bills 'eligible' for its own operations. For the old merchant banks, the result in what was already a recession-hit economy was a squeeze which, in the words of a close observer, 'decimated the profit margins on the acceptance business'. The banks continued with this long-established activity, but it grew ever more necessary for them further to work up (sometimes with extra overseas interests) their range of profitable fee-earning services.

One of these, a merchant banking activity of many years' standing, is the fixing of 'project finance' for big export and other contracts. In this, the banks devise the pattern of, and help assemble, the funds required over a number of years to give credit to the buyer, although others – typically large commercial banks – mainly provide the money. In the late 1970s and early 1980s era of big cross-border and other syndicated lending, merchant banks often played a part in arrangements for that, too.

In today's more securitised markets, where much finance is put up against tradable paper, merchant banks are active in arranging such deals. But in this they are rivalled by many larger competitors, including the United Kingdom clearers' investment bank offshoots and foreign groups.

As the Eurobond market has increasingly become the province of the big international houses, fewer United Kingdom merchant banks trade in it, though larger groups like Warburg and Kleinwort are active. Lead management of Eurobond new issues is even more dominated by big foreign banks, specialist groups such as Crédit Suisse–First Boston, and, latterly, top Japanese houses like Nomura. There is United Kingdom participation here, but the league tables of issue managers are dominated by non-British names. Consequently United Kingdom merchant banks increasingly focus on less capital-intensive services.

The field the merchant banks have made most their own is that know as corporate finance. This involves advising companies on a range of matters, among which the conduct of take-over battles is the one most in the headlines. The banks also provide guidance over share issues, whether in connection with a company's debut on the Stock Exchange, subsequent cash-raisings or in other contexts.

Corporate finance work includes devising methods for restructuring companies, in conditions of trouble or otherwise. From the mid-eighties, too, the vogue for buy-outs, by which managers purchase the companies they run from sprawling larger groupings, has generated a fresh class of activity calling for specialist advice. A number of merchant banks, among them Warburg, Morgan Grenfell and Samuel Montagu, also advise foreign governments on a range of matters.

Since the advent of the Thatcher government, privatisation has produced another rich flow of business for the banks, which, with brokers, have handled many share offers, including the multi-billion pound ones for British Telecom and British Gas. The banks specialising in this work tender for the assignments in so-called 'beauty contests' run by the relevant government departments.

Advising companies involved in take-over battles, whether as bidders or defenders, is generally viewed as the merchant banks' most glamorous activity. The experts specialising in the area pride themselves on the cleverness and creativeness with which, like chess players, they plot their clients' moves in the most complex tussles. Nor are the needed skills only cerebral ones. A woman merchant banker says a large part of her job is soothing the nerves and bolstering the courage of directors at bid-target companies who are terrified at the prospect of having new bosses imposed on them.

Each take-over contest can have only one victor. But the participants, all needing specialist advice, can include more than one bidder as well as the defender. In some cases where much is at stake a client may employ more than one bank adviser. Standard Chartered, in successfully fighting off Lloyds Bank's offer in 1986, had the American house Goldman Sachs, as well as Schroders, advising it. Charterhouse and Samuel Montagu both acted for Argyll Group in its unsuccessful tussle with Guinness for Distillers. In buy-out situations, there can also be multiple players, the selling group, the management and perhaps a rival corporate bidder. All these need professional banking help, so that 'M & A' – merger and acquisition – activity altogether throws up much rewarding business for the merchant banks.

A by-product of the M & A boom in recent times has been the emergence of corporate finance 'stars', front-line bid strategists planning clients' moves in big battles and often winning their banks multi-million pound fees. Such stars may enjoy power and pay out of proportion to their ranking in a bank's hierarchy, a situation often seen lately as unhealthy for an organisation's morale. One – subsequently fallen – star was Mr Roger Seelig of Morgan Grenfell, who advised Guinness over its successful £2·5bn bid for Distillers and who, in the wake of the later scandal around the affair, resigned early in 1987.

All in all, take-over and other corporate finance business has been very lucrative for merchant banks in recent years. It has contributed important proportions of their profits, particularly in years like 1986, when mega contested bids, like those for Distillers, Imperial Group and Pilkington, were raging. Yet here, as in other parts of the banking field, competition has been spreading, pressuring profitability and making fees and rewards more dependent on the outcome of take-over battles. Not only has there been tougher rivalry for business among the City's long-established banks, but some of London's newer banks are trying to break into the market. Newcomers include offshoots of some of the large commercial banks,

British and foreign. And although these may lack the long experience of the old United Kingdom merchant banks, they have the advantage of large resources behind them. A bank with strong financial muscle may back its advice in a bid battle by purchasing its client's shares or, in a buy-out, get its parent commercial bank to finance the deal.

American commercial banks including Citicorp, Bankers Trust and Manufacturers Hanover, and securities houses such as Merrill Lynch, Goldmann Sachs and Salomon Brothers, are among foreign groups increasingly active in corporate finance, often with loans as well as advice. And, among British players, accepting houses with wealthy bank parents, such as Samuel Montagu (owned by Midland Bank) and Charterhouse (in the Royal Bank of Scotland Group), have been helped in their corporate finance role by their ability to put their group money where their advisory mouth is.

Fees earned from take-over advisory work vary much according to circumstances. Sometimes a fee of ½ per cent of the sum involved may be paid. But the bill following bid services nowadays often depends not only on the scale of the affair and the work involved but on the outcome of the take-over situation, boards being keener to pay well after a favourable result. Fees are, in short, growing more 'sculpted', according to a leading merchant banker, who says: 'Clients quite like that because they want the bank to be as committed as they are to the success of the transaction.' An extra fee will be forthcoming if the bank's job has included fixing up underwriting, such as to provide a cash alternative to an offer in shares for investors preferring to be paid in money.

Arranging underwriting provides a considerable part of a merchant bank's work, and fees, in various contexts. What is involved is the fixing up, with a Stock Exchange broker, for a group of investing institutions to buy any shares available – whether through a rights issue, privatisation or otherwise – but not wanted by those to whom they are on offer. Normally, the bank's fee is ½ per cent, the broker's ¼ per cent and that of the institutional 'sub-underwriters', who take on some risk, 1¼ per cent. But even this standard fee pattern has been squeezed through competition arrangements in some big privatisations and there has been some support for a more competitive approach to underwriting generally.[2] Also, there have been experiments under which institutions underwriting the cash value of an exceptionally large proportion of the shares offered in a major take-over get paid an extra fee – if the deal goes through.

Charterhouse and Samuel Montagu made such an arrangement for a 'core' group to underwrite Argyll's offer for Distillers, but the bid did not come off.

Despite the signs of rising competition, the traditional United Kingdom merchant banks still retain the bulk of the take-over advisory work which is the source of much lucrative fee income. In 1987 the top ten bank advisers on bids in the United Kingdom and those by British companies abroad were, in order of value of business handled: S. G. Warburg, Schroder Wagg, Morgan Grenfell, Charterhouse, Samuel Montagu, Lazard, Kleinwort Benson, Goldman Sachs, BZW and County NatWest.[3] Of these, the first seven are British accepting houses of long standing, the eighth is an American investment bank and the last two are the investment bank arms of the largest two United Kingdom clearers. Thus, in the vital corporate finance field, the competitive challenge to the well-entrenched City operators has so far been quite well contained.

When the British merchant banks worry about competition, their anxieties sometimes fix on the chances of a switch one day to the United States system of 'bought deals' through which companies raise cash. Under this, an industrial or commercial company wanting to obtain funds against new shares or bonds will invite investment banks to bid it for the whole issue. The successful tenderer then at once pays the company and takes all the stock, hoping to pass it on at some profit to investors. It is sometimes claimed that this procedure would be cheaper for companies than the British practice of making an underwritten offer to existing shareholders. The apprehension in London is that any switch to the American-style system would favour the highly-capitalised foreign houses now in the City which would be better able than the United Kingdom merchant banks to afford the risk of buying a full issue. For the present, opposition from the institutions, and the Stock Exchange's broad support for the 'pre-emption' rule under which existing shareholders must, in general, be given first pick at an issue, have fended off the prospect of change. Any transition to the United States-type arrangement would deprive merchant banks of profitable underwriting, to their detriment unless they had grown big enough to buy whole issues themselves. They therefore dislike the idea of any move towards Americanisation of the cash-raising method. But were the change still to take place one day, it would bring fresh experience of the ways in which competition could erode merchant banks' profitability.

Another lucrative service strongly developed by the merchant banks in recent years is fund management, which some insiders think probably contributes nearer to a half than a third of the banks' profits in aggregate. Just how important and buoyant this business has been in the eighties is illustrated by the fact that Warburg's separately quoted subsidiary in this field, Mercury Asset Management, raised its profits from £2·7m to £22·8m before tax in the five years to 1986–7. As further evidence of the prominence of this source of income, when the £777m TSB bid for Hill Samuel was announced in 1987, it was estimated in the Press that as much as £400m of the price was attributable to the investment management side.[4]

The surging growth in United Kingdom pension funds, which multiplied many times over to £200bn in the two decades to 1986, has been one rich source of fund management business in which the merchant banks have shared well. Even where they are not the direct discretionary managers, as they are for the pension money of many sizeable and smaller firms, the banks often provide additional advice, for instance to large companies and to nationalised industries which have their own in-house pension fund managements. Moreover, as investment has grown more international, London fund managers – and the merchant banks prominently among them – have increasingly guided British investors' move into foreign markets as well as overseas buying of United Kingdom shares.

And it is not only pension and other institutional cash that is so handled. The merchant banks also discreetly manage investments for many potentates and tycoons world-wide, as well as for numerous of the rich, if less well known, from five continents. One client of Morgan Grenfell, for instance, is the fabulously wealthy Sultan of oil-rich Brunei, while Barings acts for wealthy Arab interests, in addition to providing advisers to the Saudi Arabian Monetary Agency. The personally rich of the United States, Europe, Latin America, the Middle East, the Far East and elsewhere entrust funds to these and other accepting houses, Warburgs, Schroders and Flemings among them. Warburgs, probably – via Mercury Asset – the largest manager in the sector, saw the resources under its management climb from £4·5bn to £21·4bn in the four years to March 1987.

The merchant banks' prominent role in investment management was highlighted in a 1985 Bank of England study, which showed that at the end of the previous year the accepting house merchant banks handled 41 per cent of the funds managed in Britain for United Kingdom clients and 47 per cent of those handled for overseas investors.[5] It was notable too that the accounts they dealt with were larger on average than those of competing managers, including the clearing banks, insurance companies, stockbrokers and others.

The merchant banks' fund management profits have benefited trebly in recent years, from the increase in the range and volume of client funds, from the increase in share values and because of favourable cost trends. The Bank of England found that, in 1984, the accepting houses' investment management earned them some £120m, a figure which will have risen sharply in most of the succeeding three years, when soaring share prices will have boosted the funds' value, to which fees are geared. However, the share slump of late 1987 must, by contrast, have meant a drop in revenues, with falling values. Fees were put in the Bank's survey at an average 0·2 per cent of the funds managed, though the rate will be higher on small funds and lower on the largest. The profitability of investment management may also have gained lately from a squeeze on costs with the drop in dealing bills following Big Bang.

In the fund management field, as in others, however, competition to the merchant banks is growing, partly from specialist managers, including Scottish groups and London ones such as Henderson and GT. Considerable management is also done by stockbrokers. Moreover, insurance groups are also questing more widely for business: as one top manager in a big group remarks: 'We may not have the mien of a merchant banker, but by golly we have the talent.' The growth of performance measurement firms also helps pension trustees and others to track the success of their funds' management, with the result that they are increasingly ready to switch portfolios to new hands after a 'beauty contest' selection procedure.

The latest arm added to merchant bank activity is the very one – securities business – whose opening up to banks has led on to the creation of a new 'investment banking' sector and made outmoded the traditional houses' former exclusive grouping. Only the biggest three merchant banks, Kleinwort, Warburg and Morgan Grenfell, have invested very largely in the stock market. But their consequent evolution towards being wide-range investment banks, alongside those of the clearers and foreign groups, has produced a realignment of categories on the City's banking scene.

Thus, during the year 1988, the old sixteen-member Accepting Houses Committee 'club' is being succeeded by the broader British

Merchant Banking and Securities Houses Association (BMBSHA), which is likely to have a much larger number of participants. This arrangement recognises reality by bringing together the specialist banking groups outside mainstream retail commercial banking and embraces those concerns, large and small, which are engaged in the fields of investment banking, corporate finance, asset management and securities trading. A number of the groups in this whole area will now be briefly reviewed, the long-established merchant banks, on which some figures are given in Table 8.1 at the end of this chapter, being considered first.

Kleinwort, the largest of the accepting houses and one of the most prestigious, has a major corporate finance business and has handled key privatisations, including British Telecom's. Like some others, it has been known on occasion to pick and choose a little among the companies it advises, withdrawing where it felt it could not sympathise with a client firm's policy. Its interests include Sharps Pixley, one of the City's five leading bullion dealers, a fact that led its chairman, Mr Michael Hawkes, to be closely involved in discussions on the 1984 crisis at another gold firm, Johnson Matthey Bankers, which resulted in the latter's being the subject of a rescue take-over by the Bank of England. Kleinwort is known for the number of peers among its top people, including the Earl of Limerick, Lord Rockley and the younger Viscount Chandos, grandson of Oliver Lyttleton, a member of Churchill's wartime Cabinet. Viscount Tenby, grandson of the First World War Premier, David Lloyd George, was for many years until 1987 the group's public relations adviser.

Under Mr Hawkes' guidance, Kleinwort has set out to become a player in the international investment bank league, having built its stock market interests through the purchase of the stockbroker Grieveson Grant, through recruitment and by expansion in the United States, Japan and elsewhere. Its initial losses through the settlement clog-up of 1987 have not dampened its resolve. Kleinwort's shares have for many years been closely enough held by its founding dynasties for the group to have seemed bid-proof. But, following a £145m rights issue in 1987, the family stake fell to 25 per cent, a fact that has stimulated occasional talk of a possible take-over.

Warburg has also long been of prominent status in corporate finance and fund management and has made a very major drive into securities business with its purchases of the leading jobber, Akroyd, and of two stockbrokers. Its decision to buy on a big scale in the field gave it a head start in the post-Big Bang markets. Founded by the late

Sir Siegmund Warburg, a refugee from the Nazis who sprang from a Hamburg banking clan, the group was the biggest postwar addition to the City's top merchant bank echelons and made history pioneering take-over tactics and inventing the Eurobond. The house, which is nowadays chaired by Sir David Scholey, also a non-executive director of the Bank of England, is known for its work ethic and lack of ostentatious luxury in its building, catering and annual report. The group was perturbed when the aggressive American financier Mr Saul Steinberg built up a near-15 per cent shareholding, and correspondingly relieved when this stake was placed in 1987 with an investing institution, Canadian National Railway Pension Fund.

The third of the biggest three is Morgan Grenfell, which was formerly linked with the big United States commercial bank group J. P. Morgan, founded by J. Pierpont Morgan, though this tie was unwound some years back. In 1986 Morgan Grenfell's shares were floated on the stock market through a tender offer which fixed them at an initial price so high that they did not easily later regain it. Morgan is active in fund management and has moved into the stock market with purchases of a broker and a jobber, though on a much smaller scale than Warburg's. Its securities build-up has taken time and it has made some limited cut-backs. Morgan's most publicised activity of recent years, its corporate finance expansion as an aggressive adviser to bidders, also generated its biggest problem, the crisis triggered by the official probe into Guinness, on whose controversial battle for Distillers it had advised. Consequent resignations included those of the chief executive, Mr Christopher Reeves, and the corporate finance chief, Mr Graham Walsh, on whose departure, as those who had to carry ultimate responsibility, the Bank of England insisted. The group, now chaired by a former senior Civil Servant, Sir Peter Carey, appointed as its new chief executive Mr John Craven, the banker who had created the City marriage-broker firm Phoenix Securities. Share stakes in Morgan, which is recurrently the subject of bid rumours, include the 21 per cent holding of Willis Faber, the big insurance broker, and a near-5 per cent interest held by Germany's large Deutsche Bank.

At the rather smaller but sizeable Schroders, which is very active in corporate finance and fund management and has extensive overseas interests, securities and capital markets business is mainly equity-related. In London the group, whose J. Henry Schroder Wagg bank is run by a German national, Mr Win Bischoff, decided against market-making in gilts and concentrates its securities business on research, market-making and trading in small companies, particularly those whose launch it has sponsored. Schroders has in recent years looked increasingly abroad. It owns half the Wall Street investment bank Wertheim and its other overseas businesses include securities operations in Tokyo and Hong Kong. Over half its assets and earnings are outside the United Kingdom. Some 50 per cent of the Schroders shares are controlled by the family, which is represented on the board by Mr Bruno Schroder and by his brother-in-law, Mr George Mallinckrodt, the group chairman.

At Hambros, relatively lower in the merchant banks' size league than at one time but still of substantial scale, there has been important diversification in recent years into estate agency, while there is no longer a controlling family shareholding. The unquoted Robert Fleming, best known as a fund management house, has moved into equity, but not gilts, market-making.

The privately-owned Barings and N. M. Rothschild have accepted the capital limitations of non-quoted status and do not strive to be all-purpose in the investment bank sense. Both are active in corporate finance – Rothschild having handled several privatisations – and fund management. Among other capital market operations, Barings specialises in sterling bond issues and market-making. Rothschild has a large minority stake in the quoted Smith New Court equity market-making and stockbroking group. Rothschild – whose chief, Mr Evelyn de Rothschild, was the last chairman of the old Accepting Houses Committee and may head the new British Merchant Banking and Securities Houses Association – includes a major bullion business. Lazard has deliberately kept clear of securities trading, but is prominent in corporate finance.

Certain smaller but quoted merchant banks, including Brown Shipley and Singer & Friedlander, cover a range of activities and sometimes attract bid rumours. Rea Brothers, the smallest accepting house, was formerly headed by the late Sir Walter Salomon, an outspoken banker who came to Britain from Germany in the thirties but, following his death, it is sometimes thought that the bank could in due course change hands. Guinness Mahon, now controlled by Equiticorp of New Zealand, is separately quoted as from June 1988.

The main examples of new British investment banks built by the clearers are Barclays BZW (Barclays de Zoete Wedd) and National Westminster's NatWest Investment Bank embracing County Nat-West. The latter's chairman and chief executive, Mr Charles Villiers, and Mr Jonathan Cohen, resigned early in 1988 following the losses and some problems that attended the firm's rapid build-up. Midland Montagu has some characteristics of an investment bank, though equities are missing from its securities range, and incorporates the traditional Samuel Montagu merchant bank which is active in corporate finance. Another group is being built around Charterhouse, now owned by Royal Bank of Scotland.

Salomon Brothers and Goldman Sachs are both instances of major United States investment bank-securities houses which have expanded world wide and particularly in London, from previously more localised Wall Street bases. Salomon is New York's biggest bond trader and Goldman Sachs more notably equity-oriented. Both have long been active in Eurobonds and more recently in international equities. Each is a United Kingdom gilt market-maker and trades in United Kingdom and other equities in London. Goldman, which dealt considerably in United Kingdom shares in London even before Big Bang, has made a strong drive into United Kingdom corporate finance.

Both these large United States houses decided against purchasing a London Stock Exchange firm as the basis for their United Kingdom expansion. Salomon, for instance, did not feel confident it could 'fold' such a concern into its own culture, as Mr Charles McVeigh, who is its London chief and also a member of the international Stock Exchange's Council, explains. Instead, it built up rapidly through recruitment, and early in 1988 had a London staff of some 750, three times the figure a few years earlier, after some reduction, made in a group strategic review, from a still higher level. Salomon runs an expanding British home loans business via its Mortgage Corporation. The group uses London, with its convenient time-zone position, to co-ordinate its world-wide trading in bonds and equities: 'The international business of any major firm should be run out of London, not out of New York', Mr McVeigh comments.[6]

Morgan Stanley runs a big investment banking business in the City. And another large United States investment bank, Drexel Burnham Lambert, best known for fostering 'junk' – less than high grade – bonds in the States, is also building up in London. Though it decided not to venture into United Kingdom gilt market-making, it is an equity trader and is developing a corporate finance operation headed by Mr Trevor Swete, a former Hill Samuel man. DBL sees itself as having a significant future as a City investment bank.

Among United States houses which are based on stockbroking, but are expanding into broader operations making them also London investment banks, is Merrill Lynch, America's largest stockbroker with a big retail network world-wide. Merrill, which has some United Kingdom corporate finance activity, is a market-maker in over a hundred United Kingdom shares but does not aim to be a frontline trader, its dealing being regarded not so much as a main profit centre as to back up its services to clients. Mr Stanislas Yassukovich, chairman of Merrill Lynch Europe and also a deputy chairman of the International Stock Exchange and chairman of the latter's sister regulatory organisation, the Securities Association, says:

> Our philosophy on this matter is perhaps different from others'. Dealing for us is really dominated by what we call 'facilitation trading': we are not traders for trading's sake, but to facilitate the execution of the orders of our clients. Market share is less important, because we're not just there to turn positions between professionals. We're there to ensure liquidity for our investment clients, whether they be institutional or private.

In gilts Merrill traded aggressively ahead of Big Bang with the aim of establishing its name in the United Kingdom bond market and probably won a temporary 15–20 per cent share of the market. But its current strategy is more modest, as is its proportion of the market: the earlier approach 'obviously took us to a higher market share than we necessarily want or feel appropriate on a long-term basis', according to Mr Yassukovich.[7] Merrill's pre-Big Bang gilts market incursion probably cost it some £10m, including around £3·5m spent to buy the jobber Giles & Cresswell, rather than the larger sums occasionally rumoured.

Other broad London business built by groups of United Kingdom stockbrokers include those of Shearson Lehman, in which American Express has a controlling stake, and Prudential-Bache. Shearson bought the large London broker L. Messel and is a gilts market-maker. Pru-Bache, owned by America's big Prudential Insurance (unrelated to Britain's Prudential), has corporate finance and discount house interests, as well as some securities business, although it has withdrawn from gilts market-making.

Several American commercial banks, already well represented in banking in Britain, have focussed a considerable part of their recent development on the securities side and, with the help of purchased stock market firms, are often well entrenched on the post-Big Bang scene. Security Pacific-Hoare Govett is among the larger traders in gilts and equities, and both Citicorp Scrimgeour and Chase Manhattan are prominent, also both in gilts and equities.

Others of London's previously independent big stockbrokers have also formed the base for broad-range investment banks, one being Phillips & Drew, now owned by Union Bank of Switzerland. The new UBS-Phillips & Drew, long known as a broker to institutions and local authorities and for fixed-interest issues, has greatly widened its range, having added, among other activities, large gilt and equity market-making and an increased role as broker to companies. Already one of the top securities market players, it could expand further on the corporate finance side, where in 1987 it considered buying Hill Samuel but did not do so. Crédit Lyonnais, France's second largest bank, has plans to create an investment bank founded on its purchase of Alexanders Laing & Cruickshank, which includes securities and discount house interests.

James Capel, the London-based subsidiary of Hongkong & Shanghai Banking Corporation, which embraces the latter's merchant bank activities, has many of the characteristics of an all-purpose investment bank-securities house, although it eschews equity market-making. But the latter fact, combined with the large scale of its agency broking, make this group's business pattern unique among the larger City houses. To date at least, its lack of continuous market-making in shares has been no handicap to Capel, whose size guarantees its being well served by others which do perform this role. But its activity mix did not protect it from exposure to the October 1987 crash, when its trading in convertible securities and its lack of profitability in gilts market-making contributed to its overall 1987 operating loss of £14m.

Among the Japanese houses, Nomura, the world's biggest brokerage group, is firmly set on the path towards becoming a global investment bank. It has moved determinedly, if sedately, into the City forum, where its financial strength has helped carry it to around the top of the big league of Eurobond issuers. Having previously specialised in acting for British and other purchasers of Japanese shares, it is now increasingly, with the aid of research, serving Japanese investors in their growing interest in foreign stock markets. A further arm of its United Kingdom business offers corporate advice, notably to firms seeking share listings in Tokyo. In 1987 the group began market-making in United Kingdom shares in a modest way and also declared itself a would-be new gilts primary dealer, a role in which it was later accepted by the Bank of England.

Nomura, whose London business is chaired by Sir Douglas Wass, formerly Permanent Secretary to the Treasury, has handled its City expansion in a style suggesting long-term rather than short-run objectives. It makes much of the philosophy of 'dochakuka', the desirability of putting down roots and growing into the landscape of markets it is entering. In tune with this, it has not rushed to hire teams of dealers from other houses, but has recruited many young British graduates and trained them in Nomura ways with the idea of giving more top London jobs to Britons in due course. Despite its low-profile style, Nomura clearly sees London as a key centre in its world expansion and as an important link with its Continental offices.

Daiwa, the next in size among the Japanese groups, has also expanded strongly in London, where it too seeks to be a gilt market-maker. The other two of Japan's main securities firms, Nikko and Yamaichi, are also active in the City. How far the Japanese houses' further ambitions in Britain are fully realised may, however, depend partly on the welcome reciprocally available to United Kingdom firms in Tokyo.

Experience since Big Bang has underlined how volatile fortunes can be, particularly in wildly veering markets like those of late 1987. And it is not just securities trading whose results depend on the stock market. Fees from fund management and even corporate finance are also swayed by market conditions. It is therefore not surprising that many of the new broad-range London ventures suffered in the October 1987 share crash and incurred substantial losses, sometimes prompting cost cutting and staff sackings. Moreover, in the subsequent slack climate, more economies may be needed. Since a key feature of the Big Bang restructuring was that new groups should be well capitalised, no failures followed the price slump. But the shake-out must test the investment houses' ability and resolve to stay active in London – or rather their parent groups' willingness to bankroll them in doing so. There is a chance that some ventures which have been imperfectly planned or lack resolute backers may be withdrawn or cut back. Others may limit their objectives over a narrower front than that first aimed at. But many of the main groups seem not to have been deterred by the market upsets from pursuing their long-term ambitions in London.

One large business which seems very much set to stay, but which does not exactly fit the investment bank mould, is Mr John Gunn's expansive British & Commonwealth, with a range of money broking, fund management, investment and other interests. Another is Mr Jacob Rothschild's extensive investment-oriented group, J. Rothschild Holdings, formerly Rothschild Investment Trust.

This chapter has so far been chiefly concerned with London's specialist merchant and investment banks, just as Chapters 6 and 7 dealt with Britain's own large clearing banks. But the city is also host to numerous commerical banks from throughout the world, all of which need a presence in what is widely viewed as the globe's financial capital. Pedestrians in the Square Mile have long grown used to seeing a foreign bank on every other street corner. Over 500 overseas banking groups are represented in London, most directly but some through partnership ventures.

These banks span the alphabet from Holland's large Algemene Bank Nederland to Zambia National Commercial Bank. They range in size[8] from the world's biggest bank, Japan's Dai-ichi Kangyo, with $241bn total assets at the end of 1986, and America's largest, Citicorp, to Spain's Banco de Sadabell, the 500th with $3·7bn, and smaller groups. The London foreign bank community's geographical reach extends from Afghanistan to Argentina and its political span from China to South Africa.

While most major foreign banks had long had correspondent links with London and, in the case of the biggest, branches established there, the big inrush dates from the sixties. The growth of the Euromarket from that time drew in hundreds of overseas banks wanting to participate in this new international market. The gathering practice of major syndicated cross-border lending which followed the 'petro-money' recycling from the mid-seventies attracted a fresh wave of newcomers, while the later 'securitisation' trend, and the stock market reforms, proved a magnet for securities groups. The whole internationalisation of the City's banking fraternity has been actively fostered by the Bank of England's open-door policy designed to make the City Britain's great 'invisible' export industry of the late twentieth century.

Nowadays sixty-three banks from the United States, forty-three from Japan and hundreds in all from over seventy other nations[9] are

active in London's financial centre. They busily tap the resources of
the City's huge pool of internationally mobile funds, mostly in leading
overseas currencies like the dollar, yen and Deutschmark, and
engage in a host of transactions, from overnight depositing in the
money market to longer-term lending.

The great bulk of the activity of the foreign banks in London is in
non-sterling currency, as Table 8.2 shows. But, as already briefly
noted in Chapter 6, there is also an important element of sterling
activity by the overseas banks, in both the consumer and corporate
markets. The foreign groups thus account for as much as 85 per cent
of all foreign currency deposits in banks in Britain and for a smaller
28 per cent of sterling deposits. They have a 77 per cent share of
advances in foreign currency and 23 per cent of those in pounds.

The Japanese banks make very great use of London as a centre for
their deposit-handling arrangements as well as other business.
Together they had, in mid-1987, 38 per cent of all United Kingdom
foreign currency deposits, more than double the American banks' 14
per cent share.

Table 8.1   UK accepting house merchant banks 1986* (prev. yrs. in bkts.)

	Disclosed net profit (£m)	Share capital & reserves† (£m)	Gross assets at year end (£bn)	Acceptances at year end (£m)
Barings	7.5 (5.0)	100 (75)	2.3 (1.5)	336 (243)
Brown Shipley (Q)	4.0[1] (3.1)	44 (48)	0.8 (0.6)	74 (72)
Charterhouse	12.5 (7.4)	81 (79)	1.1 (1.3)	163 (148)
Robert Fleming	22.3[2] (18.5)	195 (118)	1.5 (1.0)	69 (39)
Guinness Mahon (Q)	2.5 (2.4)	36 (30)	0.7 (0.6)	10 (17)
Hambros (Q)	37.0 (28.5)[3]	236 (198)	3.7 (3.4)	504 (445)
Hill Samuel	42.9 (40.7)	191 (179)	3.0 (3.0)	88 (137)
Kleinwort B (Q)	50.7[4] (40.5)	365 (286)	9.7 (6.4)	798 (702)
Lazard Bros	6.2 (4.9)	77 (75)	1.5 (1.4)	146 (125)
Morgan Grenfell (Q)	54.9 (41.4)	371 (229)	6.0 (4.0)	514 (414)
Rea Brothers (Q)	1.7 (1.2)[5]	19 (9)	0.2 (0.2)	38 (35)
N. M. Rothschild	3.5[6] (3.3)	120 (90)	3.2 (2.8)	399 (351)
Samuel Montagu	14.0 (11.0)[7]	147 (139)	3.6 (3.0)	376 (287)
Schroders (Q)	21.0 (16.3)[8]	221 (172)	2.7 (2.2)	132 (166)
Singer & Friedlander (Q)	7.0 (6.4)	48 (43)	0.6 (0.6)	120 (121)
S. G. Warburg (Q)	67.2 (55.1)	382 (321)	12.5 (7.6)	316 (410)

*Or 1986–7, according to accounting year.
†Loan capital, etc., additional.
(Q) = shares quoted on the Stock Exchange. (Guinness Mahon quoted from June 1988.)
Disclosed net profit is after transactions with inner reserves, where relevant.
[1] Before extraordinary deduction of £0.5m.
[2] Before extraordinary gain of £3.5m.
[3] Before extraordinary items (addition) of £8.4m (£0.3m).
[4] Before extraordinary credit of £43.2m.
[5] 1985 figure before extraordinary debit of £1.7m.
[6] Before exceptional net credit of £15m.
[7] 1985 figure before extraordinary profit of £41.8m.
[8] Before extraordinary net credit of £51.3m (£12.9m).
Source: 1986 (or 1986–87) reports and accounts.

Table 8.2   Foreign banks' share of UK market, 30 June 1987 (£ billions)

	Sterling		Currency	
	Deposits (share %)	Advances (share %)	Deposits (share %)	Advances (share %)
US banks	14.7 (5.2)	10.2 (5.7)	80.2 (13.8)	24.8 (18.8)
Japanese banks	15.1 (5.4)	4.8 (2.7)	219.9 (37.9)	33.0 (25.0)
Other foreign banks	47.2 (16.8)	24.2 (13.6)	179.4 (30.9)	38.4 (29.1)
Consortium banks	2.5 (0.9)	1.1 (0.6)	12.6 (2.2)	5.2 (3.9)
Total	79.5 (28.3)	40.3 (22.6)	492.1 (84.8)	101.4 (76.8)

Note: The figures in brackets are the percentage shares of the totals for all banks in the UK.
Source: *Bank of England Quarterly Bulletin*, August 1987.

9 Investing Institutions

Pension funds now probably hold about a third of listed UK equities (ordinary shares).

Mr David Walker, Director of
the Bank of England.[1]

Because of the diversified nature of our portfolio, we are investing in UK plc.

Manager of a major pension fund.

I doubt whether the institutions have fully realised the tremendous responsibilities they now hold.

Lord Benson, former Adviser to
Governor of the Bank of England.[2]

Stock markets would be nothing without investors. So the spotlight must now switch to who buys, holds and sells the shares, bonds and other assets that make up the securities markets' stock-in-trade: on the users of the services the markets already surveyed provide.

Here another revolution has happened. For, where once the private capitalist was king, now some two-third of all shares in British companies are held by the investing institutions, the pension funds, insurance groups and investment and unit trusts. These impersonal bodies, acting for millions of pensioners and employees, policy-holders and small investors, are today's market mammoths with, between them, vast potential power to affect the markets and the companies they invest in. How they approach their task of deploying hundreds of billions of pounds on behalf of those they represent, and with what success, is therefore a key aspect of any look at the City.

On the further question as to how far they use their power to foster good performance by the companies in which they hold shares, many would say the investor giants are as yet pretty ineffective. Certainly, something has been done in recent years, notably by the biggest institutions, to ginger up laggard groups. But the eclipse of the major private shareholder – the Forsyte-type family guiding a business –

has meant something of a vacuum of control over managements. It is arguable that this has left the average board of directors of large groups running companies in which they may have little personal stake, with no real accountability to a highly fragmented body of shareholders – in short, unsupervised and in practice answerable to nobody if things start to go wrong.

Highlighting the responsibilities of institutions for poorly performing companies in which they are shareholders, Mr David Walker, a Bank of England executive director, called early in 1987 for a more positive approach. 'I think it would be a justifiable criticism that institutional shareholders have not been active enough', he said. 'They have if anything been insufficiently critical and insufficiently ready to exert their influence in a timely manner, so that drift in performance has tended to continue.'[3] His speech, significantly, was made to the National Association of Pension Funds, representing the biggest group of investing institutions with £200bn under their control, a figure which strikingly underlines the awesome power of these funds.

The transformation in the balance of the shareholding community over the past quarter-century is indeed largely the result of a huge build-up in the size of the pension funds in Britain, as in other advanced countries. Changes of law and practice, coupled with greater prosperity and willingness to save, boosted the scale of these funds out of all recognition between the sixties and the eighties, while the present decade's stock market boom has enlarged the funds still more. Altogether, the market worth of United Kingdom pension fund assets rocketed from only £4·5bn in 1963 to £40bn in 1979 and all but £200bn by the end of 1986. At the same time the big long-term funds of the life insurance groups – large companies like the Prudential and the Legal & General, and non-shareholder 'mutuals' such as Standard life and Scottish Widows – have climbed strongly, though less dramatically, as the habit of saving from larger incomes has grown.

Of the other main institutional groups, investment trusts ('closed-end' quoted companies, giving their shareholders stakes in the spread of the company's investments proportionate to their holdings), have grown too, though more slowly. And unit trusts ('open-end', or flexible-size, funds in which unit holders have an interest according to their numbers of units) have increased sharply, because of market upswings and a much increased public following. Unit trusts are run by management companies for profit, under rules hitherto administered by the Department of Trade and Industry and intended to be run in future by the City's new watchdog, the Securities and Investments Board (SIB). Unit holders can buy and sell as they wish at prices reflecting the trust's current value. They pay certain charges, again regulated by the watchdog authority.

In round terms, the four groups of investing institutions had assets of some £440bn between them at the end of 1986. The pension funds, including those of giants like British Telecom, the Electricity Council, the Post Office, British Rail, and British Coal, with billions of pounds apiece, accounted for some £200bn and the funds of the insurance groups, long- and short-term, for about £185bn. Unit trusts and investment trusts totalled well over £30bn and £20bn respectively. Although the early 1987 surge in equities, in which well over half the funds were invested, pushed these values much higher, the later market tumble brought them back to not far from the end of 1986 level.

Investment policies of the institutions have changed much down the years, notably because postwar falls in money values encouraged the 'cult of the equity', the theory that shares are an inflation hedge and should rise with price levels. At the same time, gilts and other bonds, through which funds had traditionally provided for pensioners' and policyholders' needs, were allotted a lesser place. But even shares showed up disappointingly in the seventies, when property grew more popular, only to be dethroned in its turn after the 1974 crash and worries about its marketability. The newest vogue for the big funds has been that for investment in foreign shares as a hedge against currency fluctuations: since the end of exchange control in 1979, the institutions have amassed shareholdings abroad equal to between a sixth and a fifth of their assets.

Tastes concerning the balance of investments vary among types of institutions, just as fashions for all have shifted over time. Investment trusts are very largely invested in shares, with almost a half of assets held overseas, while unit trusts are also quite heavily equity-oriented. Pension funds, with their long view ahead, are more substantially in equities (69 per cent at the close of 1986) than insurance groups, which use bonds to fund certain guaranteed commitments but which still hold 58 per cent in shares to back endowment policies and similar liabilities.

The result of all this for the two biggest institutional groups, pension funds and life insurance long-term funds, appears in Table 9.1, which shows that at the end of 1986 these two sets of giants held

64 per cent of their assets in shares (51 per cent in the United Kingdom and 13 per cent abroad), 22 per cent in gilts and other bonds, 11 per cent in property and just 3 per cent in cash.

During the fresh price boom through much of 1987, the pension funds were so carried away by the charms of equities that they poured substantial new funds into shares, British and foreign, while pulling money out of gilts. With this new investment, and price rises, the proportion of pension fund assets in equities rose to near some 80 per cent by the autumn of 1987, but it probably reverted to under 70 per cent after the October crash. Insurance funds went more heavily into shares than gilts in 1987, but made some net investment in the latter.

Table 9.1   Long-term investing institutions

Distribution of assets at end 1986	Total pension funds		Life insurance groups		Total	
	£bn	%	£bn	%	£bn	%
UK fixed interest	29.2	15	41.9	26	71.1	20
Index-linked gilts	5.6	3	1.6	1	7.2	2
Equities – UK	104.5	53	77.4	48	181.9	51
– overseas	32.4	16	16.2	10	48.6	13
Cash	7.7	4	3.2	2	10.9	3
Property	18.4	9	21.0	13	39.4	11
Total	197.8	100	161.3	100	359.1	100

Source: Phillips & Drew Fund Management, *Pension Fund Indicators: A long-term perspective on Pension Fund Investment*, July 1987.

Allowing for these dispositions, and for the sharp share price swings, up and then down, in 1987, however, the broad balance of the two sectors' investments was probably not greatly changed in the year to the beginning of 1988. Tables 9.1 and 9.2, showing the end of 1986 position, thus remain of interest.

The proportion of institutional funds invested in shares has grown dramatically with the years, as the funds themselves have expanded, to the point where institutional holdings now dominate among all shareholdngs in United Kingdom equities. This in itself has meant a complete change-round in the relative ownership of Britain's quoted companies, as shown in Table 9.2. While as recently as 1963 the four main institutional groups – certain financial companies being grouped

Table 9.2   Ownership of UK equities: percentages

31 December Source	1963 Diamond	1975 DoI	1978 Wilson*	1981 SE	1986 P & D
Pension funds	7.0	16.8	20.4	26.7	31
Insurance co	10.6	15.9	17.2	20.5	25
Investment trusts & fin cos	9.0	10.1	9.4	7.1	4
Unit trusts	1.2	4.1	4.1	3.6	5
Total institutions	27.8	46.9	51.1	57.9	65
Persons	58.7	37.5	33.2	28.2	18
Charities	2.7	2.3	2.6	2.2	2
Industrial & comm	4.8	4.1	4.1	5.1	5
Government	1.6	3.6	4.0	3.0	4
Overseas	4.4	5.6	5.0	3.6	6
Total %	100.0	100.0	100.0	100.0	100
Value £bn	27	45	63	92	301

* P & D research estimates for non-institutional holdings
Source: as for Table 9.1.

with investment trusts – owned under 28 per cent of United Kingdom shares, the figure had risen by the end of 1986 to 65 per cent. In other words, the institutions together own two-thirds of the £300m-plus value of British shares. Over the same period, the importance of the direct private shareholder has ebbed steadily, from a dominant role at 59 per cent in 1963 to only 18 per cent in 1986. Under the 1980s' privatisation policy of the Conservative government, personal share-holding has widened, but it is clearly so thinly spread (with many simply having small stakes in, say, British Telecom, British Gas and TSB) as to have little impact on the total ownership proportions. And although undoubtedly many wealthy private shareholders have grown richer in the 1980s' market boom their relative stake seems not to have kept pace with that of the big institutions investing for millions of smaller beneficiaries. Another point of interest in Table 9.2 is the still fairly minor proportion of British shares, only 6 per cent, held from abroad.

Although the institutions seem set to remain the predominant investors, they will hardly continue to gain on the other owner categories at their earlier pace. For new funds flowing into the largest group, the pension funds, have slowed notably, in the last few years, from 20 per cent of existing assets on average in 1977 to under 6 per cent in 1985. There are several reasons for this, one being the slimming of the pension schemes' membership with unemployment and redundancies. Funds are also 'maturing' as the ageing trend in Britain's population – pensioners will number 13·2m in 2035, against 9·3m in 1985[4] – increases the numbers receiving pensions compared with younger workers contributing for them.

But a factor of still greater recent importance has been that the stock market boom has boosted the values of pension funds, making many better off than they need to be to provide the intended benefits. Such 'over-funding' has allowed employer companies to cut their contributions – or even to take 'contributions holidays' – to the benefit of their own profits. This situation contrasts with much 'under-funding' in the drab market conditions of the seventies, when many groups had to 'top up' their pension scheme funds. Both phenomena show that, with pension funds heavily in equities, companies' profits can be influenced by fortunes of their pension schemes, as would not be the case in inflation-free conditions when fixed-interest investments could be relied on to yield needed real returns. Ironically, some companies with large staffs have also found their pension funds – widely invested in equities – worth more than their own shares' market value. Midland Bank was among others in this position when its shares were under a cloud in the mid-eighties.

Of the other institutional sectors, insurance groups' long-term funds, which have grown steadily, if at a less hectic pace than the pension funds', seem likely to continue their expansion, partly helped by government encouragement of personal pensions. Investment trusts have shown the most modest growth of the four groups, in part because some have disappeared from the sector as a result of take-overs attracted by the discount at which their shares stand below asset-value. A few have been unitised, that is, converted into 'open-end' unit trusts. Unit trusts in general seem likely to extend their long-term expansion as they continue pulling in savings from an increasingly prosperous working population. Such trends, taken all together, should maintain the investing institutions in a commanding position on the investment scene.

It should be noted here that some big institutional investors do not fit into any of the four main categories. For instance, the Kuwait Investment Office (KIO), operating multi-billion pound portfolios world-wide on behalf of the wealthy oil state of Kuwait, is based in London and holds a wide range of United Kingdom equities. The KIO is shy of publicity but is a force on the City scene. Certain other major overseas funds are managed through City specialists like the merchant banks.

Varying management arrangements apply to the handling of the huge £440bn or so of United Kingdom institutional funds. Certainly this is a substantial task, calling, as it does, not only for considerable administration, but for major strategic decisions on the disposition of resources among market sectors and the choice of shares and other holdings within these areas. There are also policy decisions to be made on how far funds should be invested or cautiously held in 'cash', which means placed in short-term, capital-safe, holdings like bills. Institutions tend as a rule to be pretty fully invested: as Table 9.1 shows they had only 3 per cent in cash at the end of 1986, a time of still strongly rising share markets. Being heavily invested is good when the market is climbing, but cash is comfortable when prices are falling or low. Institutional managers know, however, that it is hard to off-load large holdings on a tumbling market on acceptable price terms. Therefore they often try to adjust their positions in uncertain conditions, not so much by selling as by holding back from investing new inflows of funds. This is the tactic described in stock market reports as 'the institutions staying on the sidelines'.

The post-Big Bang market has, though, made it easier for institutions to sell large amounts with little price sacrifice, as some which made precautionary switches to cash before the October 1987 market crash attest. But, in a rapidly collapsing market, large disposals are less easy on anything like reasonable terms. 'Some expected to sell very large quantities in the downturn, but this was not realistic', comments one manager who presciently started selling before the October fall. In dire conditions, managers of large, not easily manoeuvrable funds tend to sit it out quietly, awaiting better times.

Of the pension funds, the very largest, including those of present and former nationalised industries, mostly have their own in-house management teams, though they often also receive advice from City specialists. PosTel Investment Management, the biggest such group, which runs the Post Office and British Telecom superannuation funds, by whose trustees it is owned, has the merchant banks Schroders and Warburgs as external investment managers. Big insurance companies manage many company pension funds, as well as their own life funds, their in-house unit trusts (if any) and certain funds for other clients. Then there are the City merchant banks which, as noted earlier, do an increasing range of fund management for pension schemes, wealthy private and other clients, and charities. Finally, a number of specialist investment management houses, Scottish as well as English, participate in the same market. Managers normally have a high degree of discretionary authority, that is, power to make many decisions without reference back to a fund's trustees or owners.

In recent years there has been some trend for the trustees of even large pension schemes to farm out the job of managing their funds to professional City houses, not least because soaring salary and other costs have rendered in-house handling less suitable. One which made the switch was British Rail's pension fund, which had been in the news some years back when its major foray into buying Old Master paintings prompted queries as to whether such incomeless investment was right for railwaymen's pension money. However, that policy had long been halted when the decision to transfer management was made. BR's fund was dispersed in 1986 between Mercury Asset, the Prudential, Robert Fleming, Morgan Grenfell, Phillips & Drew and the Scottish management group Martin Currie. The big Unilever company has similarly transferred most of the task of managing its pension fund to the City.

Over time, this trend of contracting out pension fund management to professional houses may continue. But in many cases, in-house handling will remain the best course. A fair-minded expert who manages billions for others concedes that this may save money: 'A good team can do the job at lower cost.'

The institutions, as the City's biggest investors, are generally keen on the City system by which they act for a fee as sub-underwriters of share issues, promising to buy up left-over shares not wanted by those to whom they are first offered. Though they carry the risk of losses in the case of a share market slump after they have made their commitment, the practice usually leaves them in pocket over time. Given the popularity of the system, there is something like a recognised tariff of allocations of underwriting: observers say, for instance, that the big Prudential would generally be offered about 3½ per cent on average of what was available. It is broadly understood, though, that institutions will not pick and choose much among underwriting offered them by the arranging brokers or they may not find as much coming their way next time.

Another form of City activity which, like sub-underwriting, brings extra revenue to institutions is the lending of gilts to market-makers through Stock Exchange money brokers, as described in Chapter 5, at a usual interest rate of ½ per cent.

Judging the overall investment success of the institutions and fund managers is difficult because of the impossibility of fixing an objective benchmark test of performance in the varied outlets – United Kingdom and foreign shares, bonds, property and more – that they put funds in. Yet the practice of monitoring and assessment of investment results has greatly spread of late, with the growth of measurement agencies such as WM, formerly part of stockbrokers Wood Mackenzie and now owned by Bankers Trust. WM found, for example, that in 1986 the average United Kingdom pension fund earned 22·5 per cent in capital gain and income, [5] as against a slightly larger 27·4 per cent return on the FT-Actuaries index of British equities. The comparison – not exactly of like with like – suggests that, while there was nothing remarkable about the results of the diversified pension investment, they were reasonable, given the uncertainties inseparable from any widely spread portfolio.

Certainly pressures for good performance have been increasing, particularly on 'outside' pension fund managers and on those handling unit and investment trusts, according to a Bank of England study of investment management on the basis of a survey of funds holding a fifth of all British shares. [6] The implicit sanction behind the close watch on an investment manager's success is the threat of a transfer of the fund elsewhere if performance is not up to standard. One consequence of this atmosphere has been more intensive management of portfolios, in other words, greater switching from one stock to another in quest of return. Turnover, in the sense of purchases and sales as a percentage of total holdings, nearly doubled from 35 per cent to 61 per cent between 1981 and 1986, a tendency likely to have been confirmed by the lower post-Big Bang dealing costs. It is less apparent, though, whether the more hectic activity has done any good. As the Bank of England drily remarked: 'It was not clear whether the higher turnover was in general reflected in a higher return.' [7]

Some funds' trustees retreat into indexing, that is, investing their resources to match the big indices, such as the FT 30 share, the FT-SE ('Footsie' 100), or wider world measures, so that they cannot be accused of underperforming the market. This virtually eliminates the need for, and cost of, switching. But such a defensive policy is not suited to all and indeed would lead to absurdity, and the throwing up of massive bargains elsewhere, were it to be too widely followed. Discussing its findings, the Bank commented: 'Outside managers did not do it [indexing] because they were employed to beat the index.'[8]

The Bank's enquiry also brought out the very high degree of support fund managers give to the boards of companies defending themselves against take-over bids, even if this means rejecting tempting offers. Whether this stance comes from good judgment, instincts of loyalty, shortage of administrative time or mere inertia is a matter of opinion. But the subject leads on to a wider one, the whole attitude institutional managers take towards the ways in which the companies they invest in are run.

Given their size and dominance, the point inevitably arises of how the new institutional mammoths now owning some two-thirds of United Kingdom companies' shares exert their power. If the question is formulated as: 'The investing institutions have replaced the personal shareholder – what is their influence?' the answer would probably be 'Not much.' There would be truth in this, yet it would not be the whole truth. If the institutions are largely passive shareholders, practical considerations partly explain it. Many self-administered pension funds, notably nationalised industry ones, are run on tight budgets, while commerical fund managers must also watch their costs. It would thus hardly be feasible for most of them minutely to monitor the performance of the long lists of companies in which each holds interests.

Indeed the institutions, perhaps to a degree for practical reasons, rationalised into principle, recoil from any idea of 'second guessing' the managements of the groups in which they invest. They do not seek to sit on the companies' boards, in quest of the influence such a role confers. Their own available time would hardly allow this, nor are their stakes individually enough to justify it. Yet, between them, the institutions often hold a majority of a firm's shares. So, although most of these holdings are themselves of small percentages, their votes, were they used together, could have great weight. Yet in reality the institutions' influence has been more remarkable for its absence than its presence, save in a few scattered, notable cases.

If all goes well, of course, and the interests of shareholders are respected, a passive role seems unobjectionable. The question is what happens if things go wrong. One option is to vote with one's feet

– to sell and get out on signs of adversity – and this is sometimes done. Yet where shareholdings are sizeable, this is scarcely feasible, since a start to substantial selling may well knock the price of the rest of the holding. Once in, therefore, the large investors tend to stick with a deteriorating situation and, on occasion, make a joint effort to ameliorate it.

Campaigns of this sort are usually conducted by a few of the larger institutions, such as the biggest, the Prudential, which has over £27bn of investments. It was, after all, the Pru's Mr Leslie Brown who, in 1962, pioneered institutional shareholder intervention when he lodged an effective protest about the way the company was being run at a shareholders' meeting of the old BSA. Among pension funds, PosTel is remembered for its stand against a controversial proposed six-figure golden handshake to a former Associated Communications Corporation chief executive in 1981. Other large insurance groups such as Legal & General, and big pension funds like British Coal's, are active too. Usually, discreet representations, which may eventually become known, are made by small, specially assembled groups of institutional chiefs to the managements concerned.

On occasion the institutions pick up a general point raised by a particular case. An example is their demand, in the seventies, that shareholders should, as a matter of principle, be consulted if a sufficiently major new move is proposed by a company. The case that was the trigger of these representations was Allied Breweries' planned take-over of the large J. Lyons. The outcome was a tightening of the Stock Exchange's listing rules, which now require shareholders' consent to be obtained in advance for an acquisition that would materially alter the character of the buyer's business.

A major episode came with the 'industrial lifeboat' affair in the early eighties (further discussed in chapter 10), when the Bank of England pressed institutional shareholders, as well as the banks, to help distressed industrial firms through the recession. In some cases institutions put up fresh capital, or diluted the rights on their existing shares, to aid the recovery process. This experience led both these classes of financial institution to concern themselves increasingly with the performance, strategy and running of the companies in question, many of which underwent dramatic slimming and management shake-ups.

As time has gone on, several leading institutions have grown more accustomed to exerting discreet concerted pressure in conditions where change, particularly at the top, seems needed to restore a troubled company's fortunes. In some cases, a laggardly showing by profits or shares has attracted their attention, as at Burton, where they were instrumental in encouraging moves which put Sir Ralph Halpern in charge, and at Rank Organisation, where they fostered developments leading to Mr Michael Gifford's becoming chief executive. Vickers took over Rolls-Royce Motors, obtaining the services of the highly-regarded Sir David Plastow, with institutional blessing. The big investors also closely followed the problems which ended with the break-up of Dunlop. The appointment of a new chairman at a struggling group is often a sequel to bank and institutional interest, as when Sir John Cuckney, a celebrated company doctor, became chief of Westland, the helicopter firm that was afterwards, in 1986, to be caught up in a political crisis. The changes at T & N, the former Turner & Newall, which was hard hit in the early eighties, were also ones in which the institutions took an interest.

One significant recent trend has been that certain merchant banks, now increasingly prominent as fund managers, have shown more willingness than previously to be associated with, or to take an interest in, institutional representations to troubled companies.

Just how far investing institutions may on occasion be ready to press their wish for change is shown by the remark of one leading institutional chief about a campaign for key management changes at a large group: 'We let it be known that, in the absence of action, the company's impending annual meeting was going to be more interesting than usual', he later recalled laconically. In the event, the changes sought in the case in question were made by the board in time to avoid such threatened fireworks.

Ought institutions to take on a much more vigorous role in exercise of their powers as the major shareholders they are? Certainly some authorities think so. Lord Benson, the leading accountant who acted as Adviser to the Governor of the Bank of England throughout the 'industrial lifeboat' phase, believes – as shown in the remark quoted at the head of this chapter – that they are still too little conscious of their responsibilities. 'They [the institutional investors] ought to be well informed about the companies they invest in and base their policies on two factors – first, the long-term plans and strategies in the different sectors and industries and, second, the strength and composition of the management',[9] he went on to say. Just how passive the institutions' investor role still often is has been underlined by findings that even the major fund managers do not, as a matter of course, exercise their votes at shareholders' meetings of the companies they invest in.[10]

The Bank of England director Mr David Walker delivered a broadside on the responsibilities of institutional shareholders when he addressed the National Association of Pension Funds in February 1987. Recalling how institutions were benefiting from the cheaper and more liquid post-Big Bang markets, he commented: 'This accumulation of investor power in the hands of fund managers and the continued enjoyment of relatively free market conditions represents substantial privileges.' One point he underlined was the need for institutions to keep some eye on the nature of a company's top management: 'The reciprocal of the accountability of the board to shareholders is the duty of the shareholder to satisfy himself as to the quality and composition of the board.' And he hinted that the deluge of large bids in 1986 might have been due in part to an excessively hands-off attitude by big investors: 'One major reason for the recent spate of merger and acquisition activity is that, as a result of board and shareholder inertia, assets become undermanaged and thus lowly valued in the market place.'[11]

The Bank's Governor, Mr Robin Leigh-Pemberton, focussed at much the same time on the need for thought about the 'nature of the relationship that ought to exist between the major investing institutions and the companies in which they invest'. And his semi-jocular remark on the same occasion that 'many industrial boards view shareholders as an unpredictable and dangerous group'[12] captured the very real point, which would be confirmed by institutions that have striven to 'intervene', that entrenched top managements can prove highly resistant to pressure for change.

Of the past few years' trend of rather quickened institutional shareholder activity, one experienced investment chief sums up: 'There's certainly a greater degree of nagging and of willingness to be seen nagging [company managements] than there was in the mid-seventies.' Another thinks: 'There probably is some greater degree of special relationship between the institutions as shareholders and the banks than there was at the beginning of the whole [industrial lifeboat] process.' But another points out that such consultation is not formalised: 'There still isn't a method whereby the banks and institutional equity holders can have a dialogue about the future of a company with which they are connected as lenders and investors.'

Up to now, institutional intervention has been essentially directed towards rectifying what have been perceived as management short-comings. But in principle it would be open to the big investors to seek a far more active share in companies' regular judgments on their strategies. Such a drive by those who indisputably now make up the major sector of United Kingdom corporate ownership would, however, inevitably open up more far-reaching matters of principle.

For it is not too much to say that questions on the right role for the investing institutions lead on to deeper issues about the whole character of Britain's mixed economy and indeed the nature of the capitalist system. How actively or passively should the institutions that are now, in total, the predominant owners of British industry deploy their power? How, when they do so, should they balance the long and short term interests of shareholders, and weigh these against the needs of existing employees, senior and junior, and of the economy at large? And how would the effort involved in a far more hands-on approach be financed? These are just some of the obvious points arising.

Such questions are not likely to be swiftly answered, since they call for fundamental philosophical, practical and political judgments. Yet they will have to be faced some day if the new dominant owners of Britain's business are not to abdicate their responsibilities. Associated with these points also are the matters, raised by the Wilson committee in 1980, on the accountability of the trustees of the major institutional sector, the pension funds.[13]

Part III
Policing the City: The Watchdogs

10 Bank of England

> We are heading for a Bank of England like the Banque de France: a poodle of the Treasury. That, I thought, not just the City, but all of us (including the Treasury) might live to regret. I still do.
>
> Lord Bruce-Gardyne, Minister of State and Economic Secretary to the Treasury, 1981–3.[1]

> I do not get the impression that our powers have waned.
>
> Mr Robin Leigh-Pemberton, Governor of the Bank of England.[2]

The Bank of England is 'not a nationalised industry, [it is] a national institution', proudly claimed Lord O'Brien, the then Governor of that august body, to a House of Commons committee in 1970.[3] His second claim was indisputable and, as to the first, Lord O'Brien was making the point that the Bank should not be equated with such usual subjects of the then Select Committee on Nationalised Industries as the Coal Board and British Rail. Altogether his dictum reflected the Bank's belief that, in a very real sense, it enjoyed some independence, notwithstanding its purchase by the State under Labour in 1946.

Since 1979, however, things have seemed subtly different, as the Thatcher administration has given every appearance of seeking to strengthen its authority over the central bank. 'Lawson thinks he has got the upper hand with the Bank', is one City appraisal of Mr Nigel Lawson who, first as the Treasury's Financial Secretary and later as Chancellor of the Exchequer, has crucially influenced government–Bank relations. In so far as the government's grip has thus tightened, it is ironic in the extreme that the nationalisation which had little practical effect after it was put through by a Labour government should have been given reality by a Conservative one.

Like other countries' central banks, the Bank of England looms large on the financial, economic and political scene, though its formal responsibilities are easier to define than its real power. Certainly it has amassed numerous roles in its near-300-year evolution from a private company financing William III's troops in 1694, through its receipt of exclusive note-issue powers in 1844 to its multi-functional status, with 5245 staff, today. The Bank manages, and through its printing works produces, a £13bn note issue. It handles for the government a national Debt of over £130bn, a task involving repeated new issues and redemptions of gilt-edged stock, as well as routine interest payments and transfers. It also provides custody for the nation's nest-egg of gold (and currency) reserves, as well as for other gold stocks, in vaults some think hold more bullion than America's famed Fort Knox.

It is, too, banker to the government and the commercial banks, domestic and foreign. It smoothes the daily flow of cash through the financial system, watches the money supply and appropriately intervenes in the money markets and foreign exchanges. In addition, it advises the government over a wide range of economic and financial matters, domestic and international, and keeps a close watch over the prosperity, organisation and conduct of the City and the numerous concerns working within it. Internationally, the Bank maintains important liaison with overseas central banks, whose chiefs the Governor meets, not only in many exchanges of visits but at the monthly sessions in Basle of the central bankers' 'club', the Bank of International Settlements. Top Bank men are also well to the fore at the annual autumn meetings of the International Monetary Fund and World Bank, sometimes there conducting key discussions 'in the corridors' with their foreign counterparts, as happened when the third-world debt crisis erupted in 1982. The Bank, with the aid of its United Kingdom regional branches, also closely monitors the financial health of British industry.

The scrapping of exchange control in 1979 brought an end to the Bank's forty-year-old task of administering this curb over international payments on the Treasury's behalf. But from the same year, it shouldered the formalised role of watchdog over the banking system under the new Banking Act 1979, now updated in the Banking Act 1987. Previously, the Bank, which had stepped in down the years to control bank crises – for instance in 1866 and 1890, and then in the major secondary banking crisis of the mid-seventies – had exercised its surveillance informally with no more sanction than the Governor's 'raised eyebrows'. But the magnitude of the secondary bank affair, necessitating a huge 'lifeboat' rescue costing the Bank £100m, had led the government to seek bank-policing powers by law, notwithstanding some Bank misgivings about a shift from the old informal system.

Outwardly, the Bank of England, the 'Old Lady of Threadneedle Street', with its imposing building on an island site in the heart of the

City, has all the look and trappings of authority. Its lofty halls, red-coated functionaries and stately offices, its elegant directors' Court Room and enclosed garden with Europe's most valuable half-acre of lawn, all symbolise the Bank's eminence at home and prestige abroad. Its true power is harder to assess, dependent as it is on a mix of legal ground-rules, evolving practice and ever-changing interplay between its own top people and those in government.

One fixed factor setting the Bank's public status in place is the 1946 Bank of England Act which transferred its ownership to the Treasury, to which it pays annual dividends. To a degree, this formalised the conventional right of Ministers to prevail in any showdown with the Bank which had been successfully asserted in 1917 when the coalition government slapped down an independent move by the then Governor, Lord Cunliffe. As a piece of national-isation, however, it certainly went further than that. Yet the circumstances of the Act's conception and its brevity left as much unsettled as it determined about the Bank's relationship with the government.

'We're going to nationalise the Bank. We don't know how, but we're going to do it. Get the appropriate fellow to draw up the plans', the new Labour Chancellor, Hugh Dalton, told his Private Secretary within a week of his appointment in July 1945,[4] and this was quickly done. As well as shifting the Bank's ownership to the State, the Act gave the Treasury power, after consultation with the Governor, to issue directions to the Bank if it thought this necessary in the public interest. In addition, the Bank was empowered to give directions, with the Treasury's approval, to the commercial banks, though no sanctions were prescribed for non-compliance with such orders. Neither of these powers has ever been used, though they have inevitable relevance to the Bank's position *vis-à-vis* the Treasury and to the commercial banks' responsiveness to Bank requests, such as those for loan ceilings in the 1950s and 1960s.

The 1946 Act was soon sometimes shrugged off as likely to make little practical difference. A few years after its passage, the Gov-ernor, Lord Cobbold, bridled at a reference by the Chancellor, Sir Stafford Cripps, to the Bank as 'my creature' and had to be soothed by the government. A decade on, the high-powered Radcliffe committee remarked, of the Treasury's powers under the legislation:

It would be very difficult to say whether the conferment of this direct authority brought about any actual change in the accepted

existing relationship between Bank and Treasury ... Both parties
have been trying to evolve and practise an allocation of their
respective functions which, while recognising the clear implication
of the 1946 Act that the will of the Government, formally
expressed in the form of a direction, is paramount, yet accepts the
advantages of retaining in the Bank a separate organisation with a
life of its own, capable of generating advice, views and proposals
that are something more than a mere implementation of its
superior's instructions.[5]

Later the Select Committee on Nationalised Industries was warned
(presumably by the Labour government) in 1967–8 that, 'if the Bank
of England showed any sign of wanting to conduct a policy
independent from, or in contradiction to, the policy of the Government, directions [under the Bank of England Act] would be pretty
smartly forthcoming'. But, in recalling this a few years later, the same
committee spoke emolliently on relative Bank–Treasury powers:
'Control is not the essence of the relationship, as the Treasury said', it
reported. ' "Co-operation" is the key word. The relationship between
the Treasury and the Bank may ... depend very much on the
personalities of the Chancellor and the Governor of the time. There
is no doubt that the key relationship between the Chancellor and the
Governor has plenty of opportunity for developing.'[6] This was to
prove an accurate reading, as tests of strength between the two
authorities in the seventies and eighties showed.

An important and little-discussed aspect of the Bank is the way in
which it is financed. This has to be the subject of special arrangements since earnings from the Bank's limited number of customers
could not yield anything like the income needed to pay for its work
over a wide field as Britain's central bank.

Until the early eighties a major part of the Bank's resources came
from income obtained on the substantial deposits left with it, free of
interest, by the main clearing banks. The big clearers deposited some
1½ per cent of their liabilities in this way with the Bank, which
invested the cash in Treasury bills and otherwise to earn required
revenue. The resources in question also served as a convenient
medium for the Bank's money market operations. However, under
changes in monetary policy mechanisms in 1981, the market interven-

tion was differently catered for and the clearing banks were no longer called on to leave such large sums interest-free with the Bank.

It then became a crucial question how the Bank's future income needs were to be assured. The matter was naturally one of deep importance for the central bank, to whose status, confidence and comfort an independent source of revenue was felt vital. In the event, it was arranged[7] that the whole 600-strong community of banks in Britain should place non-interest bearing deposits with the Bank, in a prescribed ratio to their deposits. With a far wider range of banks participating, the 'cash ratio deposits' were set at a slender 0·5 per cent of liabilities, a porportion cut in 1986 to 0·45 per cent.[8]

The cash ratio deposits system makes the Bank largely City-financed and avoids the need for it to seek government funding, something which, if provided, would surely bring tight control. It also has the merit of flexibility, since the rate can be adjusted, either downward, as in 1986, or upwards, should the Bank for any reason need more cash for its own operations. The latter possibility was thought of in confidential debates after the Bank's rescue of the troubled Johnson Matthey Bankers in 1984.

The successful setting up of the new arrangement was the work of the Bank's former Governor, Lord Richardson, and some insiders view his negotiation of it as one of his most notable achievements.

The cash ratio deposits, totally £913m in early 1988, are held in the Bank's 'own' accounts, those of its Banking Department, and contribute to that department's profit, out of which a dividend is paid to the Treasury. The Bank charged the costs of its operations in the secondary banking and JMB affairs to the Banking Department.

Existing separately from the Banking Department is the Issue Department, through which the Bank's note issue business for the government is handled. The £1·4bn annual profit from this side, which in effect conducts an agency business for the government and which one expert jokes was 'nationalised' by Sir Robert Peel's 1844 Bank Charter Act revamping the Bank, goes to the Treasury.

When some big-scale exceptional operation is undertaken by the bank in the national interest it is handled through the Issue Department. When the BP shareholding of the crisis-hit Burmah Oil was bought by the Bank in connection with its rescue package for Burmah in 1975, that purchase was done through the Issue Department and the ultimate profit passed to the Treasury, which would equally have borne any loss. Ironically, the latest special role for the Issue Department also concerned BP and arose after the last block of the government's BP shares had been underwritten for sale and when the 1987 market crash occurred before deals began. The Bank's temporary 70p a share 'safety net' offer for the part-paid BP shares was handled through the Department and the final financial outcome will accrue to the Treasury. More generally, the government repays the Bank's 'own' Banking Department for the three services the Bank conducts for it, in connection with the note issue, debt management and the reserves (the Exchange Equalisation Account).

The elements of the Bank's operations – from monetary and exchange policy to markets, City organisation, the state of the banks and industry, and much more – are so wide that any government feels an interest in many of them. But how far the Treasury, on the government's behalf, seeks a say in fresh decisions on each depends on many things. Much turns on the relative strengths of the personalities of successive Governors of the Bank and Chancellors of the Exchequer, and on confidence between them. The political background matters too. Where a government is driving for change, its relations with the Bank may be less tranquil than in static conditions. Again, a Labour government, expecting and getting few favours from a hostile City, may feel beholden to, and rely on, a Governor who helps ease its difficulties.

Generally speaking, governments in the past have traditionally been content to let the Bank get on with its job so long as the main lines of their money and other key policies are followed. Detailed execution of monetary, gilts and much exchange policy would thus be the unfettered province of the Bank, as would dealings with the banking community. This broad approach prevailed in the seventies, when there was reasonable government–Bank amity, despite the boiling over of growth policies under Mr Heath's premiership, and the 1976 sterling crisis and spending cuts under Labour. In the 1976 troubles, the actions of the Governor, Lord Richardson, in helping handle problems, while pressing more restrictive policies on the Chancellor, Mr Denis Healey, allowed a good working atmosphere to prevail. 'Healey's a strong man, knows his own mind and is totally confident: he could use Richardson well and wasn't afraid of being persuaded by him, wasn't trying to knock him down', a near observer noted later. At the same time, there was some discontent in the Treasury that the Bank did not take it more fully into its confidence over crises such as those affecting the Crown Agents and the secondary banks in the mid-seventies.

With the arrival of Mrs Thatcher's government in office in 1979, however, there began a period of rapid developments and of frequent disharmony between what insiders call the West End (government and Treasury) and East End (Bank) centres of official financial authority. One single fact which vividly spotlights the nature of the new age is that plans for indexed (inflation-proofed) gilt-edged stocks were later debated at top level for weeks between Treasury, Bank and Prime Minister's Office, before being agreed on – against the Governor's opposition. In the old days the Treasury would rarely even have queried the terms of a gilts issue.

The Thatcher government took over with a pronounced dedication to monetarist policies, a marked reliance on economists sharing its views, a resolve on what it saw as necessary change at all costs and a less than perfect grasp of the City markets' workings. These were ingredients for a spell of possible turbulence ahead. Indeed, for much of its first two years the new administration embraced what many saw as a highly simplistic version of monetarist ideology. It even flirted with the idea of a mechanistic money base system that would have fixed the amount of cash in the economy on an almost automatic basis, regardless of changing needs. Such approaches were at odds with the more subtle, Keynesian methods by which the economy had long been steered, by governments of both complexions, through a mix of influences, monetary, tax, State spending and exhortatory.

The new economic thinking, unveiled in the 'medium-term financial strategy' in the Spring 1980 Budget, rested on the concept that the growth in money supply should fall steadily over the years, while the Budget deficit was also to be cut. The twin objectives were to reduce inflation and to lower the relative amount of wealth-recycling by the State. Efforts made in the past to influence other quantities, such as the exchange rate and pay rises, were firmly stopped.

The times were made more troubled by the fact that the actual money supply targets set for 1980–1 – growth of only 7–11 per cent – contrasted with an inflation rate which, boosted by VAT rises and pay awards, more than doubled to 21·9 per cent in the first Thatcher year to May 1980. The gap between these rates implied a great degree of squeeze, because the intended expansion of money supply was much smaller than the pace at which prices were rising. Interest rates had early on been pushed up in an attempt to enforce the planned restriction on money supply, and the Bank of England Minimum Lending Rate (MLR), the key to all rates, stood in May 1980 at a steep 17 per cent. Such a lucrative return proved a magnet drawing world cash to London, with the result that the pound also shot up in the foreign exchanges, reaching some $2·40 US dollars at the end of 1980. In terms of its average value, as adjusted for inflation, sterling soared by 43 per cent, from 106·5 at the end of 1978 to 152·4 by January 1981,[9] a vastly higher rise than that of any other leading currency. But at the same time British industry began to groan under the double burdens of lofty interest rate bills and the competitive handicap in world markets of a much dearer pound. Collapses of small firms escalated and large ones neared the brink of destruction.

In this national predicament, the Bank told the government that, in its view, interest rates were too high for the economy's good. It was also concerned for industry's competitiveness as the pound climbed higher, but the government's view at the time was that this was not the quantity to be worked upon: its view was rather that sterling's strength was at least partly due to the growing flow of North Sea oil revenues. Meanwhile, the Bank tried to control industrial distress by urging the commercial banks to extend credit to hard-pressed firms in the emerging recession.

Alongside all this, philosophical debates were under way in which the Bank was seeking to persuade the government against a switch to a mechanistic money base system, an idea outlined as a possibility in a March 1980 'Green Paper'[10] discussion document. Such an arrangement would have gone far towards surrendering control over events to market forces and so risked wild interest swings.

The time was a difficult one for the Bank's Governor, Lord Richardson, who had persuaded the previous Labour government to pay more attention to money supply, but who was never exclusively enough dedicated to its use as a regulator to be regarded by the Thatcher government as 'one of us'.

As its worries over the economy deepened in the summer of 1980, there also loomed for the Bank the embarrassment that the M3 measure of money supply, so closely targeted by the government, would soon leap for largely technical reasons. The surge, which turned out to be of 8 per cent in July and August alone, against the 9 per cent or so full-year target set in the Budget, was to a substantial extent because of the scrapping, at the end of June 1980, of the former 'corset' control on bank lending. That change caused credit previously diverted via bill finance to be rerouted back into the direct lending which was captured in the statistics. Distress loans to troubled industry also raised the money supply increase.

In July, Mrs Thatcher, the Prime Minister, who took the closest interest in financial policy, agreed, on the Bank's pressing, to a one per cent cut in the key MLR to 16 per cent. A few weeks later, the Premier left with her husband for a short summer holiday in Switzerland. There she talked with one of the high priests of monetarism, the Swiss-born Professor Karl Brunner, whom she met through Dr Fritz Leutwiler, then President of the Swiss National Bank, and from whom she seems to have gained increased enthusiasm for money supply control measures. (The Bank was hurt that the Swiss had not, via the central bank network, given them the customary notice of the encounter, allowing them to provide suitable briefing: presumably the meeting was viewed as private.) The later weeks of the autumn saw Professor Brunner at the Prime Minister's headquarters at 10 Downing Street, whither Treasury and Bank of England personnel were called to hear his monetarist views.

Mrs Thatcher's return to London coincided with the second monthly post-'corset' jump in money supply, again causing her to fear that the Bank was inadequately enforcing the monetary policy she had at heart. The Prime Minister sent for the Governor, but in that mid-September both he and the Deputy Governor, Sir Kit McMahon, were abroad at conferences. Two other senior Bank officials, at that time unknown to the Premier, Mr John Fforde, executive director on the home side, and Mr Eddie George, called in answer to the summons and, according to Whitehall legend, felt the full force of Mrs Thatcher's annoyance. Yet, so far from its being suitable to boost interests rates yet higher in a bid to crush down the money supply figures, United Kingdom industry's increasing distress rather indicated, many felt, the need for a cut. One pointer to the pressure came when ICI, Britain's largest industrial company, reported heavily reduced second-quarter profits and afterwards cut its dividend for the first time in over forty years.

A piquant occasion occurred around this time when the Prime Minister was at a businessman-of-the-year lunch at the Savoy Hotel, attended by eminent people including Mr Robin Leigh-Pemberton, then chairman of the National Westminster Bank. As the guests were assembling, the NatWest chief was talking to a government Minister, Mr John Biffen, the Chief Secretary to the Treasury. Presently, Mrs

Thatcher came up to her Treasury colleague, asking him what on earth was happening to the recently announced money supply figures, which she described as out of control. The Prime Minister then turned to Mr Leigh-Pemberton and suggested it was his responsibility, since money was pouring forth from his bank in a way that was completely defeating her policy. So forceful was she on the subject that the NatWest chairman was provoked to reply with equal robustness, saying this was nonsense and that the matter needed to be seen in perspective. At this stage the lunchers were called to their places and Mr Leigh-Pembeton remarked to Mr Biffen: 'Well, that's torn it. I suppose you oughtn't to talk to Prime Ministers like that.' But Mr Biffen said: 'Oh, you'd be surprised. She'd be very interested in your reaction', and predicted that the PM would return before leaving to resume the exchange.

Sure enough, this proved to be the case and on her way out Mrs Thatcher got hold of the bank chairman and said: 'Now, I want to know what those loan figures are.' Mr Leigh-Pemberton suggested that, as he was coming to a reception given by the Prime Minister in the next day or so, he should verify the exact figures and let her have them then. Accordingly, he set out for the party with the fully-checked figures on a card in his pocket.

While he was chatting at the reception, at the Prime Minister's official residence, Mrs Thatcher came up and immediately asked if he had got the promised figures. 'Yes, Prime Minister, here they are', the chairman responded, taking out the card and preparing to explain its contents. But the Premier interrupted, saying, 'Thank you very much', taking the card from his hand, putting it in her handbag and soon moving on to other guests. As it happened, Mr Leigh-Pemberton had at that moment been talking to the Governor of the Bank of England, Lord Richardson, who now asked: 'What's this? What are your doing passing figures to the Prime Minister like that?' 'They are figures of the increases in lending by the National Westminster Bank, which are not anything like as high as they are alleged to be', was the answer. It is interesting to speculate whether it was on this day that the first thought of Mr Leigh-Pemberton's appointment as a future Governor entered the Premier's mind.

As the autumn of 1980 wore on, a rather more fruitful dialogue of the monetary situation developed within the official sector. The Prime Minister, the cutting edge of whose style was growing more familiar in the Bank as elsewhere, demanded detailed defences of

Bank opinions on interest rate levels, more mechanistic money systems and other matters. These were provided and lengthily debated at Downing Street summits chaired by Mrs Thatcher and attended by Treasury and Bank chiefs and various advisers. The Treasury side included the Chancellor, Sir Geoffrey Howe, the Financial Secretary, Mr Nigel Lawson, Sir Douglas Wass, the Permanent Secretary since 1973, and Sir Peter Middleton, who was to succeed him in 1983 and become an important interpreter of the government's policies and link with the Bank. The latter's team embraced the Governor, Lord Richardson, and among others Mr Eddie George (later a director), who played a key part in the re-examination and explanation of points which were at issue.

These discussions were gradually productive of more mutual understanding and constructive decision-making. It was settled that, in acknowledgment of the importance of market forces, the Bank was to conduct more of its intervention in the money markets indirectly through bill transactions and the later phasing-out of the officially-influenced MLR was envisaged. However, any idea of a purely mechanistic money base system of control was shelved. An announcement was made accordingly in November.[11]

As to the Bank's view that monetary contraction had grown too severe, quarters near the government sought an opinion – from another Swiss, Professor Jürg Niehans, of Berne University – on the situation, to the background of a still rising pound and an increasingly stricken industrial climate. After Professor Niehans had reported, and Mrs Thatcher's new economic adviser, Sir Alan Walters, had opined that the squeeze was indeed too tight,[12] interest rates dropped further, to 12 per cent in March 1981. But pressure then shifted onto the fiscal leg of policy in the Budget of that month, which provided for a slimmed fiscal deficit after fresh public spending cuts. This dismayed the Cabinet 'wets', who felt the ideology of monetary rigour was being continued by other methods.

Later, monetary policy grew more subtle. Less total dependence was placed on the efficacy of controlling money supply as the cure-all for economic ills. Indeed in time the M3 broad measure of money stock was dethroned as the sacred guide to policy, not least because in the exchange control-free situation created by the Tories it was too maverick an indicator to be relied on. More attention was paid to the exchange rate and a sharp drop in sterling in 1981 eased exporters' handicaps. Also, any idea that short-term interest rates should be set entirely by market forces was scrapped. Now, indeed, signals by the

Bank of England calling for rate changes are openly acknowledged as government decisions.

Eventually the government could congratulate itself that inflation was much reduced and post-recession industry's productivity up. But the price for these changes was high, since unemployment had more than doubled since 1979 and manufacturing output had fallen by a fifth in the eighteen months to late 1980.

For the Bank, the 1979–81 period was a difficult one. It interpreted its role, not as a blind executant of government policies, but as an adviser which had on occasion to press contrary, unwelcome, views, while still accepting that Ministers had the final say. It was proved right as to the excessive level of 1980 rates, which produced too tight a squeeze, the relevance of the exchange rate and the undesirability of a mechanistic-type money control system. The government carried its insistence on a tough policy to force down inflation, at high cost in worklessness and lost output, but in time modified its methods on some points in response to the Bank's views.

The monetary policy wrangle left a residue of coolness between the Bank and government. In this context, the Prime Minister's well-known fear of being over-persuaded played a part. 'It is her nightmare to be manipulated by officials', one of these recalls. And it seems that the diverse personalities of the forceful, direct Premier and the subtle, highly financially-tutored Governor, Lord Richardson, prevented their dealings developing personal warmth. 'She was the dog, he the cat', is how somebody closely involved remembers it.

An imperturbable insider sums up by saying: 'It was a really bad year, but other governments have had dreadful initial years,' and draws attention to the benefits from the generally more consistent policies since 1979. Meanwhile, a framework had been marked out for detailed future discussion on monetary matters between the Bank and a government unprecedentedly keen to track even the details of policy.

Relations between the Bank and the Treasury underwent some fresh strain in 1981, in connection with the two rival take-over offers for Royal Bank of Scotland Group. In line with long-hallowed tradition, the Governor expected his prior assent to be obtained by any would-be bidder for a sizeable British bank, most of all for a clearer. And he was not accustomed to being defied if he opposed such a move. But this was just the situation that soon confronted Lord Richardson, and in which he enjoyed little Treasury sympathy.

Hongkong and Shanghai Banking Corporation, which needed to expand internationally, had been eyeing Royal Bank as a suitable flagship for its European expansion. But, busy with absorbing its American purchase of Marine Midland Banks, it had not followed up its ambitions when, in March 1981, Standard Chartered Bank bid for Royal Bank, with the latter's agreement and the Bank of England's blessing for what it approved of as a willing union of two United Kingdom banks. Sir Michael Sandberg, Hongkong Bank's then chairman, sought Lord Richardson's approval for his bank's staging a counter-offer. This consent was refused, but the Eastern bank went ahead none the less. The Bank of England was appalled by this unprecedented flouting of its authority. But Hongkong Bank, sensing some shift towards more permissive views on bids in Whitehall, where Hong Kong free market ways were now admired, felt emboldened to proceed further. In the eyes of Hongkong Bank's chiefs, there was a parallel between Lord Richardson's reaction and the knot-tying in the marriage ceremony. 'It was as though he were saying, "Those whom God hath joined together let no man put asunder" ', one said later, referring to the approval of a Standard-Royal Bank union. 'He was the marriage broker and there was no way he could accept his plans should be changed.'

The Governor and the Bank saw matters very differently. As they perceived it, a would-be rival bidder who had not even got his target board's consent was effectively saying to a Bank chief whose warning 'raised eyebrows' were never ignored in the City: 'Times change, Governor, and we're going ahead.' Not only did the Hongkong Bank's bid lack support from Royal Bank's board; there was no precedent for a clearing bank passing under overseas control. For one thing, the Bank feared that such a distancing of ownership might make a clearer less susceptible to its influence in future. There were worries too about the then state of bank supervision in Hong Kong.

Beyond all this, the Bank was also concerned that, if it failed to sustain its position in the affair, its sway in the City, resting on its informal authority, would be undermined, with dangerous consequences. It explored with the Treasury the idea of its being given new legal powers to control overseas take-overs of British banks, but this idea was rejected by the government. Nor was much understanding of the Bank's predicament evident in Whitehall. 'It was a bad case of the Bank of England going out on a limb', one senior Treasury man afterwards commented, highlighting what must have been something of a dialogue of the deaf between these two authorities on the issue. The months in which the Monopolies Commission scrutinised both bids were unhappy ones for the Bank. Fortunately for it, though, the Commission was more understanding, recommending, by a majority, the blocking of both bids, a course the Government accepted. 'A consequence of [Hongkong Bank's] proceeding with its bid is that the Bank's authority would be seen by others to be weakened', its report stated. [13]

This whole affair was an instance of the awkwardness created for the Bank as the Thatcher government's free-market thinking filtered into the area of bank take-overs without its precise implications having been tackled and formulated. In the event, the Bank's authority was little impaired and, as Bank and Treasury co-operated more actively in planning later shifts towards easements in bank take-over curbs, nobody ventured on further defiance of it.

In the early eighties, when the world met recession as restrictive policies were adopted to protect the West's foreign accounts in face of the second oil price leap, the Bank mounted a quiet 'industrial lifeboat' operation. This was aimed at mobilising commercial bank and other financial aid for companies threatened by the interest and exchange rate squeeze which was particularly sharp in Britain, and at persuading firms to get more competitive. Banks were encouraged to extend credit lines, rather than cutting them off and forcing ailing businesses into failure. Investing institutions with sizeable shareholdings were often also urged to provide support. But, though the Bank busily orchestrated rescues, it put no money into the operation itself. This was in contrast to its mid-seventies secondary banking lifeboat rescue action, for which it shouldered the £100m bill (£350m at today's prices) mentioned earlier.

The Bank had a department of about twelve officials dedicated for some years to the industrial lifeboat work, which was superintended by Mr David Walker, the executive director who later played an influential part in relation to the stock market revolution. Two Advisers to the Governor, both of great experience, Lord Benson, who had retired as chief of the prominent accountants Coopers & Lybrand, and Lord Croham, who had in turn headed the Treasury and the Civil Service, also performed a crucial role.

The Bank closely concerned itself with the problems of some 200 troubled companies, many already weighed down by large borrowings from banks, domestic and foreign, and facing crisis in the harsher trading climate. Often the problem-vexed concerns had complex agreements with many banks, any of which would have been entitled to call in its part of a loan which was not being serviced and so push the debtor firm into collapse. At lengthy 'case' meetings, the Bank urged that this should not be done and foreign bank creditors learned that a readiness to go easy with debtors in crisis was part of the price of being welcome guests in London. The United Kingdom clearing banks, for their part, responded readily, often easing their normal standards to extend further credit and co-operating with other banks and parties connected with a troubled customer. On occasion the Bank looked to institutional shareholders to help out a company in which they had a significant investment by putting up new capital. Troubled companies, on their side, were expected to take necessary remedial measures of economy and change, often after examination by specialist accountants.

There were few industrial sectors where the early-eighties recession was not felt and even the giants of British industry – such as ICI, BP, GKN, and Courtaulds – adopted their own major belt-tightening measures.

In many firms throughout Britain, fresh looks were taken at management, product, cost, and other policies in this testing period. Company boards frequently undertook this radical work themselves, but in many cases the clearing banks played an active role as advisers, some developing special departments for the purpose. 'The recession has sorted out the men from the boys', one banker remarked, while another said: 'It's not just industrialists and businessmen who've learned: it's also the bankers.' Some banks ran 'intensive care units' to give special life-support to badly tottering companies.

It was a feature of the recession, with its banking support measures, that relatively few sizeable firms collapsed. In the early stages the failure of the large Stone-Platt Industries textile machinery group stood out as an isolated event. Yet eventually the toll of casualties mounted, with well-known names like Acrow, Laker Airways and others, as well as numerous little firms, going out of business.

The identities of some companies which faced crisis but survived have never been revealed, but those whose (later solved) problems are known to have been of interest to the Bank of England include

Weir Group and Thos Borthwick. Turner & Newall was another troubled business with whose affairs the Bank of England concerned itself, as was Dunlop, whose ultimate fate it was to have most of its elements dispersed to new owners.

In conducting its discreet rescue mission, the Bank was following a precedent of the thirties when, under Montagu Norman's Governorship, it sponsored amalgamations in the steel, cotton, armaments and other industries, also in a depressed economy. [14] It looks on this type of activity as an occasional one only, although it keeps a constant watch on industrial trends through its regional Agents.

A further highlight for the Bank in the year 1982 was the Governor's role, which won plaudits, in the handling of the international debt crisis discussed in Chapter 6 above. Towards the end of that year the question arose of a successor to Lord Richardson, who was due to complete his second five-year term as the Bank's chief in mid-1983.

The Bank's Governor has, since the 1946 nationalisation Act, been appointed by the Crown on the advice of the Prime Minister, who thus has as much control over the post's filling as over any in the Cabinet itself. Once in office, however, the Governor, unlike a Minister, enjoys security during his five-year term. This protects him against removal should he offend Ministers with unpalatable advice but cannot safeguard him against the subtler harassments with which the government of the day may seek to assert its sway. How a Governor then develops his role in the context of the Bank's ill-defined constitutional position depends very much on himself, on the surrounding political and economic situation, and on other personalities involved.

Lord Richardson, a barrister and former merchant banker who had chaired Schroders before going to the Bank, had had an eventful ten years at the Bank. One of his earlier actions had been the successful handling of the secondary banking crisis from the end of 1973. Apart from other episodes of his Governorship which have already been discussed, Lord Richardson had, in 1980, put through a major reorganisation of the Bank which gave line management responsibilities to the four executive directors who previously had more advisory functions. New, younger holders were at much the same stage moved into most of these posts, notably Mr Eddie George on the monetary policy side, Mr David Walker handling City and industrial matters, and Mr Anthony Loehnis with responsibilities for international matters. A little later Mr Rodney Galpin became the director concerned with bank supervision.

Somewhat reserved by nature, Lord Richardson had been slow at first to make public pronouncements, and had initially been labelled 'the unknown Governor', an inappropriate sobriquet given his later flow of impressive speeches and energetic tenure of his post. As conscious as any of his predecessors of the status and dignity of his office, he liked, as Governor, to keep the reins of affairs quite closely in his own hands. And, on the crucial and delicate question of relations with the Treasury, he again had a bent towards handling things himself: he was not overly keen on the creation of the multi-level links with which that Department sought, particularly as the Thatcher government proceeded, to strengthen its contact with, and influence over, the Bank.

In his first, 1973–8, term and just afterwards, Lord Richardson enjoyed fairly harmonious relations with the Heath, Wilson and Callaghan governments. 'Richardson was a very successful Governor', sums up an acute observer conversant with the whole scene. 'He had his problems with Chancellors, but by and large they came to respect him. He became established as an international figure. The series of his lectures while he was Governor are an interesting source. His influence grew with experience.'

But the latter years of his Governorship were sometimes clouded, as the Thatcher government pursued its narrowly-focussed, highly controversial early brand of monetarist policy, showing little appreciation of views at variance from its own thinking. The Royal Bank affair also for a time cast a shadow.

Lord Richardson, though sixty-seven, would have been willing, if asked, to stay on at the Bank into a third term, but Mrs Thatcher decided on a change. By-passing a number of possibles, she picked Mr Robin Leigh-Pemberton, the National Westminster Bank chairman, whom she had consulted, along with some other senior City people, on two or three occasions since the exchange in 1980. He was her first choice and was preferred to some bank chairmen whose names had been canvassed and to the Deputy Governor, Sir Kit McMahon, then best known for his part in negotiations for the release of the American embassy hostages in Iran in 1981. But Sir Kit was often said to be insufficiently 'monetarist' in inclination to suit the Thatcher thinking. In fact, had the first preference not been available, it is likely that the Governorship would have gone in 1983 to Sir George Blunden, a highly experienced executive director who was then, at 60, about to retire from full-time duties and who later became a most influential Deputy Governor.

Mr Leigh-Pemberton, who had not been considered a front-runner for the post, accepted the Governorship and so became the first chairman of a clearing bank ever to head the Bank of England. (Lord Franks had been offered the Governorship by Mr Harold Macmillan in 1961, when he was leaving the chairmanship of Lloyds Bank, but had declined it as he was about to become Provost of Worcester College, Oxford.)

There was some criticism of the appointment of Mr Leigh-Pemberton, a scholar, barrister and country landowner, with business experience, who had served a spell in his youth as an officer in the Brigade of Guards, on the ground that he had insufficient experience of international finance. The new Governor had not been a full-time banker before becoming the NatWest's chief in 1977. It was also suggested in some quarters that the appointment was too political because Mr Leigh-Pemberton had earlier been the Conservative leader of Kent County Council. While this was not generally thought to make the appointment unsuitable, it was widely felt that the new Governor had been chosen as likely to be more in tune that his predecessor with the Thatcher government's stance and more disposed to work closely with the grain of its policy.

Comparing the two Governors – both fine-looking men, with presence, as a colleague remarked early on – was soon a favourite City pastime. One initial inside comment was: 'Gordon [Richardson] has a mind that never accepts the simple. Robin has an equally fine mind, but he looks for the simple.' Lord Richardson, it was widely agreed, had frequently taken a long time to make up his mind, through a wish to consider all the complexities of a matter, and the preparation and checking of his speeches was a legendary process, one reputedly running to thirty-four drafts.

Mr Leigh-Pemberton's swift dispatch of business was in such sharp contrast that, after his arrival, one official remembers: 'We wondered how one submission was going and, on enquiring, were surprised to find the letter drafted had already been sent.' Since detailed discussion of any subject of moment had been a feature of the Richardson régime, the contrast came as something of a jolt. 'Gordon was certainly a towering intellect but he got into a degree of detail that was excessive. Everything had to be debated at enormous length, which put a burden on everybody', is one not wholly sympathetic recollection. But another close observer sees the same tendency in a different light: 'Gordon believes things are complicated and that you don't get anywhere by pretending they're not. You've got to do a lot of hard work to find your way through and identify the policy that takes account of the complexities.'

There is general agreement that both these latest two Governors have been good, in their own ways, at encouraging their staffs, and well liked in the Bank. One early report after the change of Governorship was that relations with the Treasury had improved because they were getting quicker answers to questions, presumably since matters were not being so much referred up to the top through the chain of command. Another point is that Mr Leigh-Pemberton's being a natural delegator has meant a welcome shouldering of greater responsibilities by the several high-powered youngish executive directors advanced in the 1980 reorganisation. The Bank's fostering of the major City restructuring ahead of Big Bang may also have been smoothed under the new Governor's more devolutionary management style. 'If anybody's the creator of the City revolution, David Walker is', a senior colleague remarks. And during the past few years, Mr Eddie George, the Bank's maestro on monetary policy and gilts, has developed excellent working relations with the Treasury, where his advice is highly regarded – almost embarrassingly so, according to a story that he was once bidden to talk to the Chancellor in preference to the Governor and Deputy Governor, who had to insist they must accompany him.[15]

It was not long after the change of Governorship that it began to be said that the new Governor was assuming a more 'hands off' role, like that of a chairman of a board, while the Deputy Governor, Sir Kit McMahon, effectively became in many ways like the Bank's managing director. This was further explicable, not only because of the Governor's preference for delegating, but because of the other claims on his time. Before he went to the Bank, Mr Leigh-Pemberton had become Lord-Lieutenant of Kent, a position of honour that involves being the Queen's representative in the County, welcoming royal visitors there and performing other ceremonial duties. It was understood that this role would continue after its holder's appointment to the Bank. In addition to the time so required, any Governor spends a considerable part of the year abroad, on bilateral trips to foreign central banks and at many international meetings.

Against this background, an earlier initiative by Sir Kit McMahon to form an executive committee, chaired by the Deputy Governor and comprising executive directors and some other key personnel, to steer much of the Bank's business, soon developed into an important reality. A meeting of this body, now known as the Deputy Governor's committee and chaired by the present Deputy, Sir George Blunden, is held each Thursday morning, followed by a session of the bank supervisory committee, also chaired by Sir George. Later the Bank's Court (its board, including twelve part-time directors) meets under the chairmanship of the Governor and later lunches in the stately Court Room. The non-executive Court members include bankers, industrialists and some others, one being a trade unionist, Mr Gavin Laird, general secretary of the engineering workers union.

The arrival of a new Governor who was the appointee of the government in power did not, however, prevent the outbreak of fresh ructions between the Bank and the Treasury. Little more than a year after Mr Leigh-Pemberton's move into the Governor's chair, there occurred an event, the threatened collapse of the gold bank Johnson Matthey Bankers (JMB), which inflicted some of the greatest scars ever on the relationship between the two bodies. At one later moment even the likelihood of the Governor's continuing in office seemed to be under query, so great was the controversy stirred by the case. Yet JMB was by no means the first bank to have tottered and been rescued with central bank aid in Britain, let alone abroad. The secondary banking affair ten years earlier had been far larger and graver, and yet had been handled with smoothness and amity between Bank and Treasury. And, further back in history, lay the affair of Baring Brothers, the top merchant bank whose 1890 crisis had been met with aid arranged from other City banks by the Bank of England and backed by a promise of government support if needed. Across the Atlantic the large Continental Illinois, one of America's top ten banks, had earlier in 1984 been bailed out of disaster by the United States Federal authorities. The fact that the JMB matter so inflamed the Bank of England's relations with the Treasury, and to a lesser extent those with the large clearing banks, is thus significant for the Bank's recent story.

   Johnson Matthey Bankers was one of the five London gold-dealing banks and was a subsidiary of the Johnson Matthey gold refiners of Hatton Garden. It had come satisfactorily through the secondary banking crisis, despite some earlier upsets, and under the Banking Act 1979, which gave legal backing to the Bank's supervision of the commercial banks, it was classed as one of the upper tier of more lightly regulated 'recognised banks'. Another interesting aspect was that the big mining finance group Charter Consolidated had a sizeable minority shareholding in the quoted Johnson Matthey parent.

However, in the eighties JMB had, with little publicity, been grafting onto its gold business a rapidly growing lending side. In the four and a half years to September 1984, as emerged in due course, JMB's loans multiplied many times, from £34m to £450m. Moreover, a great deal of the lending was in a few large lumps – always a risky business, but often a feature of swift loan growth – to a handful of borrowers. Most of the latter turned out to be businessmen with links to the Indian sub-continent and traders connected with Nigeria.

None of this was fully apparent on the face of JMB's accounts, but, from the returns they often belatedly received, the Bank of England's supervisors grew concerned and asked more and more questions as 1984 progressed. Eventually, in late September of that year, the crisis burst forth.

The matter was brought to the attention of the Deputy Governor, Sir Kit McMahon, on Tuesday, 25 September 1984. The previous month JMB had, after an expression of concern by the Bank, asked its auditors, Arthur Young, more fully to investigate its largest loans. The result of this probe had just shown the need for large new loss provisions which, with others identified by the auditors as necessary, would have virtually wiped out JMB's capital and left it, in the absence of fresh aid, forced to close its doors. Fresh scrutiny by a team from the clearing banks, with whom the Bank urgently canvassed the chance of cash aid for JMB, and by other accountants, commissioned by the Bank, quickly confirmed that the position was quite as dire as this and probably still worse.

The matter was of acute concern to the Bank as watchdog over the City's health. The fear was that a JMB crisis (though the trouble was not on the gold side) could not be confined to that bank itself and that a JMB failure could infect other gold banks, given that the gold market members had numerous dealings with each other.

Possible rescue purchases of JMB by various parties were explored but none of those approached would shoulder a task whose ultimate cost was unpredictable. The urgent crisis was confronted at a crowded summit at the Bank through the night of Sunday, 30 September to Monday, 1 October 1984. This was attended by over a hundred people, including representatives of JMB and its associates, possible bidders, and other gold banks, merchant banks and clearing banks who were looked to to help in some way. The gold banks, particularly through N. M. Rothschild's chairman, Mr Evelyn de Rothschild, and Mr Michael Hawkes, head of Kleinwort Benson, owner of the Sharps Pixley bullion firm, urgently pressed for action to safeguard their market and offered certain help.

By the morning the Bank had decided there was no safe way of staving off the crisis except by itself taking over JMB. Alarm had been heightened during the night by telexes from the Far East markets, already open for Monday business, showing worrying awareness of a London gold bank's troubles and reluctance to deal with a City bank. It subsequently proved, too, that at the time of the crisis JMB had £1·94bn of deposits, and £4·6bn of forward contracts in the foreign exchange, bullion and other metals markets, on all of which it would, unaided, have gone into default. [16] The outcome was that the Bank bought JMB for just £1, the Johnson Matthey parent having agreed first to channel £50m, the most it felt it could afford (it raised extra capital from shareholders including Charter Consolidated), into the subsidiary it was parting with. The other banks, including the clearers, promised, with greater or less reluctance, to help, though the details were left for negotiation later.

Before down most of the exhausted crowd of City bigwigs dispersed to home or offices to snatch some brief sleep. The chairman of one major merchant bank stretched out on the sofa by his desk, only to be awakened early by a formidable cleaning lady demanding: 'What do you think you're doing in here: this is the Chairman's room?'

The Deputy Governor of the Bank, Sir Kit McMahon, who had taken the lead in the emergency, as his predecessor, Sir Jasper Hollom, had in the earlier secondary banks 'lifeboat' affair, went, after a sleepless night, with the Governor, Mr Leigh-Pemberton – recently returned from the annual IMF summit – to call on the Chancellor of the Exchequer. They saw Mr Lawson at his residence, 11 Downing Street, at 8 am, following at least one telephone call to the Chancellor during the night. Sir Kit had, over the previous few hectic days, several times telephoned the Treasury's Permanent Secretary, Sir Peter Middleton, and twice called on him. There was little Chancellor or Permanent Secretary could do further but note what had happened. Within minutes news of the rescue was announced and the markets opened calmly.

Changes at the top of JMB were quickly made and the Bank put one of its own directors, Mr Rodney Galpin, in as chairman and appointed a number of City experts, some recently retired, as JMB directors, full- or part-time. Teams of experts lent by the clearing banks were put in to sort out the loan book chaos at the troubled bank where, one expert remarked, 'the whole thing had run amok'.

A long haul of trying to get payment on overdue loans began. All told, the new management found it necessary to charge massive loss provisions of £254m against JMB's 'very poor quality' loanbook.[17] In other words, JMB had been a very soft touch. The biggest problem loan situation among a number was the near-£50m owed by the interests of Mr Mahmoud Sipra, affectionately known as 'The Cobra', head of the El Saeed group of shipping, commodity trading and film finance businesses. A number of these shipping companies were compulsorily wound up in 1984 and 1985 and in 1986 Mr Sipra was banned for twelve years by the High Court from being a director of a United Kingdom company. Various other substantial outstanding loans were also causing concern.

Later the Bank-owned JMB issued a writ alleging negligence and claiming large damages against Arthur Young, the big accountancy firm which had been JMB's auditors. This action is being contested (as at mid-1988).

In November 1984, the Bank placed a £100m deposit, on 'banking terms' with JMB to provide needed liquidity to the latter: it viewed this as not adding to its commitment to that business, for which it had become fully responsible through its take-over.

Meanwhile, the Bank, anxious to minimise the cost to itself of the bail-out, held lengthy talks with the City banks it had involved in the rescue. A £150m indemnity was thought necessary since the £254m of loss provisions required would more than absorb JMB's capital. The Bank at first aimed itself only to be responsible for 10 per cent of the indemnity, the proportion it had taken in the original secondary banking lifeboat operation. But the clearing banks objected to the large share this would have left for them. They felt the JMB trouble was little concern of theirs – 'Why drop it in *our* lap?' one queried – and blamed the Bank for faulty supervision. In the end, after tough argument at numerous meetings, the Bank had to shoulder 50 per cent (£75m) of the indemnity. The clearing banks, whose behind-the-scenes protests at being asked to contribute to the rescue did nothing to cool the whole affair, reluctantly took a £35m share, while the gold banks, which felt much involved, took £30m and the top merchant banks (accepting houses) £10m.

Eventually much less than £150m was needed, since potential losses were considerably worked down through disposals and partial debt recoveries. By April 1986, Mr David Walker, the Bank of England executive director who by then had succeeded to the chairmanship of JMB, announced that the main JMB bullion dealing business was being taken over by Australia's big Westpac bank and renamed Mase Westpac. Other subsidiaries were also disposed of and the remnants of JMB, where debt collection slowly continued, became known as Minories Finance. By March 1987 the Bank's maximum potential direct bill was down to just under £21m, with the commercial banks sharing a similar liability. The maximum notional cost to the Bank was by then not more than £30m, allowing also for interest forgone on the funds invested in the rescue. Financially, therefore, this affair which so long dominated the headlines – and sparked heated Parliamentary exchanges – shrank to relatively modest proportions.

But this stage was not reached without a period of much fresh tension between the Treasury and the Bank, some of it plainly visible to the public.

In the first place, the Bank's known attitude was that there would be no public money in the rescue, a belief that was no doubt compounded of its hope of getting the commercial banks to provide most of the guarantees, together with its ability to absorb such cost as fell on itself from its own Banking Department funds. (The Bank does not regard costs carried on its own Banking Department accounts as public expenditure, though this is debatable, since its dividends to the Treasury bear some relation to its profits.) As the autumn went on, the Bank's £100m cash deposit with JMB (later adjusted into capital) became publicly known and when Mr Nigel Lawson, the Chancellor of the Exchequer, was tackled on this supposed subsidy in the House of Commons, he was unaware of the payment and felt embarrassed. The Bank had seen the payment in of this sum to a business it already owned as a matter of course since the money was needed in JMB's continuing business, but the Chancellor's ire was aroused and the Bank acknowledged it should have put the Treasury in the picture on the point.

There were other signs that the Treasury was not giving the Bank wholehearted support: the *Financial Times* reported that 'Treasury

Ministers have made known their major reservations about the Bank's handling of the events leading up to JMB's collapse and of the rescue itself.'[18] Understandably, Mr Lawson soon set up a joint Bank–Treasury committee to examine lessons from the débâcle for the bank supervision system and to identify needed legal and other changes in the Bank's supervision arrangements. The Governor chaired this, but the presence on it of two top Treasury men, Sir Peter Middleton and Sir Frank Cassell, showed the Chancellor meant to keep a close hand on developments. Political interest in the matter was also built up, with the SDP leader, Dr David Owen, MP, focussing on the public spending aspect of the Bank's £75m share in the indemnity and raising queries, which the Bank indignantly dismissed, about JMB's bullion side. Later, when suggestions of fraud arose, allegations flew in Parliament and elsewhere.

The Leigh-Pemberton (Bank-Treasury) committee reported,[19] recommending an end to the two-tier nature of bank authorisation and proposing other improvements which, with staff additions in the Bank's supervision department, were adopted. The Bank, for its part, published a detailed account of the JMB crisis and the reasons for its rescue.[20]

Speaking in the Commons[21] in June 1985, Mr Lawson directly censured the Bank's supervision of JMB, an unusual move, since any government–Bank differences had traditionally been kept private. In measured words, but ones clearly conveying criticism, he said, 'The Bank did not on this occasion act as promptly as they should have done. They did to some extent fall down on the job.' But he affirmed his 'fullest confidence' in the Governor. There was also some further public criticism of the Bank in a reference to an already controversial point: 'On the £100m loan, I think I should have been told at the time. This is now accepted by the Governor and the Bank of England generally.' Of the events preceding the emergency, the Chancellor spoke of 'the appalling, absurd record of incompetence and mismanagement by JMB' leading to the collapse, and also said 'no prima facie evidence of fraud has so far been discovered'. Of the rescue operation itself, the Chancellor said, 'I am satisfied that the Governor was acting properly within his discretion', which sounded a less than full-hearted endorsement of the Bank's action.

Mr Lawson also contrasted the full information published about the JMB affair with the lack of that given about the earlier secondary banking crisis lifeboat mounted 'by the then Governor of the Bank of England, backed by the then Chancellor, [Labour's Mr Denis

Healey]. There was indeed such a discrepancy as to public information, though the secondary banks' 'lifeboat' had in fact been launched under the Conservative government of Mr Edward Heath, in December 1973, over two months before Labour took over in early March 1974.

A few weeks later Mr Lawson told the Commons that the City of London Police Fraud Squad had been called in to investigate 'serious and unexplained gaps in the records of JMB, including the possibility of missing documents relating to substantial past transactions on certain accounts that are the subject of large losses'. Although this statement was consistent with the previous one, the swift new turn of events on the fraud probe triggered a fresh Treasury display of irritation with the Bank.

At the end of July 1985, in an ill-tempered Commons debate just before the summer recess, some Labour members called for the Bank Governor's resignation because of the 'awesome' collapse of JMB, about some of whose borrowers vivid allegations were made.[22] At this stage, so far from riding to the Governor's defence, there were signs that Whitehall was maintaining a certain detachment. On the morning of the debate, *The Economist* reported: 'Senior Whitehall officials were suggesting this week that Mr Leigh-Pemberton's chances of riding out the storm are only a stingy better than even.'[23] This was reminiscent of an episode some months earlier when, as Sir Kit McMahon's term as Deputy Governor was within months of ending, a Press report suggested his reappointment was 'in the balance', adding that 'some Treasury officials have been highly critical of Mr McMahon, in view of his central role in masterminding the rescue of JMB'.[24] On that occasion, after Press comment on the adverse effect for sterling of the seeming Treasury–Bank rift and pressure from Mr Leigh-Pemberton for a quick announcement, Sir Kit was duly reappointed.

Such apparent 'leaks' led observers to feel that some at the 'West End of Town' – whether Ministers or officials – were inspiring ideas likely to shake the Bank's morale and perhaps make it more susceptible to government pressure. Somebody close to the scene was later asked whether he thought Ministers in any way desired the Governor's resignation – an event that would, given the circumstances, have amounted to being hounded from office, and so been unprecedented – in July 1985. The answer was carefully phrased: 'If it had got so that the Chancellor's own position was in jeopardy, I've no doubt who he'd have preferred to resign. That's natural, isn't it?'

Yet it is difficult to think that Mr Lawson's own office was in any way at risk through the matter.

Mr Leigh-Pemberton saw no occasion to resign and let it be known that he was not proposing to do so. He did not think, in all the circumstances, that any doctrine of 'ministerial' responsibility required him to step down; he even spoke along these lines to the Permanent Secretary to the Treasury, Sir Peter Middleton, who agreed. Some years afterwards, he recalled:

I took the view that there was no reason why either of us [the Chancellor or himself] should resign. I thought the general media onslaught was unjustified and I didn't see the situation as the political or financial disaster that people were making it out to be. I saw it as my duty, having taken JMB over, to put it back into good order and restore it to the private sector at the minimum cost to the capital and reserves of the Bank of England. I emphasise that because there was no taxpayers' money in this. I felt that that was what was required and I'm very pleased to say that we succeeded in doing that in both a timescale and at a cost that were an improvement on my expectations. I felt sure that we could do it: I had thought it might take longer. [25]

At about this time, the Governor successfully carried an important point in a difference with the Chancellor and the Treasury, who had favoured setting up a formal Department of Trade investigation into JMB. Mr Leigh-Pemberton considered such a move would undesirably and unnecessarily prolong the whole unsettling affair and this opinion prevailed at the highest level. Insiders remember Mrs Thatcher's expressing the view that it would be better if Whitehall saw the attacking Labour MPs, rather than the Bank, as the adversary.

From this stage, in the late summer of 1985, the heat started to go out of the JMB affair, whose costs emerged as less heavy than had previously seemed likely. Of Mr Leigh-Pemberton's deportment during this fraught time, a senior banker said: 'He has very good soldierly virtues and really does know how to lead his troops – in the sense of encouraging them and then not betraying them, not throwing them to the wolves, if they've let him down.' The same observer felt the Governor's very stable personality had helped him withstand the flak. Another insider thinks the affair upset Mr Leigh-Pemberton less than it might have hit his perhaps more sensitive predecessor: 'Robin has ridden it. Some of it has obviously been highly distasteful, but he's never let it affect him. For Gordon [Richardson] to have been called – what was it, a "useless deadbeat" [a term used in the July 1985 Commons debate] – it would have been terrible.'

Could the JMB rescue have been better handled, aside from the question whether the danger signs should have been spotted and acted on more quickly? There has been no great dispute over the Bank's decision, once it had failed to find a rescue bidder, to buy the ailing concern in order to fend off the dangerous repercussions its failure would have had on the banking system. Some say that the other gold banks could (perhaps with some notice) have made credit and other arrangements to render themselves invulnerable – but there would still have been risks.

The most contentious point was that, in the effort to limit the cost falling on itself, the Bank pressed the little-connected clearing banks to take an important share of the indemnity burden for the broad purpose of sharing in the solution of a City problem. There was this difference compared with the secondary banking crisis – when the big banks were mobilised to provide cash-recycling aid – that the situation of JMB was so bad at the moment of crisis that the commercial banks were bound to lose something under the indemnity. In the secondary banking affair the clearers had essentially provided large credit, while the costly rescues involving the main losses had been financed by the Bank alone.

There are real problems about the financing of necessary bank rescues and, as the mounting of these in order to avoid damage to the financial system can be seen as in the public interest, the issue remains one of general concern, of which the government cannot wash its hands. After all, it would be a lucky country that never had another bank crisis calling for action, so the matter is worth keeping on the national agenda.

It has been suggested that the Bank might have been wiser to have made itself fully responsible for the JMB bail-out, subject to accepting the aid proffered by the closely concerned gold market. On this view, the Bank could have provided itself with any extra required income by, in due course, raising the commercial banks' interest-free cash ratio deposits with it. This would have meant, in effect, spreading the burden thinly across 600 City banks, rather than concentrating it on far fewer clearers and merchant banks. The idea is worth remembering for any future bank crisis, though if the cost were very high even this method of financing could prove inadequate.

Although relations between the Bank on the one hand, and the Treasury and government on the other, have never since been as fraught as they were in the JMB affair and have very much improved, there have been occasional recurrences of strain. One such arose over the 1986 Budget, when Mr Lawson announced a 5 per cent tax on issues of ADRs, the system by which British shares are repackaged for trading in dollar terms. The idea was to heighten the relative attraction of ordinary Stock Exchange sterling trading in United Kingdom equities ahead of Big Bang, but in fact the move sparked loud complaints from big companies fearful of a shrinkage in total global demand for their shares. It seems these protests came as an unexpected shock to the Chancellor, who was disposed to blame the Bank for not forewarning him. So far as events can be reconstructed, it appears that the Bank, on being made aware that the government wanted the tax, favoured a lower rate than that first announced. Despite this, the Bank found itself, following the Budget speech and reactions to it, in the firing-line for not having brought home to the Chancellor the full implications, and likely unpopularity, of the tax. This affair is further evidence of the low explosion threshold then still existing in Treasury relations with the Bank. It can also be seen as an illustration of the consequences of a climate inhospitable to the offering of unwelcome advice, which may thus not always be pressed hard enough. The ADR tax rate was later cut to only 1½ per cent. Changes to the Banking Act 1987 during its course through Parliament so that there should be a majority of outsiders, as compared with Bank people, on the new advisory Board of Banking Supervision have sometimes been seen as a further pinprick administered by the Treasury to the Bank.

A later episode, sometimes viewed as a further case of friction, probably, however, amounted to little, despite some brief overt signs of fracas. When the question arose of whether the government's £7bn sale of BP shares in October 1987 should, although already under way, be called off because of the market share crash, the Bank offered advice, as it had been arranged that it would in the case of any unexpected development. With shares slumping all round, it recommended that the sale should go ahead, provided there was an arrangement by which the Bank would stand ready to buy up any offered shares at a lowish fixed price in order to give worried underwriters who wanted to offload their holdings some floor to their losses. The suggested price at which this 'safety net' would operate was 90p compared with the 130p offer price. The idea was that the operation, to impart a degree of reassurance to the market, should be conducted via the Bank's Issue Department, so that any final loss, or gain, would be for the government's account. Mr Lawson accepted the concept of the 'safety net', which was put into effect, but decided on a lower support figure of 70p a share, which would be less protective of the underwriters. The Bank immediately accepted this and was quite happy with the outcome. Impressions that later arose of a Bank–Treasury rift as to who had dreamed up the idea seem to have been based on a misunderstanding.

Around the mid-eighties, there appeared for a time to be a trend for the Bank to get less closely caught up than in the previous recent past in the affairs of the City as a whole. It seemed as though, after its bruising experience over JMB, it was keen to be seen not to be everybody's keeper and preferred somewhat to draw back from optional involvements. For instance, under Lord Richardson's Governorship, the Bank had taken a strong line in pressing for changes at the scandal-hit Lloyd's insurance market and had urged the appointment to the new post of chief executive there of the leading accountant Mr Ian Hay-Davison. The latter's tenure, though valuable and effective, was, however, of limited duration and the Bank did not press for its longer continuance. Rather, having seen important changes launched, it appeared satisfied with the position reached. It now concerns itself less closely with the affairs of Lloyd's, although one of its former non-executive directors, Mr Alan Lord, is now chief executive there.

The Bank also seemed anxious at that time to have it understood that the improved supervision of the securities industry would be the responsibility of the new Securities and Investments Board (SIB), while it itself was concerned with the separate matter of bank supervision. It was sometimes pointed out at this stage that, traditionally, the Bank and the securities industry, as represented in the Stock Exchange, had had relatively little to do with each other and that, as evidence of this, the Bank's Governor and the Exchange's chairman had, in the past, only met regularly once a year at the Stock Exchange Christmas lunch. There would naturally be liaison where SIB was concerned with a securities business owned by a bank – a major section of all cases, in fact – but, the impression was, the two supervisors would remain very separate authorities.

But there are limits to the extent to which the Bank can ever be hands-off with the City generally. It has all along had some inevitable involvement with the new securities industry's watchdog structure because of the number of stock market firms now owned by the banks it directly supervises. It is itself, under the Financial Services Act 1986, closely overseeing the 'wholesale' (foreign exchange, gold, commodities and money) markets. And many City people voice confidence that the Bank would always intervene afresh if a new bank or industrial crisis, or some fresh scandal, made this necessary.

In fact, something of a turning of the tide towards a more hands-on approach to the City again dated from the winter of 1986–7, when the Bank took an active role in exacting top-level changes at Morgan Grenfell, after the start of the official probe into Guinness, which that merchant bank had advised. There were signs, too, that it was with government approval that this shake-up had been encouraged.

Then, in the following year and afterwards, the Bank became increasingly interested in the City's worries over the alleged excessive complexity of the supervision arrangements being planned for the securities industry by SIB (see Chapter 11). Eventually this concern culminated in the joint decision by the Governor, Mr Leigh-Pemberton and the government Minister responsible, Lord Young, the Trade and Industry Secretary, to pick a new chairman for SIB when the initial term of its first chairman, Sir Kenneth Berrill, expired in May 1988. The choice, made known in late February 1988, fell on none other than Mr David Walker, the influential Bank of England executive director who had played a crucial part in shaping the City revolution and whose appointment to head SIB signalled strong Bank concern that the securities watchdog system should function smoothly. As often before, and in line with the views of many in the City, the Bank had taken a hand over a significant shift in City affairs. Meanwhile, since the JMB affair, important changes had been occurring in the Bank's own upper reaches.

In the autumn of 1985, Sir Kit McMahon, the Bank's Deputy Governor, received an invitation, which he found irresistible, to join the Midland Bank as its future executive chairman, with the task of guiding the group on a new post-Crocker path to prosperity. He accordingly resigned from the Bank, in which he had formerly worked closely with Lord Richardson and where he had later played a part as something like the Bank's administrative chief under the new Governor's more devolutionary régime.

Despite the fact that many people had thought Sir Kit – an international expert of long experience in the Bank – well fitted for the Governorship himself, this latter relationship had worked smoothly and Mr Leigh-Pemberton spoke appreciatively of his colleague as a most loyal Deputy Governor.[26] But still, Sir Kit was not only much the same age as, but in many ways more knowledge-able on Bank matters than, his new chief, which led many observers to think the Deputy would one day take up a new challenge elsewhere. As somebody near the scene has said of the situation from 1983 to 1985: 'It must have been difficult for [Mr Leigh-Pemberton] to be aware that the man in the next room probably felt he was rather better equipped for the Governorship than he was himself and that much of the rest of the world also thought so.'

On Sir Kit's departure, Sir George Blunden, who had been high on the short-list for the Governorship itself in 1983, was brought back from partial retirement at the age of 63 to fill the Deputy post. In the event, Sir George has proved a highly active and influential Deputy Governor, whose benign, white-haired appearance accompanies a personality of considerable firmness as well as subtlety. With unrivalled knowledge of the Bank and of the City, Sir George has proved an effective complement to the Governor. His chairmanship of the Bank's key internal committees makes him the nearest a Deputy Governor has yet come to being chief executive of the Bank.

From 1986 onwards the relationship between the government and the Bank appears to have settled down onto a more relaxed basis after earlier upsets. Having got its own carefully selected nominees into both top Bank posts, the Thatcher administration seems happier with Threadneedle Street. Sir George Blunden and the Treasury's Permanent Secretary, Sir Peter Middleton – under whom the Treasury's contact with the City has further increased – keep closely in touch, which assists the despatch of business. Consultation between the two bodies on monetary matters is also continuous.

It has often been argued that the Bank's independent power and status has been somewhat weakened under the Thatcher regime, that the organisation has passed more under the government's sway, become its 'poodle' in one phrase. And certainly the Bank has seemed at times under some pressure in seeking to sustain its traditionally proud and confident stance. The extreme tightness of monetary policy in 1980, despite the Bank's worries, Mr Lawson's public criticism of it over JMB, even the ADRs affair, are examples of episodes that scarcely enhanced the central bank's standing. The Treasury's seeming unconcern about upholding the Bank's authority in the Royal Bank of Scotland affair hardly testified to the Bank's influence.

As to the conduct of monetary policy, there can be no doubt of the closer involvement nowadays of the government and the Treasury in decisions that would once have been considered details for the Bank alone.

But a number of present and previous Bank people think worries about all this out of place. What matters, they reason, is how effectively Bank arguments register in the formation of final decisions – and, it is claimed, they do so to the greatest extent when the 'East End' and 'West End' co-operate well. As one former Bank man sums up about this complex relationship: 'If you want independence, you lose influence and if you want influence, you don't have independence.'

The Thatcher administration's record of asserting itself with all the public bodies with which it has to deal – including the BBC and the Church of England as the established church – is also a significant part of the broader context in which Bank–government relations must be seen.

The position of the talented and assertive Mr Nigel Lawson as Chancellor of the Exchequer for five years since 1983 and before that as the Treasury's Financial Secretary in 1979–81 has also been an important factor in the balance of power between the government and the Bank in the past decade. The JMB affair showed Mr Lawson's sharpness when displeased, a sharpness in part openly revealed. Going public in criticism of the Bank was something new for Ministers, even if clashes with the central bank were not. Winston Churchill, for instance, taxed his Governor, Montagu Norman, in 1927 with treachery for wooing a high Treasury official away to the Bank's Court, but that 'terrible scene'[27] occurred behind closed doors. In today's world, though, any disputes, whether or not played out in the light of day, have a way of publicly surfacing.

Mr Lawson, as a long-time City expert and former financial editor, came to his task unusually well equipped with expertise to enhance his influence. This makes him an effective protagonist in discussion with the Bank, though the latter too deploys much knowledge and skill. Chancellor and Governor regularly get together for an informal talk once a fortnight over lunch. At more formal policy sessions, the Chancellor and his advisers meet a formidable Bank team consisting of the Governor, the Deputy Governor and some executive directors, normally Mr Eddie George, the monetary specialist, and Mr Anthony Loehnis, the overseas director. Mr Lawson's own financial talents doubtless reinforce his power in debate with Threadneedle Street, although the Prime Minister's well-known liking for getting her own way may at times be as influential in determining who wins if Treasury and Bank differ.

Yet, for all this, to suggest that a long-term switch in the centre of gravity of power and influence from the Bank to the Treasury has taken place would be to assert what is far from clear or proven. For time and circumstance continue much to affect the complex and ever-evolving relationship between the 'East' and 'West' ends of the axis of the financial authorities.

The personalities and tactics of different Governors in pressing the influence of themselves and their organisation must always, of course, be important in the sum total of the Bank's relationship with Whitehall, and each Governor has his own style. There can also be important changes in the balance of influence over a span of years. One knowledgeable observer described Lord Richardson, who had his own rugged time with the Thatcher government, as having 'the virtues of immense dediction, real imagination and energy – and a great sense of the Bank's standing *vis-à-vis* the Treasury and of having an independent position'. But while this approach made for success under two governments of different parties in the seventies, it was less effective under Mrs Thatcher's in the eighties.

Similarly, the Governorship of the present holder, Mr Leigh-Pemberton, can be seen as having gone through phases. The JMB affair broke out in his first eighteen months of office and, following the remarkably inflamed atmosphere which attended it, the Bank for a time kept something of a low profile, concentrating its energies on improvements to its banking supervision structure. Bank chiefs have referred to the 'sheer wall of prejudice' that appeared to stand against them in the JMB episode. And one remembers a consciousness then that 'the Treasury felt the Bank of England had caused them great embarrassment and they weren't minded to make life any easier for us'.

seemed on the rise, compared with the low watermark reached during the JMB affair. One example is the way in which it has created, without as all-embracing powers as it once wanted, and in agreement with the Treasury, a promising-looking system under the Banking Act 1987 for regulating bank take-overs in the public interest (see Chapter 11). A more active interest has also been taken in relation to the regulation of the securities markets, now to be overseen by one of the Bank's own directors, Mr David Walker. The Governor and the Bank have, too, played a prominent and successful part in negotiating the international 'convergence' pact – also described in the next chapter – aimed at creating a fairer competitive environment among leading world banks.

Mr Leigh-Pemberton has interpreted his role as Governor in the light of the ultimate predominance the law accords the government of the day, while asserting his views as he thinks appropriate, both publicly and in dialogue with Ministers. He has the advantage of a natural sympathy with the Thatcher government's broad monetarist approach, as was confirmed when, in his 1987 Mais Lecture to the City University Business School, he endorsed the interest-exchange rate squeeze of the controversial 1980–81 period as having been 'necessary to break the inflationary psychology'.[28]

As Governor, Mr Leigh-Pemberton works closely with a talented top Bank team of senior executives consisting of the Deputy Governor and executive directors, to whom he gives much scope. A satisfactory working atmosphere has prevailed between the City-wise Chancellor and the land-owner, barrister Governor, even if they could not be called twin souls. As one insider remarks: 'The Governor has a very good relationship with the Chancellor. They are not, and never have been, bosom friends.'

The Governor's reappointment early in 1988 for a second five-year term from mid-1988 has strengthened his position. A chief of the Bank can count on an attentive hearing from a government that has twice picked him for the post with secure tenure and Mr Leigh-Pemberton has latterly spoken out with increasing plainness and eloquence on subjects where opinions may differ, such as the level of interest rates, Stock Exchange account arrangements and other matters. One sign of his enlarging influence came when his and the Bank's view in favour of 'uncapping' sterling and letting it rise above DM3·00 against the German currency was upheld by the Prime Minister in March 1988 in debate with the Chancellor.

Mr Leigh-Pemberton does not accept suggestions that have at times been made over recent years that the Bank of England's power and influence have diminished since his Governorship began in 1983. 'I do not get the impression that our powers have waned', he says. 'They may be different. They may be greater in some respects and less in others. But I've never had the feeling of a gradual impoverishment of power.'[29]

The question of the Bank's ability to win in a difference with the Treasury is a difficult one for him to discuss in detail. But, speaking generally, he says on this issue: 'I can think of occasions where we have taken a view and thought one particular line of action right, knowing at the outset that the Treasury felt the opposite. And more than once we persuaded the Treasury to change their stand: either they accepted our argument at the time or, a little later, one noticed that their position had changed.' Identifiable successes include the March 1988 'uncapping' of the pound and the earlier decision not to launch an official investigation into JMB.

In an interesting illustration of his philosophy, the Governor also says: 'On the whole, in this life, if you have a good case, you probably prevail. I like to think that principle applies. Your confidence may not always be fulfilled. But if you don't believe that good cases have a chance of succeeding, you might as well give up.'

In his youthful spell in the army, Mr Leigh-Pemberton won the sword of honour at Sandhurst as the best officer cadet, an achievement which foreshadowed the plaudits he was to earn in his difficult first term as Governor – a period he has described as 'tempestuous' – for 'soldierly virtues' and 'being nice with people'. Whether he has the generalship to assert the Bank's power still further will become clearer as his second term in the City's top post unfolds.

When the office of the Bank's chief is considered in a broad span of history, it is a fair inference that a Governor needs to be a strategist – perhaps a mean and crafty strategist – adept at far-sighted planning and with a politician's skills if he is to gain the maximum clout for the body he heads. At the same time, Ministers should beware of the Bank's ever being downgraded to the status of a mere executant vassal. Otherwise they would risk denying themselves the judicious and sometimes unwelcome advice which an organisation with some sense of independent authority can best provide and which no wise government should be without.

In the next few years, as the Bank moves towards its 300th anniversary in 1994, further changes in its top echelons are inevitable and will arouse wide interest. When Sir George Blunden retires, perhaps in his 67th year in 1989, after a distinguished Deputy Governorship, a successor is virtually certain to be chosen from within the Bank. This would be in line with all precedent and, what is perhaps more important, would ensure valuable continutiy. Mr Eddie George, the executive director who heads the monetary and gilts side of the Bank, and who keeps close touch on these subjects with the Treasury, is a well-fancied choice for the post. A previously also much-discussed possibility, Mr David Walker, is now out of the running for the Deputy role with his appointment to chair the City's SIB watchdog until April, 1992. Mr Walker, however, continues on the Bank's Court, as a non-executive director in his new capacity, and is often spoken of as a very possible choice for the Governorship itself later on.

Mr Leigh-Pemberton's second term as Governor runs until mid-1993 and, if he completes it, his successor would probably be appointed around the end of 1992. But by then there will be a new government, whose Prime Minister – whoever he or she may be – would pick the succeeding Governor, since the next general election must, at the latest, take place by mid-1992.

However, should Mr Leigh-Pemberton choose not to serve all his second term, it might well fall to the present government to select the next Governor. Should Mrs Thatcher thus appoint two Governors, she would be the first Prime Minister to do so, which would be a fact of some political significance. For a Premier – herself of record tenure of her own office in the twentieth century – would be influencing the Bank's character for some years into the future. Whether or not, if this happened, the present Prime Minister would choose a Governor with the aim of providing a strong counterpoise to the Treasury would be one of the more interesting aspects of the appointment.

11 Protecting Investors and Users

Thou shalt not steal; an empty feat, When it's so lucrative to cheat.
Arthur Hugh Clough.[1]

Greed is all right, by the way. I want you to know that. You can be greedy and still feel good about yourself.[2]
Mr Ivan Boesky, United States financier later disgraced in insider trading scandal.

Self-regulation . . . involves something more than trusting people to behave themselves.
Professor Jim Gower.[3]

Most modern markets have some form of watchdog system to ensure that investors and users are fairly dealt with and protected from fraud. Such safeguarding arrangements, which embrace banking as well as stock and other markets, also aim to check the financial health and capability, as well as the probity, of the operating firms. For, after all, it is little more comfort to feel one's money has evaporated through the misjudgments of the most honest incompetent than because of deliberate 'white collar' theft.

Britain now has an extensive and much reformed legally-backed regulatory system covering almost all City markets as well as the banking system. But the creation of the novel and elaborate structure has involved much effort, caused some controversy and been subject to such delay it has not yet been fully tested in practice. How well it works is likely to depend not only on its own nature but on how whole-heartedly the City desires the success of what is in reality a powerful mechanism to foster high standards of business ethics and prudence.

From long before Big Bang, the great bulk of London's stock and share trading (save that in the little-regulated Eurobond market) has gone through the Stock Exchange, which has been accustomed to enforcing a highly regarded standard of business conduct on its own members. Rules against 'market-rigging', the code of professional behaviour and other arrangements, including those for verifying the financial strength of member firms, have been administered by the ruling Council and its cluster of satellite committees, with the aid of a skilled staff.

Down the years, occasional Stock Exchange miscreants have been hauled up to be reprimanded or, in aggravated cases, expelled, while, from time to time, an instance of alleged fraud or other criminality has reached the Courts. But these have been rare events. Generally the Exchange's rules have been well observed, even if, when conditions were changing, some could be strained at (see Chapter 2) by methods passing muster as legitimate. The Exchange also helps the investor through the extensive requirements which its Listing Agreement – the conditions for a full quotation of shares – imposes on companies to disclose the information, on trading results and other developments, needed for an informed market. It cannot, of course, safeguard the investor against losses due to his own folly, misjudgment or ill-luck. Further, a compensation fund long guaranteed that, if Exchange firms were 'hammered' – collapsed – as some did in the mid-seventies and later, investors would not lose money. All these arrangements, at intervals improved in response to need, were given effect on a 'club' basis without legal underpinning, since the Stock Exchange, alone among the world's major bourses, was subject to virtually no statutory control.[4] The general law of agency as to fair dealing by brokers as agents was, though, naturally applicable, as elsewhere, and the Companies Acts,[5] with their requirements on the conduct of companies and other matters, were and remain relevant.

Outside the Exchange, however, matters were often less satisfactory. Certain off-Exchange securities transactions took place through dealers licensed by the Department of Trade and Industry under the Prevention of Fraud (Investments) Act 1958 but subject to little, if any, continuing supervision. Also, the early eighties brought a crop of scandals in which firms managing investments failed in controversial circumstances, losing investors their life savings. These unfortunate occurrences included disasters in the little-regulated commodities markets. In one case a Judge spoke of the world of commodity dealing as 'a jungle suitable for hunting for large and experienced animals but one in which the small animal is at very serious risk', and as revealing 'a most perilous state of affairs which merits attention by Parliament'.[6]

Such events led the Trade Secretary, then Mr John Biffen, in July 1981 to ask a distinguished legal expert, Professor L. C. B. (Jim)

Gower, to consider the statutory protection and control needed for investors, personal and business, in a wide field, including unit trusts, and to advise on needed new legislation. As it happened, before Professor Gower's task was complete, the Government–Stock Exchange accord of July 1983 and its aftermath highlighted the impending need for investor protection. For it was clear the scrapping of the old single-capacity stock market system, and the creation of new financial conglomerates, would mean new conflicts of interest, calling for extra safeguards. For instance, investment advisers would often in future co-exist in groupings with market-makers highly interested in the investment taking certain directions. Moreover, as London's securities markets grew more international following Big Bang, the old club-ethic mode of maintaining standards might not always win obedience from, say, new foreign players more used to asking 'Is it legal?' than 'Is it moral?' In short, the looming of a new market era redoubled the case for reforming an already unacceptably inadequate and fragmentary City watchdog system.

Professor Gower interpreted his remit in a broad way and in his full report[7] in November 1983 proposed major reforms to build a far more comprehensive and consistent structure of investor protection. This would sit alongside the Bank of England's arrangements, themselves much improved since the mid-seventies secondary banking crisis, for supervising the banks.

The essence of the Gower scheme, which was to form the foundation of the radically reformed system, was that supervision should be via a small group of 'self-regulatory organisations' – the Stock Exchange being an obvious example – for different sectors, enforcing appropriate rules under the watch of some form of governmental super-body. Under a new Act of Parliament, all 'practitioners' in the investment business would have to be authorised in order to operate legally. Professor Gower made it clear that he was not after regulation for regulation's sake and was recommending just that degree of investor protection that was 'no greater than ... necessary to protect reasonable people from being made fools of'.[8] The question of whether the top supervisory body should be a Government Department or a 'self-standing commission' was left to some degree open in the report but it was made clear that the State should in some way remain responsible for the new system's overall surveillance.

The essential character of the proposed new watchdog structure would thus be one of considerable reliance on self-regulation, but with ultimate oversight of the structure, on the State's behalf, in some form. The plan avoided an official supervisory body corresponding to the America's statutory Securities and Exchange Commission (SEC), an idea that would probably have been unwelcome to the Thatcher Government with its dislike of avoidable governmental controls. The concept was rather of a hybrid system, involving substantial self-regulation by representatives of practitioners in the investment business, but with some form of State back-up to stiffen it.

As a next step, in 1984, the Governor of the Bank of England, Mr Robin Leigh-Pemberton, appointed a 'ten wise men' group of City notables, chaired by Sir Martin Jacomb, then a vice-chairman of Kleinwort Benson and now chairman of BZW, to advise on the new structure for the securities markets. In essence this body – the 'Governor's group', which also included the Stock Exchange's chief, Sir Nicholas Goodison – was asked to say whether the City could deliver an effective self-regulatory system for the new environment. Its report was never published but it is believed to have told the Governor that self-regulation could work but that it would need statutory underpinning. A minority view was that the Bank of England should play the key role in the stock market's regulation. A parallel body to the Governor's group undertook a similar study for the sectors, such as unit trusts and insurance, where collectively managed investment products are marketed to a large extent outside the City. This was chaired by Mr Marshall Field, who was chairman of the Life Offices Association.

The eventual outcome was a system marrying the elements of the statutory and self-regulatory on Gower-type lines. Underlying the whole edifice is a legal requirement that all those engaged in investment business must be authorised – it is a criminal offence to operate otherwise – and subject to continuing regulation. The case-to-case administration, and general arrangements, in each investment sector are run by one of the five sector 'self-regulating organisations' (SROs) under an overseeing top body, the Securities and Investments Board (SIB). The curiosity of the British system lies in the status of the latter, which is a private company (not a government department or a United States-style official body), but still one to which a government Minister, the Secretary of State for Trade and Industry, has delegated important powers given to him by law. The SROs have all now been recognised by SIB as suitable for their task, following which they, in their turn, have become responsible for authorising, and keeping tabs on, the investment businesses in their own bailiwicks. SIB would also be able to withdraw its recognition from an SRO if things were to go badly wrong there. This would be what one top City person calls a 'nuclear sanction' and is an event highly unlikely to occur. But the fact that it is possible serves to underscore the powerful nature of SIB's control, in principle at least, over the regulatory system. How the balance of influence between it and the different SROs works out in practice only time will show. SROs, for their part, can also withdraw authorisation of a member whom they judge to have become unfit to continue in business. Some operators are authorised by SIB directly, but this happens in only a minority of cases.

The law governing this whole extensive watchdog structure, the Financial Services Act 1986, is a sizeable tome, weighing nearly a pound, which defines the new arrangements and prescribes many of the ways in which they should be operated in the interest of protecting investors. Indeed, during the passage of the measure through Parliament, the legal teeth prescribed for SIB were sharpened, notably with the result that it has power to direct changes of rules at the SROs. The Act as passed also specifically provides for powers of the Secretary of State to be devolved to SIB by name (not just to a 'designated agency', as intended at first) and this was done in 1987.

The Act lays down certain requirements for investment businesses, such as that they must be 'fit and proper'. It also provides for SIB to make detailed 'conduct of business' rules, and prescribes that the individual rules also to be made by the SROs for their own members must be at least as protective of investors as SIB's. This requirement has become known as the equivalence principle. Areas covered by the rule-books include the manner of market-making, the content of advertisements, the disclosure of payments or commissions, 'Chinese walls' (separating parts of firms where conflicts of interest can arise), the keeping of records and capital adequacy.[9] The Act, which embraces the marketing of life insurance but without affecting arrangements under the Insurance Companies Act 1982, provides further for recognition of investment exchanges. Additionally, and in order to prevent each sector's rule-books from importing unacceptable new restraints on competition, the Act provides for these to be vetted by the Director General of Fair Trading.

In further significant provisions, the Act tightens the enforcement arrangements of the earlier legislation which made 'insider trading' – misuse of privileged information for personal gain – a criminal offence by stiffening the authorities' power to require co-operation in their investigations. It also provides for exchanges of 'regulatory' information, not only within the United Kingdom supervisory régime (that of the banks and building societies included) but, in certain circumstances, between British and overseas authorities. The latter power was swiftly acted on, in late 1986, when a new 'memorandum of understanding' between the British and American securities market regulators was also invoked. It was information from the United States authorities concerning the insider trading case involving the American financier Mr Ivan Boesky which alerted the United Kingdom authorities to the affair of alleged rigging of Guinness shares and led the Trade and Industry Department, in late 1986, to appoint inspectors to investigate Guinness. This was in due course followed by a number of arrests in the course of what is proving one of the longest-running scandal sagas of recent times.

Although it took City people some time to realise it, the new watchdog system has little or nothing voluntary about it. The fact that the law, in the shape of the Financial Services Act 1986, has moulded it and stands as its backing, means that it has a marked legal flavour about it. As one leading City personality says: 'This was going to be practitioner regulation under statute. But what has turned out is that the practitioner element is virtually nil and what we're starting with is a highly bureaucratic and legalistic system.' But this is in fact scarcely surprising, given the framework of law which is sufficiently robust to make City firms' lawyers put even the rule-books of the sector self-regulating organisations under their legal microscope. Many City people now take the view that there is little to choose between the United States regulatory system, under the supervision of an undoubtedly statutory body, the Securities and Exchange Commission (SEC), and Britain's new structure.

Sir Kenneth Berrill, the former academic, government 'think tank' chief and stockbroker, who became the first chairman of the watchdog system's (SIB) top body, said in 1986: 'The SIB and the [American] SEC in reality stand very close to each other in terms of their powers and duties.' He was stressing the degree of resemblance as an answer to those with little confidence in SIB's ability to keep order: 'There remains in many quarters a deep-rooted mistrust of what may be called City self-regulation and [a view] that the SIB's nominal private status appears to identify it with the old club-like ways of running the City.'[10] In the event, SIB has come to face more discontent in the City for being too powerful, with its complex and legally-backed structure, than too feeble in protecting investors.

There have been protests that its rules, and the related ones of its sector self-regulating organisations, are too complicated and obscure, that the structure could inhibit business and that it could cost the City £100m a year to administer, given the need for numerous in-house 'compliance officers' to see rules are obeyed. Yet none of this is surprising since it was, after all, Parliament's and the government's aim to have an effective control, even if the full implications of the system were not foreseen.

In many ways, the mixed and controversial nature of the system chosen is due to the conflicting motives which prompted its design. The structure was devised to be at the same time effective and yet to avoid State control of the kind thought at odds with the ideology of the free market-minded Thatcher government. Yet these may be incompatible objectives, the compromise an impossible one. The invoking of legal powers and sanctions in a very real sense means that the law permeates the structure. Or so it seems to many in early 1988. Time will be needed for a demonstration of how flexibly or otherwise the system can work.

The important self-regulating organisations (SROs), which are crucial to the running of the new system, and which will come under the general oversight of SIB, are five in number. The first represents the enlarged Stock Exchange. After the link-up between the old Stock Exchange and the International Securities Regulatory Organisation (ISRO) – the body rapidly formed to represent the previously little-regulated Eurobond operators (including many large foreign houses), as new regulation loomed – the resultant amalgam assumed a twinned form. It contained both the International Stock Exchange (ISE), the broadened exchange itself, and its supervisory accompaniment, known as The Securities Association (TSA), which has taken the form of an SRO. Just how international the Stock Exchange body has become, now that the Eurobond market has been absorbed, is illustrated by the fact that TSA's first chairman was Mr Andrew Large from the international banking group Swiss Bank Corporation. On his resignation to take up new business duties, the chair was assumed by Mr Stanislas Yassukovich, the London-based American who heads all the European operations of the big Merrill Lynch securities house. TSA's chief executive is Mr John Young, previously the Stock Exchange's policy and planning director, and incidentally also a former England rugby and athletics star.

The four SROs in addition to TSA are the Association of Futures Brokers and Dealers; the Investment Management Regulatory Organisation (IMRO), representing the larger and some smaller investment managers; the Financial Intermediaries, Managers and Brokers Regulatory Association (FIMBRA), made up of a host of often small operators throughout the country; and the Life Assurance and Unit Trust Regulatory Organisation (LAUTRO).

SIB itself has up to eighteen board members, appointed by the Secretary of State for Trade and Industry and the Governor of the Bank of England. In addition to the full-time chairman, there is at least one executive director – the former senior Civil Servant Mr Roy Croft has held this role for some time – and may be more. The board has two deputy chairmen, Sir Mark Weinberg, who chairs Allied Dunbar, and Mr Ralph Quartano, head of PosTel, which manages the Post Office and British Telecom pension funds, and several other 'practitioner' members, picked for their standing and experience. Then there are some 'non-practitioner' members from outside the City. Members serve in their personal capacities and SIB people are at pains to say that the practitioner appointees are not there to speak up for their own sectors' interests – though they draw attention to what these are – but to foster the creation of a proper SIB view. 'People have tended to drop their partisan approach', a SIB member claims encouragingly. It is worth noting that, whereas in the United States the authorities corresponding to the SIB board members – the commissioners of the SEC – give up their jobs as securities market operators for a period of years to serve, the majority of Britain's SIB members are current practitioners. Supporters of the United Kingdom approach say this gives them a more immediate feel for the regulatory and other needs of the City situation at any given time.

Initially the SIB chairmanship was offered to Sir Martin Jacomb, who had chaired the 'Governor's group' and is widely known and respected in the City, as well as being an old friend of the Chancellor of the Exchequer, Mr Nigel Lawson. He was, however, unable to serve. The possibility of Sir Nicholas Goodison's taking on the task was then canvassed in an approach which recognised the Stock Exchange's good standing as an enforcer of high market standards, but he too declined. The authorities then persuaded Sir Kenneth Berrill to assume the chairmanship. For a time Sir Martin served as a

SIB deputy chairman but pressure of work made it impossible for him to take on a further term and in 1987 he was succeeded by Mr Quartano. Sir Martin is a non-executive director of the Bank of England and is sometimes spoken of as a possible future Governor.

Any hope that the reformed watchdog structure might be working by the time of Big Bang in October 1986 was soon disappointed. Because of the novelty and complexity of the hybrid structure, preparations proved lengthy, timetables suffered delay and contentious matters gradually surfaced. Rule-making by SIB and the SROs was a major task, given the precision necessitated by the legal background, and controversy was stirred as to the exact degree of 'equivalence' needed between the rule-book of SIB as the apex body and those of the satellite SROs in their different fields. Restiveness at the detail of rule-books accompanied fears of 'ending up with rules so complicated even the practitioners don't fully understand them', in the words of one senior City personality. Also, all the required consultations were a very time-consuming process. In mid-1988 all the SROs are themselves recognised and are well ahead with vetting member investment bodies which, since 'A-day' in April, have had to be authorised. Interim authorisations cover applicants not fully dealt with before A-day. Certain provisions of the Financial Services Act, for example, those for compensation funds and on other matters including rules over clients' accounts, would be phased in later.

The government, via the Secretary of State, decides when the various arrangements provided for in the Act come into effect. The timing of the introduction of an important provision, Section 62 – which allows those claiming to have been injured by an investment business' breach of regulatory rules to sue for damages – has been the subject of sharp controversy. The City developed a great dislike of Section 62 and mounted a sustained campaign against it in the autumn of 1987. Earlier criticism had been muted, perhaps to avoid the impression, in the run-up to the June general election, of quibbling at the investor protection framework. The worry has not been about an aggrieved personal investor – 'Aunt Agatha' – suing a stockbroker for negligence but about the big City firms suing each other, 'on technicalities', as one practitioner puts it. The fact is, though, that the 'technicalities' would arise from the legally-based rule-books which are essential to the new structure. In any event, the ability to sue is a major means of giving reality to the new, more protective, system. In the autumn of 1987, Lord Young, the Secretary of State, shelved the problem for a while by postponing the implementation of Section 62. However, the provision remains in the Act and the timing of its introduction continues to be an important issue. Some would like Section 62 to be effectively buried, but legal advice is believed to be that this would not be constitutional, since Parliament has placed the provision in the law. There is also the political fact that the existence of an effective City watchdog structure was part of the present government's prospectus to the electorate in 1987, so that an important part of it could scarcely be permanently shelved. If Section 62 were finally judged inapt, repealing legislation would be needed to cancel it.

In the context of general City discontent about the toughness of the new regulatory structure, there was considerable muttering directed against Sir Kenneth Berrill and the SIB. This seems unfair when they are doing their best to administer the law, as it exists, through the new system. However, major doubts built up as to whether Sir Kenneth, who will be 68 in August 1988, would be reappointed for a second three years when his first term as SIB's chairman ended in the spring of this year. In the event, Sir Kenneth was thanked for his work in launching the new system and the SIB top job passed to the Bank of England director Mr David Walker for the next stage of the watchdog system's life.

Meanwhile, SIB has fought various battles in its short life. It managed to carry its demand for 'polarisation', that such bodies as banks and building societies should not both hold themselves out as providers of impartial investment advice and also sell their own unit trusts and similar investment 'products'. However, its efforts to tighten the rules over unit trust pricing and related matters in a way that would strengthen the position of investors, at some detriment to management groups' profits, have been less successful. That matter has been passed to the Trade and Industry Department, which is pursuing a compromise formula.

Although SIB presides over a very broad span of the investment field, not all City markets and activities come under its wing. For instance, Lloyd's, the London insurance market racked by scandals in the early to mid-eighties, is specifically exempted from the Financial Services Act. Its recently restructured Council has been left to continue with various reforms on a wholly self-regulatory basis and without being under SIB in the way the securities market and most other self-regulators are.[11]

A further important section of the City, the 'wholesale' money, foreign exchange and bullion markets, is now regulated by the Bank of England through a detailed system. While this lacks the direct force of law, it should be effective since any seeking to opt out of it could face problems of not being covered under the Financial Services Act. In practice, avoidance of control in such a way is not expected. Businesses dealing with investment in commodities stand to be regulated via the appropriate SRO, which will often be the Association of Futures Brokers and Dealers, or directly by SIB itself.

The City Takeover Panel, which since 1968 has closely governed the conduct of bid battles in the interest of fair play for investors on a basis of voluntary compliance, enjoys no direct legal authority to enforce its rulings. None the less, the Panel, presided over by the former chairman of the Bar Council, Lord (previously Mr Robert) Alexander QC, can now call in aid certain backing from SIB and otherwise to support its stance and help certain of its enquiries. It can also seek to make its writ run by methods including getting City concerns to 'cold shoulder' clients who ignore its decisions.

The persistence of share price jumps ahead of take-over bid announcements, suggesting leaks of confidental information and possible insider trading, remains a cause of some public worry. But the Stock Exchange's revamped Surveillance Division conducts extensive monitoring, with the aid of 'audit trails' of dealing which can now be followed from records, thanks to computerised trading. The authorities also now have fuller powers to follow up, if need be with the involvement of the police, any signs of the now criminal insider trading.

The law has prescribed a wide-ranging, legally-backed structure of City regulation and protection of investors against abuse. But how it works out will to some degree depend on the City's will to make it effective. Much is set beyond doubt by the law itself, but there must still be scope for judgment in administration and for the success of the system to be helped by a broad public attitude of support. A general climate of professional and City opinion favourable to effective results is also something without which any regulatory arrangements, particularly novel and 'hybrid' ones, could stumble. Yet such a positive approach cannot be taken for granted and may need active fostering, since watchdogs face redoubled problems if they operate in a general atmosphere where everything favours liberality rather than control. Indeed, one fact of business life familiar to all financial authorities is just how sharply the climate can veer between one hostile to their regulatory activities and a troubled atmosphere in which, by contrast, they are positively wanted. The past two decades well illustrate this.

In the boom-time following Britain's partial banking deregulation under the 1971 Competition and Credit Control policy, in a context of easy money, fringe banking mushroomed – yet the mood was all against supervisory strictness. But after the secondary banking crisis broke out in December 1973, there was nothing but welcome for stronger Bank of England surveillance, which was then widely seen as overdue. None the less, some years on, in more 'free-market' 1980, the financial community clamoured against '*dirigisme*' when the Bank of England published its guidelines to ensure prudent liquidity standards.

Later, in 1986, the exploding take-over boom in frothing stock markets brought signs of increasing ingenuity and adventurousness by some merchant banks' advisers in support of clients. The Bank of England rapped the table in February 1986 with reminders that market share purchases to back clients' bids must not top certain proportions of banks' capital, but the warning seemed not to change the atmosphere. However, this whole buccaneering movement juddered when Guinness's conduct of its battle for Distillers, with advice from the merchant bank Morgan Grenfell, climaxed in an official investigation and widespread talk of malpractices. Arrests and charges in connection with the alleged operation to rig Guinness's shares and related matters followed in 1987 and 1988. Financial markets were shaken too, around the time of Big Bang in October 1986, by revelations across the Atlantic on the insider trading activities of the United States financier Mr Ivan Boesky and others. Also near the end of 1986 there was the quite separate matter of one of the chiefs of Morgan Grenfell's securities side, Mr Geoffrey Collier, being arrested and later convicted and fined for insider trading.

Such developments – notably the spreading Guinness affair – helped to dampen the previous spirit of competitive exuberance and made way for more cautious attitudes towards business methods. This was against the background that each new unfortunate disclosure or seeming premature leak of bid intentions started to give the City a bad name in an undiscriminating, blanket way in the mind of a public often little versed in financial affairs. Then, after the world stock market crash of October 1987, some further tendency for sombre self-examination made itself manifest.

A vivid commentary on the cycle by which periods of euphoria, and tilting against authority, are followed by sobriety and new respect for convention comes from Sir Mark Weinberg, a deputy chairman of SIB. In his own business, the South African-born Sir Mark is a highly successful entrepreneur who has built two major businesses – Abbey Life, and Hambro Life (now Allied Dunbar, a broad financial services company, in the BAT group) – popularising unit-linked life insurance and actively selling it. So he is no stranger to the past decades' competitive marketing in life insurance, where a self-regulatory agreement on commissions is now in force with his strong support.

Sir Mark, a close observer of the whole financial scene as well as an experienced practitioner and an influential chief of the City's regulatory structure, reflected thus to the author on the tendency for the market atmosphere to veer between climactic and more subdued phases:

> In any market-place, whether it's, say, mergers or life assurance that's in question, whenever there is a very competitive phase, there's a tendency for people to test the system, to push at the rules, to 'inch' forward. And once one step has been taken, and been tolerated, there's an almost inevitable process of others wanting to catch up – until it's seen that somebody's gone over the top. And then a rather sharp and rude correction takes place. In this way, after developments like Guinnessgate, you get this natural tendency for those in the market-place to want a stronger discipline there. So when you get that correction, you have a 'honeymoon' from the regulators' viewpoint, when the people who were in favour of 'inching' on the way up lean over backwards not to associate themselves with it and are all behind the authority of the correction. They feel awkward, embarrassed, that their reputation's slipping somewhat and they become very conscious of the need to stick by the rules.
>
> In a more stable period, of course, people go more carefully and are more reluctant to cross or push at the mores and the law and so on. But in a very competitive, bull type of phase, you get this gung-ho atmosphere when people say 'I've got to win'. Their motivation in the 'inching' phase is to show the client that they can

do better – and you get one individual or another pressing to forward his career and the business he represents. He doesn't wake up in the morning and say 'Today I'm going to test the system.' He says 'I'm going to fight as hard as I can to win this particular case for my client.' And a significant part of the advisory bank's capital can swing on his success, just as the amounts involved for the client can be substantial too. [12]

Such thoughts do much to illumine certain trends in the City of the mid-eighties. Their implication is perhaps that City people could do with a broader time-span of vision.

More generally, the phasing in of the full regulatory system over the months and the need for experience of it in operation mean that time will be required for judging its adequacy in practice. Experience will also show how smoothly it can work in tandem with the Bank of England's longer-established supervision of the banks.

In the formal, legal sense, the Bank of England has only been responsible for bank supervision since 1979, when the first Banking Act was passed in the wake of the secondary banking crisis and in line with Common Market requirements. In reality, though, it had been actively monitoring at least part of the sector for far longer. Thus, for many years until 1974, the Bank had informally kept in close touch with the main clearing, merchant and some other banks but was in less near contact with the growing 'fringe' whose troubles triggered the crisis from late 1973.

From the mid-seventies the Bank – at first without statutory backing and later with the 1979 Banking Act's support – built a more comprehensive supervisory system. As from the passage of the 1979 Act, it was based, in a similar way to the Financial Services Act's authorisation procedure, on the requirement that no deposit-taking concern could legally operate unless authorised by the Bank. The fact that an existing authorisation can, if things go seriously amiss, be withdrawn naturally gives the Bank a powerful sanction for its continuing supervision, parallel to that implicit in the SIB–SROs system.

At first there was a distinction between upper-tier recognised banks, which were more lightly regulated, and the more closely supervised licensed deposit-takers, but this split was removed in the Banking Act 1987, leaving all concerns engaged in banking needing a single type of authorisation from the Bank.

True to its traditions, the Bank supervises the numerous brood of some 600 banks in Britain in a somewhat flexible manner, so that needed standards of capital backing and other dispositions can be considered according to a concern's own circumstances. But the central bank nevertheless works to detailed published guidelines, such as those related to the calculation of a bank's capital ratio, that is, the proportion of capital it holds in relation to its loan and other assets, the latter being 'weighted' for risk. With the growth of 'securitised' business, which may involve a refunding commitment that does not appear in the balance sheet, the Bank has also developed rules to allow for such 'off-balance sheet' business. Broadly, obligations of the kind are reckoned as having the appropriate proportion of the weight of an actual loan. Further published papers cover expected standards on such matters as liquidity and permissible degree of exposure through foreign exchange positions and by way of loans to any one borrower. The Bank has also outlined its views on the extent of provisions it thinks needed against third-world debt risks.

In its supervision, which is aimed at seeing that banks are prudently and properly run, the Bank requires regular returns from the banks supervised. It also holds periodic meetings with managements – sometimes jokingly known in the merchant banks' parlours as 'the quarterly wigging' – since the watchdog process requires it to judge the quality of those running the banks. In any event, those in charge of banks' management have, under the law, to be 'fit and proper', a parallel requirement to that in relation to investment businesses under the Financial Services Act. Also, any record of financial crime would be an almost insurmountable barrier to anybody's acceptability to the Bank as a senior bank executive. There is no system of Bank inspection of banks' books, so the supervisors have to make their judgments at one remove. The latest legislation does, however, put some extra obligations on the auditors who enjoy direct access to a company's business.

The Banking Act 1987, passed following the Johnson Matthey Bankers affair, somewhat tightened the Bank's powers, for instance concerning large loan exposures which can, as was proved in the JMB case, prove highly risky, and in other ways. Proposals to commit sums worth more than 25 per cent of a bank's capital to a single customer have to be cleared with the Bank in advance, though there are exceptions for short-term underwriting.

The control-averse Thatcher government would not grant the power the Bank wanted in the Act to allow it to bar, on 'national interest' grounds, plans to take over banks, whether from abroad or from within the United Kingdom. However, the Bank was accorded enhanced powers to vet would-be buyers of as little as a 15 per cent stake in a bank and to reject them if it viewed them as not 'fit and proper'. It is now clear that such a rejection would take place if the Bank simply thought an intending purchaser was unsuitable to run or influence a bank, although of perfectly good standing generally. All the signs are that the Bank will use these powers fully. A company whose proposal to buy into a bank was turned down could, in principle, seek to challenge the Bank by testing its interpretation of its powers through the courts. But in practice it seems improbable that such a party would do so and risk publicity around the issue of its fitness and propriety. Even were such a challenge to be made, and to succeed in showing the Bank's control power to be weaker than it apparently is, that outcome would no doubt lead to new pressure on the government for more effective policing sanctions to prevent inappropriate buyers getting a grip on United Kingdom banks.

It seems that the Bank will be particularly chary about any stake-building designed to make a bank a take-over football, or 'put it into play', as the jargon goes. It would also be down on any move that would make a major United Kingdom bank end up as the subsidiary of an industrial or other non-financial concern. The interest of the Saatchi & Saatchi advertising group in Midland Bank was discouraged for this reason. Clearing and other big bank groups should, in the Bank's view, be run by boards which are at the top of the organisation, not slotted in as some lower tier of a conglomerate. And, while the new policy may not bar all take-overs of banks as fully as in the past, it is unlikely that the Bank would let much of the banking system's 'core' – its clearing and key merchant banks – pass out of British hands. Some pointers on its approach on these matters, which seem in line with current government thinking, were given in a speech by the Governor, Mr Robin Leigh-Pemberton, late in 1987.[13]

Revised compensation arrangements giving substantial protection to small depositors – who are repaid 75 per cent of losses up to £20 000 from Deposit Protection Fund financed by the banks in the event of a bank's failure – form another feature of the Banking Act 1987. The Act also provides a formal basis for the new advisory Board of Banking Supervision, the idea of its creation being to enable the Bank to tap outside expertise in its supervisory activities.

Britain's strengthening of bank supervision over recent difficult years has gone broadly in step with a similar process in other advanced countries. The purpose in each case is to enhance the protection of depositors and minimise the chances of bank failures, with all their attendant risks to the world banking industry. An important innovation since the secondary banking crisis, which had some counterpart abroad, has been international co-operation between bank supervisors in leading countries. This is carried out via the so-called Cooke committee, which has been chaired by Mr Peter Cooke, an associate director of the Bank of England, and based at the Bank of International Settlements, the central banks' 'club', in Basle. Certain agreements among the leading industrial countries to foster improved and effective supervision of banks have been arrived at down the years. Examples of common approaches include the encouragement of adequate provisioning by banks against third-world debt and of the preparation of consolidated bank group accounts.

But 1987 saw further major steps towards the creation of a 'level playing field' world banking market. The concept is that a fair and open banking market will be promoted if all the relevant world banks work towards similar standards of capital in relation to business. This should both stop the more venturesome stealing a march on competitors by operating on a thinner-than-normal base of precautionary capital, and also help ensure that all banks maintain sufficient capital, so rendering it less likely that any one bank will be driven by excessive competitive pressures into a failure that could send shock waves through the system or necessitate a costly rescue.

At the beginning of 1987 a bilateral United Kingdom–United States pact along these lines was worked out by the Bank of England's Governor, Mr Robin Leigh-Pemberton, and his opposite number, the then chairman of the Federal Reserve, Mr Paul Volcker. By the end of the same year, plans had been hammered out for a much broader agreement of the same nature, by which the leading industrial nations would set their systems to 'converge' by the end of 1992. The aim by that time would be for all banks to maintain capital (the cushion available to meet any losses) at least equal to 8 per cent of their assets, weighted according to risk. An interim target of 7.25 per cent has been set for the end of 1990.[14]

The participant countries are Belgium, Canada, France, Germany, Italy, Japan, the Netherlands, Sweden, the United Kingdom and the United States, Switzerland, (the Group of 'Ten') and Luxembourg. Negotiations for the pact had been under way for some time and it is notable that Japanese banks, which have tended, as have French banks, to run on relatively low capital ratios, have been building up their capital ahead of the coming agreement.[15]

In Britain itself the various recent supervisory improvements have been framed so that the regulatory systems for the banks, the securities markets and the building societies (under the Building Societies Act 1986) should be compatible with each other. Detailed arrangements have been worked out for the necessary co-operation, with the concept of a 'lead regulator' – or authority most concerned – handling co-ordination. The system now seems certain to leave the Bank of England with an important influence on all matters where banks are involved, including, in the case of many, influence through their role as owners of securities houses.

Over the whole regulatory field there is a certain irony in that two contrary trends of development have been under way. On the one hand, the world's governments have been pressing on with deregulation by lowering barriers between different financial sectors and national markets and by sweeping away conventional curbs on business, such as interest rate limits. This has increased competition – which should help the consumer – but must also heighten risk for financial businesses, both through the resultant price-cutting and as groups branch out into areas where they have little experience. But at the same time, in an effort to check such dangers, official regulators, nationally and in international concert, are more closely supervising banks and imposing on them tougher prudential standards. Time will show whether the new freedom-cum-regulation mix is better than the old segregated markets whose dividing barriers brought some safeguard against the spread of troubles.

12 Lessons and Reflections

The cost of doing business in London is rising, while profit margins are under intense pressure and are coming down.

Leading American broker.

Governments must be aware that sophisticated technology and truly international markets (such as the Eurobond market) preclude them from regulating capital flows.

Securities Industry Association.[1]

If you can keep your head when all about you are losing theirs – you are not in possession of all the information available to the market.

Adapted from Kipling's 'If'.

Governments these days are like the magician who let the genie out of the bottle and could not recapture or control it. Influenced by free-market ideology and the new technology, they have removed shackles on money switches among nations and dropped barriers between markets, so unleashing vast sums to roam the globe in quest of profit. Yet risks are inseparable from these heady conditions. Nor is it difficult at the start of 1988, and after the experience of the October 1987 stock market 'meltdown', to identify areas of particular hazard.

For instance, in an open-market setting and with huge capital flows on the move, the exploitation of computer and telecommunications technology to its 'state of the art' limits has generated a crop of financial innovations and 'derivative' money products. Examples include the explosively growing futures markets through which one can speculate on, or hedge against risks in, the volatile stock market and fluctuating interest and exchange-rate environments of the 'deregulated' eighties. By so-called 'portfolio insurance', investors can seek, through 'contrary' futures and share index positions, to protect themselves if they fear markets will move adversely to their existing stance. Again, the strong swing towards the financing of companies' needs against tradable 'securitised' paper is a recent development whose full implications have yet to be weighed.

These and other new trends carry their own dangers. Mounting last-minute resort to portfolio insurance proved a major destabiliser

261

which, in October 1987, helped send Wall Street and other world stock markets plunging. Innovations like 'securitisation' have prompted competitive 'under-pricing', in other words, excessively cut-throat vying for business, with resultant risks, according to a Bank of International Settlements study.[2] Again, securitisation can, by creaming off the best business, reduce the average quality of loans resting on the books of the banks which, for their part, also shoulder potentially hazardous 'off balance sheet' liabilities if they guarantee such deals. The securitisation trend means too that investors providing the funds must rely wholly on the credit of the 'borrowing' company issuing the paper, which could prove unfortunate if that group's business ran into trouble. And, in general recession conditions, investors might find it hard to sell off securitised paper, even if the debt was sound. These are just a few of the risks that cannot be ignored in the freer market climate.

And then, above all, the very openness of the world financial system, with exchange controls largely scrapped and currency values floating – by contrast with the pre-1973 fixed rates system – carries the potential for yet further instability, notably when large nations' payments patterns are out of kilter. Today's big imbalance, America's large deficit – with the dollar's resultant slide – and Japan's surplus, has relayed far bigger shocks to the foreign exchange market than the last great imbalance, OPEC's surplus and the rest of the world's deficit, did in the more regulated seventies.

The justification urged for this decade's exercise in financial deregulation is that it fosters the most efficient use of capital, just as it is held that banishing trade protection does the same for goods. Yet, as the persistence of much protectionism in trade, sheltering industries in high-cost countries, bears out, the pure milk of the principle of free trade remains, in the goods context, much diluted in practice. Not so, though, with the 'liberation' of financial markets. That the case for an unshackled world financial community has received high favour from the world's governments is attested by the amazing statistic that the money washing through the currency markets is now thirty or more times the scale of underlying trade and invisibles business.

Governments and politicians are, of course, not unaware of risks of free-market, deregulative policies and step in to counter them as they see a need, unembarrassed by considerations of consistency. Often such intervention is based on the discoveries of the now frequently derided John Maynard Keynes about the possibilities of offsetting unwanted tendencies through contrary action. For instance, the terrifying stock market meltdown of Black Monday, 19 October 1987, when New York share prices crashed 23 per cent in a day, was met by an energetic pumping out of central bank credit to encourage fresh buying. This bolstering support contrasted sharply with the situation after the 1929 market collapse, which was left to take its dire course unchecked by governments then ignorant of crisis control techniques.

The world's authorities have also grown more adept at crisis management within the financial industry. The British success in mobilising credit and cash to control the impact of the mid-seventies secondary banking crisis supplied a model for the far larger operation by key central banks in 1982 to prevent the third-world debt emergency from bringing down the global banking system. By dint of their closer supervision of banks, and through their new international 'convergence' pact, central banks have also developed a comprehensive watchdog structure to curb the chances of future bank crises. They are especially watching the growth of hidden commitments not revealed in the balance sheets of banks. As to any hazards from securitised finance, these have not as yet proved too serious in practice, though worries reflected in rising prices for some such finance are prompting a certain switching back to traditional bank borrowing. Central banks jointly tracked the 1987 stock market crash closely.

Whether it will be possible to control the more newly linked-up world stock markets against further risks of destabilisation, as well as to safeguard investors from any brokers' imprudence or malpractice, remains to be seen. Maintenance or improvement of a supervision parallel to that of the banks is moving up the advanced nations' agendas and is being tackled in Britain through the still only briefly tested SIB structure. With the new technology knowing no frontiers and laughing at controls, efforts to check any future market crises may not be easy, though fresh channelling out of liquidity would again have its effects, even at some cost in inflation. Meanwhile, some good marks must be allotted to the forces of financial law and order, when it is recalled that the world's stock markets ended unchanged over the whole of the tempestuous year 1987, the FT Actuaries World share index, in local currency terms, rounding off that year at 99.08, against 100 on 31 December 1986.[3]

Inevitably, greater uncertainty surrounds the ability of central banks and governments to achieve crowd control in the vast and turbulent foreign money markets, where the dollar's weakness was a major contributor to the late 1987 stock market crisis. In this massive and difficult-to-control forum, central banks at times intervene substantially to ease instability. And the possibility of additional control measures remains in the forefront of debate, with Britain's Chancellor of the Exchequer, Mr Nigel Lawson, having gone so far as to ventilate the idea of further moves towards managed exchange rates.[4]

Altogether, the jury is still out on whether the modern, deregulated, financially-oriented world of the eighties is better or worse than what went before it. That predecessor society lasted through the near-three decade postwar era, and during it rapid economic growth and high employment were achieved in a context of controlled, compartmentalised national markets and of exchange rates fixed under the Bretton Woods International Monetary Fund agreement. The drawbacks then experienced were rising inflation, which eventually eroded the worth of many financial assets, recurrent devaluation crises, and a consequently unsettled climate in which even shares – those supposed hedges against inflation – often did not prosper. The eighties world has restored and enhanced financial asset values, as the long stock market boom has shown, but its benefits are more unevenly apportioned, the well-off gaining much, while the property-less and unemployed have fared relatively worse.

The risks of instabilities and upsets in the free-market globe are being more and more realised since the stock market crash and the disturbing tumble in the dollar. And this growing recognition of the downside potential in the financial world of too doctrinaire free-for-all policies should sustain pragmatic official action aimed at controlling the excesses of market freedom. It may be too that free-market ideology, already diluted since the early eighties – Britain, for instance, no longer follows a pure monetarist policy – will be further qualified with a new American leader succeeding President Reagan. Short of world-wide catastrophe, a reversion to the controlled postwar economic system seems improbable, perhaps impossible, given modern technology which can crack many controls. But it is not to be excluded that in time a new synthesis will evolve after the previous rapid swing from a much-controlled system to one inspired by a radical free-for-all philosophy.

Meanwhile, for better or worse, Britain and the City remain heavily committed to the new open markets and to the drive to make London more comprehensively than ever one of the world's top three financial centres. The investment of billions of pounds in the Big Bang changes, and the increase in the work force, highlight this. So do the facts that finance and insurance provide some 10 per cent of all jobs in Britain and must now generate more than the 7 per cent of national output they accounted for in 1985.[5]

Though it is too early finally to assess the success of the reformed City stock markets, their ability to cut costs to users has already been demonstrated. The October 1987 crash afforded a further test from which one favourable outcome was that overseas investors wanting to switch their funds home in the shaken climate found they could, by and large, sell in London: the market did not seize up. But there has been some criticism of the extent to which prices then moved against shareholders. Quotations on the SEAQ screen often proved to hold only for small sales, while sizeable deals soon became the subject of price negotiation by telephone. Those few dealers who did not adjust prices downwards as quickly as others suffered losses in the exceptional conditions but may have gained reputation in clients' eyes. There are those who, looking back on the October upheaval, wonder whether there may not be greater merits in the New York system, where 'specialist' traders actively match deals and significantly absorb one-way business in unusual markets. This may continue to be a talking point, as will the complaints of small investors that their ability to deal during the crash left much to be desired.

The October turmoil and its quieter aftermath have highlighted questions about the revamped London stock market's profitability, or lack of it, for the operating firms. The huge £3bn investment by bank and other buyers, not only in costly new equipment but in buying up stockbroking firms with some £1.5bn cash which by-passed the market and went straight into selling partners' pockets, needs large earnings if it is to reap a fair return. And although the booming phase of 1987 yielded some lucrative profits, up to all of these or more were often wiped out in the autumn crash. Thereafter, turnover and revenue tailed off in uncertain conditions, again with no good result for earnings. It is thus scarcely surprising that redundancies and talk of sackings proliferated, as houses sought to lower expenses in line with sparser revenues. A competitive squeeze on the numbers in market-making and other activities may well follow the shake-out, while even strong houses will look critically at their span of activities. The big ones are well-heeled enough to be likely to stay in for the long haul, which was, after all, the Bank of England's idea in encouraging the formation of highly capitalised groups. But the total £3bn of investment in the new market only looks like yielding a full return over an extended period.

One particular danger the City needs to take seriously is that it could, because of the sheer steepness of its cost rises, lose some business to the smaller but rapidly developing, and less expensive, Continental centres. Amsterdam, Frankfurt, Paris and Zurich, for example, are, like London, also keen to exploit their European time-zone advantage to play further in the world financial village. There are some signs that these centres could benefit if groups including the Americans switched certain operations to the Continent on the ground that London expenses were too high.

One leading American points to London's heavy floor-space costs and steep salaries – including bills for overtime to facilitate twelve-hour working – as factors which could drive business off across the Channel. For the United States securities houses, the dollar's fall is an extra handicap, since it further inflates the burden of expenses incurred in sterling.

Another prominent American investment banker echoes the same points, while thus summing up the general profitability predicament: 'We, the City, have built an enormous overhead for our business, quite a bit of it simply to recruit good people who are highly mobile and opportunistic.' This reference to lofty salary, or 'compensation', figures focusses on one of the Big Bang revolution's least attractive aspects, the pay explosion created by unbalanced supply and demand which has caused remarkable differentials between City rewards and those elsewhere, prompting deep jealousy of financial 'Yuppies'. Aother uncomfortable recent feature of the City has been evidence that, here and there, the enterprise spirit was going over the top and resulting in practices pushing up against, or over, what the law allows.

Such manifestations mean that the City is striving to earn its living and increase its business without the rest of the country and of Europe at present feeling they owe it any particular favours. None the less, the chances are that, with its new investment, long-established skills, large infrastructure and the English language, Britain's unique financial centre will manage to hold its own.

Notes

(*BEQB* = *Bank of England Quarterly Bulletin*)

1 The City's Place in the World

1. 'The International Market: Growth in primary and secondary activity', Research Department: Jeffrey M. Schaefer and David G. Strongin July 1987, p. 11.
2. Euromarkets Survey, 16 May 1987.
3. Interview with Sir Timothy Bevan, 16 Apr. 1987.
4. Sir Alec Cairncross, *Years of Recovery: British Economic Policy 1945–51* (Methuen, 1985) p. 8.
5. *BEQB*, May 1988, p. 217.
6. Association of International Bond Dealers figure. (Estimate of total outstanding is the author's.)
7. Salomon Brothers, International Equity Flows – 1986 (10 June 1987).
8. InterSec estimate (interview with Mr David Booher, 13 Apr. 1987).
9. As in note 1 above, p. 21.
10. *Stock Exchange Quarterly* (London) Spring 1987, p. 15.
11. *BEQB*, Sept. 1986, pp. 379–82.
12. 'The Foreign Exchange Market in the 1980s', Group of Thirty, New York, 1985.
13. *Quality of Markets Quarterly*, Summer 1987 (The Stock Exchange, London) pp. 32–3.
14. Morgan Stanley Capital International SA, as shown in *Phillips & Drew World Investment Review*.
15. Ibid., Nov. 1987.
16. As in note 13 above.
17. As in note 7 above.
18. Ibid.
19. 'Morgan Stanley International Perspective', 4 Mar. 1987.
20. As in note 1 above, p. 14.
21. Ibid.
22. As in note 8 above.
23. *The UK Stock Exchange Survey of Share Ownership* (up to 1981).
24. *The Banker*, Nov. 1987.
25. Ibid.

2 The Government–Stock Exchange Accord

1. *The Economist*, 23 July 1983.
2. J. Dundas Hamilton, *Stockbroking Tomorrow* (Macmillan, 1986), p. 2.
3. Grossing up from the published yield of the 'charge for general services' at the rate levied in order to estimate the total revenue on

which it was levied. One element of approximation is where the rate (it has varied between ½ per cent and 2 per cent) changed during a year and it is not known how revenue was spread during the period. The years in question are the Stock Exchange ones, running to a date in late March.

4. Dundas Hamilton, pp. 26 and 169.
5. The choice of a new dealing system for equities. The Stock Exchange, 17 July 1984.
6. The exemptions were essentially where some other form of government control or influence operated.
7. Committee to Review the Functioning of Financial Institutions, Cmnd 7937 (Wilson) 1980.
8. Interview with Mr David LeRoy-Lewis, 14 Apr. 1987.
9. Interview with Lady Wood, 16 Dec. 1986.
10. Interview with Mr David LeRoy-Lewis, 14 Apr. 1987.
11. Wilson (note 7 above) paragraph 366.
12. Described in the present author's book, *The Secondary Banking Crisis, 1973–75* (Macmillan) 1982.
13. This report is referred to in the Stock Exchange document described in note 5 above.
14. Wilson, paragraph 360.
15. Interview with Sir Gordon Borrie, 29 Aug. 1984.
16. Interview with Mr Ronald Artus, 30 Mar. 1987.
17. *Financial Weekly*, 27 July 1984.
18. *The Daily Telegraph*, 28 July 1983.
19. *The Economist*, 23 July 1983.

3 City Restructuring for Big Bang

1. *The Times*, 30 July 1983.
2. Interview with Mr David Walker, 17 Apr. 1984.
3. 'The Implications of the agreement between the Stock Exchange and the Government concerning minimum commission' (paper by City Capital Markets Committee, 2 Nov. 1983).
4. Interview with Mr David LeRoy-Lewis, 14 Apr. 1987.
5. Discussion Paper on the future structure of the Stock Exchange, April 1984. See also Stock Exchange Notices: 'The choice of a new dealing system for equities' (17 July 1984) and 'The choice of a new dealing system for gilt-edged securities' (8 Aug. 1984).
6. Interview with Mr Stephen Raven, 25 Oct. 1985.
7. Interview with Mr John Robertson, 8 Oct. 1985.
8. Interview with Mr Charles Villiers, 3 Sept. 1984.
9. Quoted in an article by the author in the *Investors Chronicle*, 24 Oct. 1986.
10. Interview with Mr John Robertson, 1 July 1987.
11. *BEQB*, Mar. 1984, p. 45.
12. *Financial Times*, 10 Aug 1985.
13. Interview with Sir Martin Jacomb, 6 Aug. 1986.
14. *The Sunday Times*, 8 June 1986.

4 The Pay Explosion

1. Interview with Mr Michael Silverman, 21 Nov. 1986.
2. *Sunday Telegraph*, 7 June 1987.
3. *The Economist*, 19 July 1986.
4. *Financial Times*, 5 Mar. 1986.
5. *Financial Times*, 24 July, 1986.
6. Private information.
7. *Financial Times*, 10 June 1986.
8. Coopers & Lybrand, 'The Big Bang, Earnings and Benefits of Key Specialists' (1986).
9. Hay Management Consultants, 'Boardroom Remuneration Guide' (as reported in *The Times*, 9 Nov. 1987).
10. Interview with Sir Martin Jacomb, 6 Aug. 1986.
11. See note 8 above.
12. *Financial Times*, 7 Oct. 1987.
13. Mercury Asset Management, Report and Accounts 1986–87, and Mercury International Group, now S. G. Warburg Group, Report and Accounts 1986–87.
14. *Sunday Telegraph*, 23 Mar. 1986.
15. *BEQB*, December 1985, pp. 555–6.
16. On BBC 1, 21 Feb. 1986.
17. *The Sunday Times*, 16 Feb. 1986.
18. As in note 10 above.
19. As in note 1 above.

5 City Markets after Big Bang

1. Quoted in *The Observer*, 15 Feb. 1987.
2. Speech ('Big Bang: The Dust Settles') to Stock Exchange conference, 23 Feb. 1987.
3. Interview with Mr Michael Jenkins, 10 Oct. 1986.
4. As in note 2 above.
5. *Quality of Markets Quarterly* (The Stock Exchange) Autumn 1987, p. 11.
6. Ibid., p. 13.
7. Ibid., p. 7. For later commentary see *Quality of Markets*, Spring 1988.
8. *Quality of Markets Quarterly* (The Stock Exchange) Summer 1987, p. 8.
9. Sir Nicholas Goodison, article in *Financial Times*, 20 Jan. 1988.
10. *BEQB*, Feb. 1987, pp. 54–65.
11. *Quality of Markets Quarterly* (The Stock Exchange) Summer pp. 32ff, and Autumn pp. 28ff.
12. Mr Mick Newmarch, speech to conference on 'Technology in the Securities Markets: the Next Five Years', 9 April 1987.
13. Interview with Mr Michael Marks, 18 June 1987.
14. Interview with Mr Michael Hawkes, 3 Nov. 1987.

15. *Quality of Markets Quarterly* (The Stock Exchange) Winter 1987–8, p. 9.
16. Conversation with Mr Jim McCaughan, 9 Dec. 1987.
17. As in note 15 above, p. 14.
18. Interview with Mr Richard Westmacott, 15 Jan. 1988.
19. *Quality of Markets Quarterly* (The Stock Exchange) Autumn 1987, p. 12.
20. Interview with Mr Peter Wilmot-Sitwell, 12 Jan. 1988.
21. *Quality of Markets Quarterly* (The Stock Exchange) Summer 1987, p. 17.
22. Figures from *BEQB*s, the US Government's Federal Finance and comparable publications.
23. Bank for International Settlements. International Banking and Financial Market Developments, 30 Oct. 1987.
24. Ibid.
25. *BEQB*, Dec. 1980, pp. 440–1.
26. 'The Foreign Exchange Market in the 1980s', Group of Thirty, New York, 1985.
27. *BEQB*, Sep. 1986, pp. 379–82.
28. Interview with Mr Michael Jenkins, 10 Oct. 1986.
29. Association of British Insurers figures.

6 Clearing Banks: Business

1. This celebrated epigram occurs in a memorandum by Keynes, circulated to the United Kingdom War Cabinet on 15 May 1945, after the peace with Germany but before that with Japan. Entitled 'Overseas Financial Policy in Stage III', it dealt with Britain's future financial position in the world and referred particularly to the substantial sterling debts the country had incurred to various nations during the war. *Source: The Collected Writings of John Maynard Keynes. Volume XXIV. Activities 1944–6. The Transition to Peace*, ed. Sir Austin Robinson and Donald Moggridge. (Macmillan and Cambridge University Press for the Royal Economic Society, 1979).
2. Association of Payment Clearing Services figures.
3. *The Banker*, July 1987.
4. *BEQB*s, Table 3.1.
5. *The Times*, 7 Aug. 1987.
6. Patrick Frazer and Dimitri Vittas, *The Retail Banking Revolution* (Michael Lafferty Publications) 1982, p. 33.
7. *Building Society Fact Book 1987* (Building Societies Association).
8. Speech to Institute for International Research Conference on Consumer Credit, 7 July 1987.
9. National Westminster Bank Annual Report and Accounts, 1986.
10. Interview with Sir Philip Wilkinson, 20 Jan. 1987.
11. *Financial Times*, 30 June 1979 and 24 June 1980.
12. The oil producers' accumulated surplus at the end of 1982 was put by the Bank of England at $363bn (*BEQB*, September 1983, p. 348).

13. Speech, 'LDC Debt – The Bailout that Isn't' (The Global Financial System and LDC Debts: Four speeches, Citibank–Citicorp, issued Aug. 1983).
14. Interview with Sir Jeremy Morse, 10 Nov. 1986.
15. *Financial Times*, 7 Sept. 1987.

7 Clearing Banks: Organisation

1. From the US bank notice quoted at the head of Chapter 6.
2. Interview with Sir Timothy Bevan, 16 Apr. 1987.
3. Monopolies Commission: The Hongkong and Shanghai Banking Corporation; Standard Chartered Bank Ltd; The Royal Bank of Scotland Group Ltd; A Report on the Proposed Mergers. HMSO (Jan. 1982) Chapter 12.38.
4. *BEQB*, Nov. 1987, pp. 525–6.
5. Andrew Boyle, *Montagu Norman* (Cassell) 1967, p. 137.
6. Interview with Sir Philip Wilkinson, 20 Jan. 1987.
7. *Banking World*, Sep. 1987 (article by the author).
8. *Investors Chronicle*, 9 May, 1986 (article by the author).

8 Other Banks: Merchant, Investment and Foreign

1. John Orbell, *Baring Brothers & Co Ltd: A History to 1939* (Baring Brothers, 1985) p. 23.
2. See, for example, *Financial Times*, 10 June 1987, reporting an article in *The Treasurer* by Mr David Tucker of M & G group.
3. *Mergers & Acquisitions* magazine, list as reported in *Financial Times*, 11 Jan. 1988.
4. *Financial Times* (Lex) 3 Oct. 1987.
5. *BEQB*, June 1985, pp. 21–6.
6. Interview with Mr Charles McVeigh, 19 Aug. 1987.
7. Interview with Mr Stanislas Yassukovich, 8 Oct. 1987.
8. *The Banker*, July 1987.
9. *The Banker*, Nov. 1986.

9 Investing Institutions

1. *BEQB*, May 1987, pp. 247–51 (speech by Mr David Walker, executive director of the Bank of England, on 27 Feb. 1987).
2. *Financial Times*, 3 Dec. 1986 (article by the Editor, Mr Geoffrey Owen, based on an interview with Lord Benson).
3. *BEQB*, May 1987, p. 250.
4. Reform of Social Security (Cmnd 9518) June 1985, Table 1.2.
5. The W. M. Company, 1986 Pension Fund Service: Summary, 31 Mar. 1987.
6. *BEQB*, May 1987, pp. 253 ff.

7. Ibid., p. 257.
8. Ibid., p. 256.
9. See note 2 above.
10. *BEQB*, May 1987, p. 257.
11. See note 1 above.
12. Speech on 16 March 1987, to Industrial Society seminar on 'The City and Industry'.
13. Committee to Review the Functioning of Financial Institutions, Report (Cmnd 7937) par. 1225.

10 Bank of England

1. Jock Bruce-Gardyne, *Ministers and Mandarins* (Sidgwick & Jackson, 1986) p. 115.
2. Interview with Mr Robin Leigh-Pemberton, 9 Mar. 1988.
3. First Report of the Select Committee on Nationalised Industries, Session 1969–70 (House of Commons Papers, 258, vol. VI) Q. 188.
4. Ben Pimlott *Hugh Dalton* (Jonathan Cape, 1985) pp. 457–8.
5. Committee on the Working of the Monetary System Report (1959) Cmnd 827, par. 761.
6. As in note 3 above, pars 202 and 214 of report.
7. *BEQB*, Sep. 1981, p. 347.
8. *BEQB*, Sep. 1986, p. 346.
9. Morgan Guaranty Trust Co. of New York, World Financial Markets, September 1981, p. 14 (table on real effective exchange rates).
10. Cmnd 7858.
11. *BEQB*, Dec. 1980, pp. 428–9.
12. William Keegan, *Mrs Thatcher's Economic Experiment* (Allen Lane, 1984) pp. 156 and 159–61. Also, Sir Alan Walters *Britain's Economic Renaissance* (OUP, 1986) pp. 144–5.
13. The Monopolies and Mergers Commission (as in note 3 to Chapter 7 above) Chapter 12.29.
14. Andrew Boyle, *Montagu Norman* (Cassell, 1967) Chapter 8.
15. Stephen Fay, *Portrait of an Old Lady* (Viking, 1987) p. 184.
16. Johnson Matthey Bankers Ltd, Report and Financial Statements, 15 Months to June 1985, p. 3.
17. Ibid., p. 2.
18. *Financial Times*, 22 Oct. 1984.
19. Cmnd 9550.
20. Bank of England, Report and Accounts 1985, pp. 33–42.
21. House of Commons, Hansard, vol. 81, 20 June 1985, cols 454–65.
22. House of Commons, Hansard, vol. 83, 26 July 1985, cols 1440–8.
23. *The Economist*, 27 July 1985, p. 69.
24. *Financial Times*, 13 Dec. 1984.
25. As in note 2 above.
26. Interview with the author, 26 Oct. 1983, preparatory to an article in *Investors Chronicle*, 4 Nov. 1983.
27. As in note 14 above, p. 213.

28. *BEQB*, Aug. 1987, p. 368.
29. As in note 2 above.

11 Protecting Investors and Users

1. *The Latest Decalogue.*
2. Recalled in *Financial Times*, 17 Nov. 1986.
3. Review of Investor Protection, A Discussion Document (HMSO, Jan. 1982). The subsequent full report by Professor Gower under the same title was Cmnd 9125 (HMS0) Jan. 1984.
4. Ibid. (1982) 3.22.
5. Last consolidated in the Companies Act 1985.
6. Cmnd 9125 (see note 3 above), p. 27 (footnote).
7. Cmnd 9125 (Jan. 1984).
8. Ibid., 1.16.
9. A useful summary of the Act's provisions is given in *BEQB*, Feb. 1987, p. 60.
10. Midland Bank Review, Summer 1986.
11. Developments at Lloyd's, in particular its new regulator arrangements, are discussed, along with the nature of the earlier troubles in that market, in *A View of the Room, Lloyd's: Change and Disclosure* (Wiedenfeld & Nicolson, 1987) by Mr Ian Hay Davison, who was the first chief executive of Lloyd's between 1983 and 1986.
12. Interview with Sir Mark Weinberg, 23 Apr. 1987.
13. Speech by the Governor, Mr Robin Leigh-Pemberton, on 'Ownership and control of UK banks', *BEQB*, Nov. 1987, pp. 525–6.
14. Committee on Banking Regulations and Supervisory Practices (the Cooke Committee). Proposals for international convergence of capital measurement and capital standards (30 Nov. 1987).
15. *BEQB*, Nov. 1987, pp. 518–24.

12 Lessons and Reflections

1. As in Chaper 1, note 1, p. 45.
2. 'The Cross Report' (Bank for International Settlements, Recent Innovations in International Banking. Prepared by a Study Group established by the Central Banks of the Group of Ten Countries, chaired by Mr Sam Y. Cross of the Federal Reserve Bank of New York, Apr. 1986.)
3. *Financial Times*, 3 Jan. 1988.
4. Speech to IMF, reported in *Financial Times*, 1 Oct. 1987.
5. *Financial Times*, 8 Aug. 1987, reporting OECD Economic Surveys, 1986–87, United Kingdom, July 1987.

Index

Plc, Ltd & Co., etc., have generally been omitted from company names; 'n' denotes an end-note.

Abbey Life, 255
Abbey National Building Society, 124, 127
Accepting houses, 7, 171 (*see also* Merchant banks)
Accepting Houses Committee, 171, 177, 180
Access (credit card), 127, 132
Acrow, 219
Afghanistan, 185
Akroyd & Smithers
  capital, 37, 44
  chairman's Stock Exchange role, 28
  director's comment on jobbers' predicament, 56
  gilts market share, 64
  merger with Mercury Securities (now S. G. Warburg Group) 55–7
  profits, 25
  shares publicly launched, 37
Alexander, Lord, QC, 253
Alexanders Discount, 60, 115
Alexanders Laing & Cruickshank, 60, 116, 147, 183
Algemene Bank Nederland, 185
Allied Breweries, 199
Allied Dunbar, 250, 255
Amsterdam, 266
Angermueller, Hans, 141
Alphas (top UK share category in Stock Exchange trading system), 90
America, *see* United States of America
American Depositary Receipts (ADRs), 14, 45, 102, 233, 237
American Express, 182
American mutual funds, 97
Amro (Amsterdam–Rotterdam Bank), 73
Amsterdam, 266
Analysts (stockbrokers'), 74
Anti-Apartheid Movement, 128
Argentina, 141–2, 185
Argyll Group, 173, 175
ARIEL (Automated Realtime Investments Exchange Ltd), 40, 45
Artus, Ronald, 42

Associated Communications Corporation, 199
Association of British Travel Agents (ABTA), 33
Association of Payment Clearing services (APACS), 124
Astley & Pearce, 114
ATMs (Automated Teller Machines), *see* Cash machines
'Audit trails', 253
Australia, 5, 137

Bache (later Prudential-Bache), 44
Baker, Mrs Mary, 154
Baltic Exchange, 118
Banco de Sadabell, 184
Bank Charter Act, 1844, 209
Bank of International Settlements (BIS), 143–4, 206, 259, 262
Bank of England, 204–41 *passim*
  Banking Dept, 209–10
  banking supervision, *see* Supervision of banks and Big Bang revolution, encouragement of, 43–6, 52–3, 61, 266
  cash ratio deposits, 209, 232
  and 'Convergence pact', 259
  Deputy Governor's Committee, 224
  and discount market, 115–16
  Euromarket, 8
  and exchange market, 110–11
  and exchange rates, 210, 216
  financing, 208–9
  and gilts market, 40, 46, 63–5, 103–4
  and gold market, 113, 119
  Governor (the office and role), 143, 158, 210, 220
  'industrial lifeboat' operation, 129, 199, 218–20
  investment management studies, 176–7, 197
  Issue Dept, 209, 234
  and Johnson Matthey Bankers, 224–32, 238–9
  and monetary policies, 154, 210, 212–6, 223, 237

and money supply, 213–15
and Morgan Grenfell, 179, 235
nationalisation in 1946, 205, 207–8, 220
pay explosion, views on, 82–3
regional Agents/branches, 206, 220
relations with Chancellors, governments and Treasury, 205, 210–18, 220–1, 228–31, 233–4, 236–41
relations with City, 158–9
reorganisation, 220–1
roles, 205–7
and Royal Bank affair, 157, 216–18, 237
and secondary banking crisis, ('lifeboat' 1973–5) *see* Secondary banking crisis
and Securities & Investments Board, 235, 250, 252
supervision of banks, *see* Supervision of banks
and takeovers of banks, 157–8, 258
and Third World debt crisis, 143, 145
views on institutional investors' role, 190, 201
wholesale markets, supervision of, *see* Wholesale markets
see also under names of Governors and directors
Bank of England Act, 1946, 207, 220
Bank of Scotland, 125, 147, 166
Bank Rate, 115
Bankers Trust, 174, 197
Banking
cheque accounts, national proportions, 127–8
competitiveness, 123, 128, 175
consumer lending, 133
corporate, 126, 129, 133–5, 149–50
deposits, 126, 187
international, 8–9, 124, 134–46
mortgage business, 124, 126–31
retail, 126, 129, 149
segmentation of services, 149–50
See also Banks, clearing banks, Investment banks, Merchant banks
Banking Acts (UK), (1979), 225, 256; (1987), 119, 157, 257–8
'Banking habit', 127
Banks
in Britain, number, 17
clearing, *see* Clearing banks
foreign in London, 17, 124, 185–7, 219

help in 'industrial lifeboat', 199, 218–9
investment in and purchases of, Stock Exchange firms, 52, 55–63, 66–8
merchant, *see* Merchant banks
see also 'Convergence pact', Third World debt *and under separate names*
Banque Arabe et Internationale d'Investissement, 60
Banque Commerciale pour L'Europe du Nord, 8
Banque de France, 205
Banque Nationale de Paris, 17, 125
Barclaycard (credit card), 127–8, 132
BarclaysAmericanCorporation, 138
Barclays Bank
buys de Zoete and Wedd Durlacher Mordaunt, 57–8, 61, 66
the clearing bank, 123–5
corporate debts, 134
figures, 147
organisation, 149
overseas interests, 136–8
and South African interests, 128, 136–7
situation, 160–1
woman director appointed to board, 154
Barclays Bank of California, 138
Barclays de Zoete Wedd (BZW)
chairman, 58, 73 (*see also* Jacomb, Sir Martin)
formation and activities, 6, 58, 67, 180
loss, 1987, 160
market shares, 99, 104, 175
pay policy, 79
payments to 'marzipan level', 79
Barings, 143, 169–70, 176, 180, 187, 224
Baring Securities, 81
'Basket trades', 95 (*see also* Portfolio reorganisation)
Batten, Mary, vii
BBC, 237
'Beauty contests', 172, 177
'Belgian dentist', 17
Belgium, 259
Benson, Lord, 189, 218
Berrill, Sir Kenneth, 59, 235, 248, 250–2
Betas (share classification), 90
Bevan, Sir Timothy, 6, 126, 152, 160–1
Bickerstaffe, Rodney, 72
Biffen, the Rt Hon John, MP, 36, 213–4, 244
'Big Bang' change in City of London securities markets

some changes involved, 11, 17–19, 55
competition, new, 4
echoed abroad, 4
investment in, 66–8, 265–6
market (stock) after, 7, 89–102, 118,
    195, 201, 265
restructuring ahead of, 52, 55–68
see also Stock Exchange (The)
'Big Four' British banks, 125, 145–6
    (*see also under individual names*)
Bills (of exchange), 7, 115, 171
Bischoff, Win, 179
Bisgood Bishop, 37, 58
Black Horse estate agents (Lloyds Bank),
    127
'Black Monday' (19 October 1987), 96–8
    (*see also* Stock Market share crash of
    October 1987)
Blunden, Sir George, 222, 224, 236, 241
'Block trading', 44
Board of Banking Supervision, 233,
    258
Boardman, Lord, 163
Boesky, Ivan, 243, 248
Bond issues (government), turnover and
    outstandings, 15, 105–6
Bonuses, 23, 77, 79, 81
Booher, David, 11
Bootle, Roger, 74
Borthwick, Thos., 220
Borrie, Sir Gordon, QC, 27, 30–1, 36,
    41, 46–50
'Bought deals', 175
Boyle, Andrew, 158, 271–2n
Brazil, 141–2, 144
Bretton Woods agreement, 110, 264 (*see
    also* Exchange rates)
Britain (United Kingdom)
    financial industry, 17
    national reserves, 206
    share ownership in, 16, 193
    shares of, and in, bond and equity
        markets, 13–15, 105–6, 193
    wealth, 7
    *see also under individual markets and
        sectors and* City of London
British Coal pension fund, 191, 199
British Gas, 10, 16, 172, 193
British & Commonwealth, 60, 185
British Merchant Banking and Securities
    Houses Association (BMBA),
    177–8, 180
British Petroleum (BP), 10, 14, 209–10,
    219, 233–4
British Rail Pension Fund, 74, 191, 196

British Telecom, 10, 73, 172, 178, 191,
    193, 195
Brown, Brendan, 74
Brown, Leslie, 199
Brown Shipley, 180, 187
Bruce-Gardyne, Lord, 205
Brunei, Sultan of, 176
Brunner, Prof Karl, 213
BSA, 199
Buckmaster & Moore, 60
Budgets (UK), (1980), 211; (1981), 155;
    (1984), 155; (1986), 233
Building societies, 18–19, 21, 26, 102,
    124, 126, 130, 167
Building Societies Act, 1986, 127, 260
Bullion markets, 17, 112–13
Burmah Oil, 209
Buxton, Andrew, 161

Cairncross, Sir Alec, 267n
Callaghan of Cardiff, the Rt Hon Lord
    (formerly Mr James, MP), 28
Canada, 4, 31, 128, 259
Canadian Pacific Pension Fund, 179
Canary Wharf, 17
Capel, James, 59–60, 63, 66, 99–100,
    104, 162, 183
Capital flight, 144–5
Carey, Sir Peter, 179
Caribbean offshore centres, 9
Cash machines (ATMs), 149
Cassell, Sir Frank, 229
Cazenove, 28, 66, 100
Cedel, 108
Central banks, 13, 19, 110, 205, 263
Central Gilts Office, 64
Certificates of deposit (CDs), 114
Chandos, Viscount, 178
Charities, 193
Charlesworth, 5
Charter Consolidated, 225–6
Charterhouse, 173–5, 187
Chase Manhattan Bank, 59, 76, 104,
    183
Chicago, 12, 117
Chicago Board of Trade & Options
    Exchange, 117
Chicago Mercantile Exchange, 117
China, People's Republic of, 162,
    185
'Chinese walls', 170, 247
Church of England, 237
Churchill, Caryl, 20
Churchill, Sir Winston, 237
Citibank, 113 (*see also* Citicorp)

Citicorp
  director's remarks, 141–2
  provisioning, 144
  role in UK banking and stock market,
    59, 104, 115, 126
  size, 185
Citicorp Scrimgeour, 99, 183
Citizens Financial Group, of the US, 138
City Capital Markets Committee, 53
City of London
  atmosphere, 19–21
  costs, 266
  creation of Euromarket, 8–9
  developments, 4, 10–12, 17–20, 265–6
  earnings, invisible, 18
  employment in, 18
  history and role, 4, 7–12
  prospects, 266
  relative size in world, 12–15, 105–6,
    111–12
  representations to government, 158–9
  securities houses heavy borrowers, 96
  see also 'Big Bang' *and individual
    sectors*
City Takeover Panel, 62, 253
City University Business School, 239
Clearing banks (UK), 123–67 *passim*
  boards, 151–4
  capital, 129, 156, 257, 259
  consumer lending, 131–2
  corporate business, 126, 129, 133–5,
    149–50
  deposits with Bank of England, 208–9
  international expansion, 136–40
  investment in securities houses, 57–9, 61
  management, 150–1
  mortgage lending, 129–31
  pay, 151, 155
  profits, 129, 146–7
  provisions, 129, 145–6
  relations with government, 154–6,
    158–9
  scope and character, 123–8
  segmentation of services, 149
  takeover issues, 156–8
  tax on, 146, 154–6
  *see also particular aspects of markets
    and individual banks separately
    listed*
Clearing system (banks, etc.), 124;
    (Eurobonds), 9, 108
Clive Discount, 63
Clydesdale Bank, 125, 147, 158
Cobbold, Lord, 158, 207
Cockfield, the Rt Hon Lord, 46

Cohen, Jonathan, 180
Cold war, 8
Collier, Geoffrey, 254
Commercial Union Insurance, 120
Commodity markets, 17, 118–19, 244
Common Market (European
    Community), 127, 167, 256
Communist countries, 8
'Compensation' (pay, etc.), 77
Competition Act, 1980, 33, 46
Competition and Credit Control (CCC)
    (1971), 254
Conservative (Tory) Party, 23, 171
Consortium banks, 187
Consumer credit, 126, 131–3
Continental Bank, of Canada, 138
'Convergence pact' (international, on
    banks' capital), 239, 259–60, 263
Cook, Thomas, 127
Cooke committee, 259
Cooke, W. Peter, 259
Co-operative Bank, 125, 166
Coopers & Lybrand, 77, 80–1, 218
Corporate finance, 170, 172–5 (*see also*
    Clearing banks, Merchant banks)
'Corset' lending control, 129, 213
Cotton, 116, 220
Council for the Securities Industry (CSI),
    36
County Bank, 58 (*see also* County
    NatWest)
County NatWest, 160, 175, 180
Courtaulds, 219
Craven, John, 60, 73, 179
Crédit Agricole, 125
Credit cards, 123, 132
Crédit Lyonnais, 60, 116, 125, 183
Crédit Suisse, 60, 113
Crédit Suisse-First Boston, 65, 108, 172
Cripps, Sir Stafford, 207
Crocker National Bank, 138–9, 146
Croft, Roy, 250
Croham, Lord, 218
Crown Agents, 211
Cuckney, Sir John, 200
'Cult of the equity', 191
Cunliffe, Lord, 207
Currie, Martin, 196

Dai-ichi Kangyo, 125, 185
Daily Telegraph, 49
Daiwa, 44, 63, 105, 184
Dalton, Hugh, 207
Davies, Gavyn, 74
Dean Witter, 44

de Larosière, Jacques, 143
de Rothschild, Evelyn, 180, 226
de Zoete & Bevan, 57, 66, 69
Deltas (share classification), 90
Deposit Protection Fund, 258
Deregulation, 4, 262
'Derivative markets', 116 (*see also*
    Futures, Options *and* Swaps
    markets)
Deutsche Bank, 108, 170, 244
Director General of Fair Trading, *see*
    Fair Trading, Director General of
Discount houses, 7, 74, 104, 114–16
Disintermediation, 5
Distillers, 173, 175, 179, 254
'Dochakuka', 184
Dollar (US), 17, 110
Dow Scandia, 60
Dunlop, 200, 220

Economist, The, 3, 49, 230
Electricity Council pension fund, 191
Employment, 18, 101, 184, 265
Equiticorp, 180
Estate agents, 127, 180
Eurobond market
    City of London its centre, 12, 108
    investors, 9, 16–17
    nature, 9, 107–8
    operators, 172
    origin, 9
    size of market, 9, 106
    staffs sought after, 71, 74, 80
    Stock Exchange, houses' link with via
        ISRO, 101
Euroclear, 108
Eurocommercial paper, 107, 133
Euro-equities ('international equities'),
    10, 13–14, 109
Euromarket, 8–9, 12, 106–8, 114, 124,
    185
Euronotes, 107
European Banking, 73
European Community, 127, 167, 256
European Currency Unit (ECU), 105
Exchange control, 4, 7, 10–1, 44, 206,
    261
Exchange rates, 110–2, 117, 210, 212,
    215, 265 (*see also* Bank of England)
Exco, 77

Fair Trading Act, 1973, 26
Fair Trading, Director General of, 26–7,
    30, 36, 247 (*see also* Borrie, Sir
    Gordon, *and* Office of Fair Trading)

Far East offshore centres, 9
Fay, Stephen, 272n
Federal Reserve Board, of US, ('Fed'),
    143, 259
Fell, Robert, 31
Fforde, John, 213
Fiat, 10, 14
Field, Marshall, 246
Fielding Newson-Smith, 58
Financial futures, 116–18 (*see also*
    London International Financial
    Futures Exchange, *and* Chicago)
'Financial engineering', 118
Financial industry, 4, 263 (*see also under*
    relevant heading)
Financial Intermediaries, Managers and
    Brokers Regulatory Association
    (FIMBRA), 250
Financial Services Act, 1986, 101, 119,
    235, 247–8, 251–2
Financial Times, vii, 114, 268–73n
Financial Weekly, 268n
First Boston, 101
First Jersey National, 138
Fleming, Robert, 176, 187, 196
Floating Rate notes, 9, 107–9
'Footsie' (Financial Times-Stock
    Exchange share index), 102, 117, 197
Foreign banks, *see* Banks, foreign in
    London, *and under individual names*
Foreign exchange markets
    bank profits from, 112, 134
    scale and operations, 12–13, 109–12,
        123
Fort Knox, 112, 206
France, 128, 259
Frankfurt, 266
Franks, Lord, 222
Fraser, Sir Ian, 62
Fraud Squad, City of London Police, 230
Frazer, Patrick, 270n
French banks, 62, 260 (*see also under*
    individual names)
Frost, Tom, 137, 163–4
FT-Actuaries index, 197
FT 30 share index, 197
Fulton Prebon, 114
Fund management, 175–7, 184, 195–8
    (*see also* Merchant banks)
Furs, 118
Futures markets, 10, 116–18, 261

Galpin, Rodney, 165, 221, 227
Gammas (share classification), 90
GEC (of UK), 125

General Motors, 14
George, Edward (Eddie), 63, 213, 215, 220, 223, 238, 241
German banks, 62 (*see also under individual names*)
Germany, West, 14–15, 106, 128, 259
Gifford, Michael, 200
Giles & Cresswell, 63, 182
Gilt-edged market
  before Big Bang, 24–6, 37, 43, 64
  foreign houses in, 65
  index-linked bonds, 211
  post-Big Bang, 93, 102–5
  prices, 37
  restructuring and strengthening, 11, 55, 63–5
  scale, 15, 106
  staffs in demand, 71–3
  see also Bank of England, LIFFE, *and under individual houses*
GKN, 219
Glass-Steagall Act (US), 4
'Global village', 6
Gold banks, 112–13, 225–7, 232
Gold market, 112–13
'Golden handcuffs', 21, 69
'Golden handshakes', 21, 199
'Golden hellos', 21, 70, 79–81
'Golden parachute', 21
Goldman Sachs, 63, 101, 104, 108, 173, 175, 181
Goodison, Sir Nicholas
  and accord of Stock Exchange with government, 51, 53
  appointed TSB chairman, 166
  approached to chair SIB, 250
  approaches to government to stop OFT case, 35–6, 47
  and City salaries, 83
  dinners to City guests, 41, 48
  on 'Governor's Group', 246
  and jobbing system, 45
  and own firm, Quilter Goodison, 35, 60
  personality, 34–5
  problems confronting at Stock Exchange, 33–8
  and single capacity, 51
Government Broker, 57, 64
Gower, Prof LCB (Jim), 47, 243–6
Graham, Sir Peter, 165
Graham-Dixon, Anthony, QC, 28
Grain, 116
Greenwell, W., 59
Greenwell Montagu, 104

Greenwich Meridian, 6
Grieveson Grant, 58, 66–7, 96, 178
'Group of Ten', 259
GT, 177
Guardian, The, 48
Guinness, 61, 173, 179, 235, 248, 254
Guinness Mahon, 180, 187
'Guinnessgate', 255
Gunn, John, 185

Halifax Building Society, 124, 127
Hall, David, vii
Halpern, Sir Ralph, 200
Hambro Life, *see* Allied Dunbar
Hambros, 62, 180, 187
Hamilton, J. Dundas, 267n
Hattersley, the Rt Hon Roy, 27
Hawkes, Michael, 96, 178, 226
Hay-Davison, Ian, 234, 273n
'Head-hunters' (recruitment specialists), 72–6, 79
Healey, the Rt Hon Denis, MP, 210, 229–30
Heath, Christopher, 81
Heath, the Rt Hon Edward, MP, 26, 210, 230
Hedderwick Stirling Grumbar, 35
Henderson Administration, 177
Hill, Maxwell, 30
Hill Samuel
  capital inadequate for planned securities role, 170
  deals in Wood Mackenzie, 61–2
  figures, 187
  fund management, 176
  quits gilts market-making, 105
  taken over by TSB, 165, 170, 176
  UBS considers buying,
'HINWIES', 16
Hire purchase, 127
Hitachi, 14
Hoare Govett, 59, 66, 94, 98–9, 104
Hoechst, 14
Hoffman, Mr Justice, 30
Holmes à Court, Robert, 139
Home loans, *see* Lending, home loans
Hong Kong, 112, 217
Hongkong & Shanghai Banking Corporation (Hongkong Bank)
  acquires James Capel, 59–60, 183
  battle for Royal Bank of Scotland, 157, 217–8
  stake in Midland Bank, 139, 162, 166
Hopkinson, David, 41
Household International, 126

Howe, the Rt Hon Sir Geoffrey, QC, MP, 35, 46, 155, 215
Hue-Williams, Charles, 58
Hutton, E. F., 7

IBM, 14
Imperial Chemical Industries (ICI), 14, 136, 213, 219
Imperial Group, 173
Inland Revenue, 69, 80
Industrial firms' problems, 199, 212–13, 218–20
'Industrial lifeboat' (Bank of England-sponsored drive to help companies in recession), 129, 199, 201, 218–20
Inflation, 3, 216
Insider trading, 248, 253–4
Institutional investors, 189–202 *passim*
    attitude to previous Stock Exchange restrictions, 37–42
    and gilts investment, 39, 102
    increased role, 15–7, 189–94
    and 'industrial lifeboat', 199, 218–19
    influence on companies invested in, 189–90, 198–202
    and post-'Big Bang' conditions, 89–94, 201
Insurance
    broking, 120, 123–4, 126–7
    funds, 16–17, 191–3
    groups, 16–17, 120, 177, 189–94
    Insurance Companies Act, 1982, 121, 247
    life, 119–20, 191–3
    premiums, 120–1
    reinsurance, 120
    role, 119–22, 127
    unit-linked, 120
    see also Life Assurance and Unit Trust Regulatory Association (LAUTRO), Lloyd's, *and under individual names*
Interbank market, 114 (*see also* Wholesale markets)
Inter-dealer brokers, 103
International Business Facilities (New York), 18
International capital market, 8 (*see also* Eurobond market *and* Euromarket)
International Commodities Clearing House (ICCH), 118
International debt crisis, 141–4 (*see also* Third World debt *and* Lending)

International equity market, 12 (*see also* Euro-equities)
International Monetary Fund (IMF), 140, 142–3, 206, 226
International Petroleum Exchange, 118
International Securities Regulatory Organisation (ISRO), 101, 249 (*see also* International Stock Exchange *and* Securities Association)
International Stock Exchange, 101, 182, 240 (*see also* Stock Exchange)
InterSec Research Corporation, 11, 16
Investing Institutions, *see* Institutional investors
Investment banking, 177
Investment banks, 108, 129, 177–8, 181–5 (*see also under individual names*)
Investment management, *see under* Fund management *and* Merchant banks
Investment Management Regulatory Organisation (IMRO), 250
Investment performance, 197–8
Investment policies, 191–2
Investment trusts, 189–91, 193–4
Investors, changing balance among, 15–7, 189–91 (*see also* institutional investors)
Investors, personal/private, 9, 16–17, 176, 193
Investors Chronicle, vii, 271n, 272n
Invisible exports, 18, 185
Italy, 18, 259

Jacomb, Sir Martin
    becomes chairman of BZW, 58, 73
    chairs 'Governor's Group', 246
    on pay aspects, 69, 79, 83–4
    SIB chairmanship declined, 250 (and deputy chairmanship held, 251)
Japan, 4, 14–15, 106
Japanese banks, 17, 114, 125, 185–7, 260 (*see also under individual banks*)
Japanese securities houses, 17, 63, 171 (*see also under individual names*)
Jenkins, Michael, 89, 117
Jobbers (stock jobbers), *see* Stock Exchange (jobbers, *and* single capacity)
Johnson Matthey, 224
Johnson Matthey Bankers
    bullion side, 112, 129
    clearing banks' attitude, 226–7, 232
    crisis and Bank of England rescue, 224–33
    fraud, suggestions of, 229–30

gold banks' attitude, 226–7, 232
indemnity, 227
see also Bank of England *and*
    Supervision of banks

Keynes, Lord (John Maynard), 123, 263,
    270n
Kitcat & Aitken, 60
Kleinwort Benson
    activities and situation, 99, 169, 172,
        175, 177–8, 226
    figures, 187
    purchases of Stock Exchange firms,
        considered and made, 57–8, 67
    recruitment of 'Wedd eight', 58
    settlement problems, 96
Kuwait, 194
Kuwait Investment Office, 166, 194

Labour governments, 26, 205, 210
Laing & Cruickshank, 60 (*see also*
    Alexanders Laing & Cruickshank)
Laird, Gavin, 224
Laker Airways, 219
Large, Andrew, 249
Laurie Milbank, 59
Lawson, the Rt Hon Nigel, MP, 215, 226,
    229–31, 237–8, 264
Lazard Brothers, 62, 170, 175, 180, 187
Leasing, 127, 155
Legal & General, 120, 190, 199
Leigh-Pemberton, the Rt Hon Robin
    appointed Governor of Bank of
        England, 221 (and reappointed,
        239)
    dialogue with Mrs Thatcher, 1980,
        213–14
    on former Deputy Governor, 236
    'Governor's Group' on City regulation
        appointed, 246
    on institutional investors' attitude to
        companies invested in, 201
    and Johnson Matthey Bankers, 224,
        226, 229–32
    Leigh-Pemberton committee (on bank
        supervision), 229
    on pay explosion, 82
    negotiates international 'convergence
        pact' on bank capital, 239, 259
    relations with government, 233, 236,
        238–40
    speech approving City restructuring
        ahead of Big Bang, 61
    style, 222–4, 231–2, 238–9

talk of possible resignation (and view
    on), 224, 230–1
on takeovers of banks, 148, 258
views on Bank's standing and power,
    205, 240
see also Bank of England
Lending
    consumer, 126, 131–3
    corporate, 126, 133–5
    home loans (mortgages), 5, 128–31
    general, 9–10, 126, 134–5
    international, 8–9, 106–8, 124, 129,
        136, 140–5
    medium-term (including Euromarket
        syndicated), 107, 134, 140
    overdraft, 132, 134
    project, 134, 171
    rescheduling of, 144
    see also Banking, Banks, Euromarket
        and 'Industrial lifeboat'
LeRoy-Lewis, David, 28–9, 31–2, 54
Leutwiler, Fritz, 143–4, 213
Lewis, Stephen, 74
LIBOR (London interbank offered rate),
    107
Libya, 10
Life Assurance and Unit Trust
    Regulatory Association
    (LAUTRO), 250
Life Offices Association, 246
'Lifeboat', *see under* Bank of England
    and 'Industrial lifeboat'
Limerick, Earl of, 178
Lincoln, Mr Justice, 33
'Link argument', 29, 40, 54
Linklaters & Paines, 28
Lloyd's, 7, 119–22, 234, 252, 273n
Lloyds Bank
    chairman's remarks, *see* Morse, Sir
        Jeremy
    Latin American lending, 125, 145
    overseas interests, 136, 138
    scale, 125, and figures, 147
    situation, 161–2
    Standard Chartered Bank, bid for, 139,
        158, 165, 173
    no stock market purchase, 61
    quits Eurobond and gilts trading, 105,
        161
Lloyds Bank California, 138
Lloyds Merchant Bank, 105
Loehnis, Anthony, 221, 238
London, *see* City of London
London Bullion Market Association, 113
London Code of Conduct, 113, 119

London Futures and Options Exchange (London FOX), formerly London Commodity Exchange, 118
London International Financial Futures Exchange (LIFFE), 45, 102, 104, 117–18
London Metal Exchange, 118–19
Lord, Alan, 234
Luxembourg, 259
Lyons, J., 199

MacArthur, John, 75
MacKinnon, Neil, 74
Macmillan, Harold (later the first Earl of Stockton), 222
McCaughan, Jim, 98
McCulloch, Hugh, 123
McMahon, Sir Kit
  chairman of Midland Bank, 139, 150, 162, 236
  Deputy Governor of Bank of England, 221, 223, 230, 236
  formation of executive committee at Bank of England, 223–4
  Hongkong & Shanghai Banking Corporation's stake in Midland Bank, 139
  Johnson Matthey Bankers, rescue of by Bank of England, role in, 225–6
  on pay explosion, 82–3
  role in release of US hostages in Iran, 221
McVeigh, Charles, 181
McWilliam, Michael, 165
Mais lecture, 239
Mallinckrodt, George, 180
Manufacturers Hanover Trust, 174
Marine Midland Banks, 139, 217
Marks, Michael, 95
Marriott, Michael, 34
Marsh, Mrs Elizabeth, vii
Marshall, M. W., 114
'Marzipan layer', 68, 75
Mase Westpac, 112, 228
'Mayday' (US stock market deregulation, 1 May 1975), 25
'Medium term financial strategy', 211
Mellen, William, 58
Mercantile House Holdings, 60, 115
Merchant banking, 17 (*see also* Merchant banks)
Merchant banks
  bill business, 171
  capital, 169–70, 187

corporate finance, 170, 172–5
fund management, 104, 170, 175–7, 196
general, 7, 17, 169–81, 256
lending, 170
profits, 177, and figures, 187
stock market trading, 170, 177
takeover advisory business, 172–5
Mercury Asset Management, 81, 176, 196
Mercury International Group, *see* S. G. Warburg Group
Mercury Securities (afterwards Mercury International Group and, later, S. G. Warburg Group), 55–7
Mergers (and acquisitions) ('M & A' business), 173
Merrill Lynch, 44, 73, 101, 108, 174, 182, 249
Merton Associates, 71, 84
Messel, L., 63, 182
Mexico, 19, 141–2, 144
M & G group, 41
Middleton, Sir Peter, 215, 226, 229, 231, 236
Midland Bank
  business segmentation, 150
  chairmanship, 150, 236
  Clydesdale Bank sold, 125, 158
  Crocker bank in US, purchase of, 138–9, 146
  gains accounts, 128
  Hongkong & Shanghai Banking Corporation acquires stake in, 139, 162, 166
  Latin American lending, 145–6
  owns Thomas Cook, 127
  scale, 125, and figures, 147
  situation, 162
  stock market purchase, 59
  woman director on board, 154
Midland Montagu, 181
Minimum Lending Rate (MLR), 115, 212–13, 215
Mitford-Slade, Patrick, 28
Mocatta & Goldsmid, 112, 165
Moncreiffe, Peregrine, 73
Monetary policies, 3, 149 (*see also* Bank of England)
Money markets, 113–6, 129
Monopolies and Mergers Commission, 37, 46, 132, 157, 218
Morgan Grenfell
  activities, 99, 172, 175–6, 179, 196 (and figures, 187)
  chief executive, 61, 73

former director convicted, 254
Guinness adviser, 179
Phoenix Securities bought, 61
resignations, 179, 235
stock market purchases, 57, 67, 177
Morgan Guaranty Trust, 65, 113, 179,
272n
Morgan, J. P., 65, 179
Morgan Stanley, 14, 108, 171, 181
Morse, Sir Jeremy, 143–4, 161
Mortgage lending, *see* Lending, home
loans
Mortimer-Lee, Paul, viii
Moscow Narodny Bank, 17
Moulsdale, 59
Mullens, 57, 64
Multi-option facilities, 108, 134
Mutual funds (American), 97

NASDAQ (National Association of
Securities Dealers' Automated
Quotation), 54
National Association of Pension Funds,
190, 201
National Australia Bank, 125, 158
National Bank of North America (now
National Westminster Bank USA),
137
National Debt, 279
National Girobank, 125, 167
National reserves (UK), 206
National Westminster Bank
former chairman Governor of Bank of
England, 221
international expansion, 134, 137–8
management style and situation, 160,
163–5
organisation, 149
scale, 123–5 (and figures, 147)
stock market purchases, 58–9, 61, 160
woman director appointed to board, 154
NatWest Investment Bank (NWIB), 58,
67, 163, 180
Netherlands, The, 259
New York (financial centre), 3–4, 6–7,
43, 52
New York Stock Exchange, 31, 41, 54,
263, 265
Newmarch, Mick, 89–90, 269n
Niehans, Professor Jürg, 215
Nikko, 44, 184
Nissen, George, 28
Nomura, 6, 44, 63, 65, 105, 108, 172,
183–4
Norman, Montagu, 158, 220, 237

North Carolina National Bank, 60
North Sea oil revenues, 212
Nott, the Rt Hon Sir John, 50, 87

O'Brien of Lothbury, the Rt Hon Lord,
278
O'Cathain, Detta, 154
O'Connor, Gillian, vii
Office of Fair Trading (OFT), 26–8,
30–4, 40–3, 45–6, 49–50 *see also*
Borrie, Sir Gordon, *and* Fair
Trading, Director General of
'Offshore market', 8, 17–8, 106 (*see also*
Euromarket)
'Old Lady of Threadneedle Street' (Bank
of England) 206
Oil prices, boost to, and surpluses,
140–1, 262 (*see also* 'recycling')
OPEC (Organisation of Petroleum
Exporting Countries), *see* Oil prices
Options markets, 10, 12, 116–17
Orbell, John, 271n
Orion Royal Bank, 105
Owen, the Rt Hon Dr David, MP, 229
Owen, Geoffrey, vii, 271n

Panmure, Gordon, 60
Pao, Sir Y. K., 139
Paribas, 60
Paris, 266
Parkinson, the Rt Hon Cecil, MP, 47–9,
51–2
Pay explosion, 71–85 *passim*, 266
Pearce, John, vii
Pearson group, 170
Peel, Sir Robert, 209
Pember & Boyle, 59, 67
Pension funds
growth in, 176, 192–4
investments, 11, 16, 189, 191–3, 197
management, 176, 196
manager's comment on OFT–Stock
Exchange case, 43
role as shareholders, 190, 201
see also Institutional investors
Peru, 142
Peugeot, 14
Phibro (full name Philipp Brothers), 44
Philipp Brothers, 113
Philippines, The, 141
Phillips & Drew, 59, 66, 99, 104, 183 (*see
also* Union Bank of Switzerland)
Phillips & Drew Fund Management, 98,
192–3, 196
Phoenix Securities, 60–1, 179

Pigmeat, 118
Pilkington Group, 173
Pimlott, Ben, 272n
Pinchin Denny, 59, 67
Pitman, Brian, 161
Plastic cards, 149
Plastow, Sir David, 200
'Polarisation', 252
Portfolio insurance, 95
Portfolio reorganisation trades, 95
Post Office, The, 191, 195
Post Offices, 125
PosTel Investment Management, 195,
    199, 250
Potatoes, 118
'Pre-emption' (concerning rights issues),
    175
Prime Minister (the office), 220 (*see also
    under individual names*)
Privatisation, 3, 10, 89, 95, 172, 193
Project finance, 134, 171
Prudential-Bache, 63, 75, 105, 182
Prudential Group ('Pru')
    backed ARIEL, 40
    comments of directors, 42, 89–90, 94
    as institutional shareholder, 190, 199
    insurance business, 120
    underwriting role, 196
Prudential Insurance, 44
Public utilities, 3
'Put throughs', 40

Quartano, Ralph, 250–1
Queen, HM, The, 59
Quilter Goodison, 35, 60
Quinn, Brian, 132
Quinton, John, 160–1

Radcliffe committee on 'The Working of
    the Monetary System', 207–8
Rank Organisation, 200
Raven, Stephen, 56
Rea Brothers, 169, 180, 187
Read, Sir John, 165
Reagan, President Ronald, 264
Reaganism, 3
'Recycling' (of petro surpluses), 9, 107,
    140–1, 185
Reeves, Christopher, 179
Regulation
    of banks, *see* Supervision of banks, *and*
        Bank of England
    compliance officers, 249
    of securities markets, 243–56
    by Stock Exchange, 243–4

UK–US memorandum of
    understanding, 248
'REPOs', 104
Resale price maintenance, 26
Rescheduling of loans, 142–4
Restrictive Practices Court, 26, 28, 30,
    33, 36, 43, 46, 48
Restrictive Practices (Stock Exchange),
    Act, 1984, 49
Restrictive Trade Practices Act, 1956, 26,
    36–7
Restrictive Trade Practices (Services)
    Order, 1976, 26
Richardson of Duntisbourne, the Rt Hon
    Lord
    as Governor of Bank of England, 209–
        10, 220–1, 222–3, 236
    and monetary policy, 215–16
    and OFT–Stock Exchange case, 46
    and Royal Bank of Scotland bid affair,
        217
    style, 220–3, 238
    Third World debt crisis, role in, 143
Richelieu, Duc de, 169
Roberts, Malcolm, 74
Robertson, John, 57–8, 60
Rockley, Lord, 178
Rogers, Mrs Kathleen, viii
Rolls-Royce Motors, 200
Rothschild, the Hon Jacob, 185
Rothschild, J., Holdings, 185
Rothschild Investment Trust (now J.
    Rothschild Holdings), 37
Rothschild, N. M. & Sons, 62, 112, 169–
    70, 180, 187, 226
Rothschilds, the, 169
Rowe & Pitman, 57, 67
Royal Bank of Canada, 60
Royal Bank of Scotland Group
    bid battle for, 157, 216–18, 237
    business and situation, 125, 127, 166,
        174, 181
    buys Citizens Financial group,
        138 (Tilney, 61)
    figures, 147
Royal Dutch, 14
Royal Insurance, 120
Royal Trust of Canada, 60

Saatchi & Saatchi, 158, 258
Salomon, Sir Walter, 180
Salomon Brothers
    business, 6, 101, 108, 113, 174, 181
    growth, 44
    in London, 17, 63, 67, 113, 181

payment, 77
research estimates, 14
Samuel Montagu, 112, 162, 173–5, 181, 187
Sandberg, Sir Michael, 59–60, 217
Saudi Arabian Monetary Agency (SAMA), 176
Savory Milln, 60
Schaefer, Jeffrey M., 267n
Scholey, Sir David, 81–2, 89, 179
Schroder, Bruno, 180
Schroder Wagg, J. Henry, 175
Schroders, 46, 61, 173, 176, 179–80, 187, 195
Scottish Widows, 190
Scrimgeour Kemp-Gee, 59, 66
Sears Roebuck, 44
Seccombe Marshall Campion, 59, 115
Second World War, 7
Secondary banking crisis (1973–5), 37, 152, 206, 211, 218–20, 224, 232, 245, 254–6, 268n
Securities Association, The (TSA), 101, 187
Securities and Exchange Commission (US) (SEC), 19, 246, 248
Securities Industry Association (of the USA), 3, 11, 261
Securities & Investments Board (SIB)
    battles fought, 252
    and Bank of England, 234–5, 260
    Sir Kenneth Berrill, chairman, 59, 235, 248–9, 252
    controversy around, 251–2
    structure and operation, 19, 246–52
    and unit trusts, 252
    Walker, David, appointed chairman, 235, 252
Securities markets, regulation of, *see* Regulation, *and* Securities & Investments Board (SIB)
'Securitisation', 5, 129, 185, 261–2
Securitised instruments, 10, 107, 129, 172, 261
Security Pacific, 59, 94, 101
Security Pacific Hoare Govett, 94, 98, 183
Seelig, Roger, 173
Self-regulating organisations (SROs), 19, 246–51
Serious Money (Caryl Churchill), 20
Settlements, 75, 95
Share ownership, 16, 189–94
Share prices, 23, 89, 96
Share and bond values, 9, 13–15, 102, 105–6

Sharps Pixley, 112, 178, 226
Sheppards & Chase, 28, 60
Silverman, Michael, 71, 84
Simon & Coates, 59
Singapore, 15
Singer & Friedlander, 180, 187
Sipra, Mahmoud, 227
Skandia, 60
'Slow money', 69
Smith, David, 71
Smith Brothers, 37, 62
Smith New Court, 62, 95, 99, 180
'Soft dollars', 39
Sony, 14
South Africa, 112, 128, 136–7, 185
Soviet Union, 112 (*see also* USSR)
Spain, 136–7, 137
Spices, 118
'Square Mile', 20 (*see also* City of London)
'Stagflation', 3
Stamp Duty, 92
Standard Chartered Bank
    bid for, by Lloyds Bank, 139, 158, 161, 173
    board changes, 139, 165
    business and scale, 125, 136, 138, 165–6
    figures, 145, 147
    role in battle for Royal Bank of Scotland, 157, 217
Standard Life, 120, 166, 190
Staughton, Mr Justice, 30
Steinberg, Saul, 179
Sterling (the pound), 7, 110, 212, 215
Sterling crisis, 210
Stock Exchange (The) (later part of the International Stock Exchange of Great Britain and the Republic of Ireland)
    accord with government, 23, 48–9, 52–3
    automatic execution facility (SAEF), 102
    automated quotations system (SEAQ), 54, 90, 92, 97, 265
    brokers, 23–4, 38, 40, 45, 54, 56
    chairman, *see* Goodison, Sir Nicholas
    chairman's liaison committee, 39
    Christmas lunch, 235
    commissions tariff, 25, 28–9, 39, 47–8, 51
    commissions, 24–5, 29, 39–41, 43
    'continuation', 39
    costs of trading, 39, 89–93

council, 27, 33, 38–40, 48, 51
Daily List (SEDOL), 91, 104
defence in OFT case, 28–30, 33, 42–3
and dual capacity, 34, 56
evidence to Wilson committee, 28
firms, 25, 33, 38, 44
Floor, 20, 75, 95, 102
general service charge, 24
and gilts dealing, profits and revenue,
25–6, 55, 63–5
international trading, 33–4, 53
jobbers, 15, 24–5, 32, 37–8, 44, 56, 95
legal challenge by OFT, 25–36, 40–3,
45–50 (*see also* Fair Trading,
Director General of)
listing rules, 244
market-makers, 54, 64, 90–2, 99, 104
matched bargains, 29
merger with ISRO, 101
money brokers, 103, 197
net trading, 91, 94, 103
outside holdings in firms, 38, 45, 55–
63, 66–8 (*see also under individual
names*)
'put throughs', 40
regulation by, 243–4
rule-book, 26–7, 31–4
single capacity, 26, 29–32, 48, 51–4
surveillance dept, 253
takeover of firms, fixing of prices of, 67
traded options, 95, 102
trading system, 51, 53–5, 89–93
turnover, 89, 99
and Wilson committee, 36
see also 'Big Bang', 'Third Market',
and Unlisted Securities Market
Stock market share crash of October
1987
effects of, 13, 18, 68, 84, 195, 255
hits international equity business, 109
impact, 96–9
reflections on, 261–6
Stock markets (world), 13–15, 105–6
Stone-Platt Industries, 219
Stormonth-Darling, Peter, 81
Strauss Turnbull, 62
Strongin, David G., 267n
Sub-underwriting, *see* Underwriting
Sun Alliance Insurance, 120
Sunday Telegraph, 269n
Sunday Times, The, 83, 269n
Sunderland, Graham, 166
Supervision
of banks, 19, 156–8, 245, 256–60 (*see
also* Bank of England)

international co-operation, 259 (*see
also* Convergence pact)
of securities markets, *see* Regulation
of wholesale markets, 119, 253
Swaps market, 11–12, 81, 109, 133
Sweden, 128, 259
Swete, Trevor, 182
Swiss Bank Corporation, 60, 108, 249
Swiss banks, 62 (*see also under individual
names*)
Swiss National Bank, 213
Switzerland, 259
Syndicated lending, *see* Euromarket, *and*
Lending

Taxation
deduction ended on bonds held
overseas, 4, 105
on gains from selling Stock Exchange
firms, 69–70
on 'golden hellos', 80
'one-off levy' on banks, 154–6, 159
other affecting banks, 155–6
see also Budgets *and* Stamp Duty
Technology, 6, 18, 149, 261, 264
Tenby, Viscount, 178
Thatcher government
Bank of England, relations with, 211–
16, 218, 221, 230–1, 233–41
'corset' control dropped, 128–9
dislike of avoidable controls, 246, 249
exchange control scrapped, 4, 7, 44
favours pay demand restraint, 72
fosters wider shareholding, 16
and monetary policy, 3, 211–16, 221
rejects 'national interest' control power
on bank takeovers, 158, 258
stress on infant businesses, 135
tax on banks, 154–6
Thatcher, the Rt Hon Mrs Margaret, MP
appoints Bank of England Governor,
221–2
challenger of established practices, 3
dialogue with Mr Robin
Leigh-Pemberton, 213–14
lunch with bank chairmen, 155
and money supply, 213–5
pay explosion, reported concern on, 83
and Stock Exchange developments, 36,
48
Thatcherism, 3
'Third market' (of the Stock Exchange),
102
Third World, debt and lending to
adjustment programmes, 142

central banks' co-operation, 142–4, 259, 263
crisis, 1982, 19, 142–4, 206
impact on banks, 125, 145–6, 159, 166
loans to, 9, 107, 129, 140–2
'rescheduling', 142–4
Tilney, 61
Times, The, 268n, 269n, 270n
T & N (formerly Turner & Newall), 200, 220
Tokyo (financial centre), 3–4, 6–7, 52, 140
Tory party, 47, 171
Trade & Industry, Department of, 27, 45, 52, 76, 121–2, 191, 248, 250
Trade protectionism, 262
Trade unions, 3
Traded options, *see* Stock Exchange
Treasury, HM
and Bank of England, 210, 216, 230, 233
looses senior staff, 76
and monetary policy, 215
more powerful, 158, 207
and OFT–Stock Exchange case, 45–6
represented on Leigh-Pemberton committee, 229
Treasury bills (UK), 208
Treasury bonds (US) ('T-bonds'), 15, 17, 101, 105–6, 111, 117
Treasury Solicitor, 30
Truck Acts, 127
TSB Group, 20, 125, 147, 165–6, 170, 176, 193

Underwriting, 132, 174–5, 196
Unemployment, 216, 264
Unilever, 196
Unlisted Securities Market (USM) (of the Stock Exchange), 101
Union Bank of Switzerland, 6, 12, 16, 59, 108, 183 (*see also* Phillips & Drew)
Unit trusts, 123, 127, 189–91, 194, 252
Unit-linked life insurance, 120, 255
United Bancorp, of Arizona, 138
United Kingdom, 172, 259 (*see also* Britain)
United States of America (US), 3, 12, 15, 128, 259, 262 *see also* US banks, US brokerage and securities houses, US investment banks, Treasury bonds (US) *and under individual names*
US banks, 17, 62, 125, 142, 182–3, 185–7

US brokerage and securities houses, 62–3, 171, 181–2
US investment banks, 62, 181–2
USSR, 17 (*see also* Soviet Union)

Value Added Tax (VAT), 1979 increase, 211
Venice, 1980 summit of Group of Ten in, 140
Vickers, 200
Vickers da Costa, 59
Villiers, Charles, 58–9, 180
Vittas, Dimitri, 270n
Volcker, Paul, 143, 259
Von Clemm, Michael, 73

Walker, David
becomes Bank of England director, 221
chairman of Securities & Investments Board, 235, 252
JMB chairman, 228
and 'industrial lifeboat', 218
on institutional and pension fund investment, 190, 201
and OFT case–Stock Exchange reforms, 43, 52–3, 223
Walsh, Graham, 179
Walters, Sir Alan, 215, 272n
Warburg, Sir Siegmund, 179
Warburg Group, S. G.
City role, 172, 175, 178–9, 195
and Eurobonds, 9, 108, 172
figures, 187
and stock market mergers, 55–7, 66–7, 177
Warburg Securities, 99–100, 104
Warland, Philip, vii
Wass, Sir Douglas, 215, 184
Waterloo, battle of, 169
Wedd Durlacher Mordaunt, 37, 57–8, 60, 64, 66, 69
'Wedd eight', 58, 74
Weinberg, Sir Mark, 255–6
Weir Group, 220
Wertheim, 180
West Germany, *see* Germany, West
Westland, 200
Westmacott, Richard, 98
Westpac Bank, 112, 228
'Wets' (Cabinet), 215
Whitehall, 20, 217, 231
Wholesale markets, 113–4, 119, 126, 235, 253 (*see also* Discount market, Euromarket, Gold market, *and* Money markets)

Wilkinson, Sir Philip, 134, 137, 163–5
William III, King, 205
Willis Faber, 179
Wills, Peter, 28
Wilmot-Sitwell, Peter, 100
Wilson of Rievaulx, the Rt Hon Lord
    (formerly Sir Harold Wilson, MP),
    28, 36
Wilson committee, 28, 36, 154, 202
WM, 197
Wood, Sir Frank, 30
Wood, Lady (Olive), 30–1
Wood Mackenzie, 58, 62, 160, 197
Worcester College, Oxford, 222
World Bank, 206

Wriston, Walter, 140

Yamaichi, 44, 184
Yassukovich, Stanislas, 73, 101, 182, 249
Yeats, W. B., 42–3
Yen (Japanese), 106, 110
Yorkshire Bank, 125, 166
Young, the Rt Hon Baroness, 154
Young, of Graffham, the Rt Hon Lord,
    235, 252
Young, John, 28, 249–50
'Yuppies', 76, 266

Zambia National Commercial Bank, 185
Zurich, 112, 266